Nameless Offences

Nameless Offences

Homosexual Desire in the Nineteenth Century

H.G. Cocks

I.B. TAURIS
LONDON · NEW YORK

Paperback edition published in 2010 by I.B.Tauris & Co Ltd

6 Salem Road, London W2 4BU
175 Fifth Avenue, New York NY 10010
www.ibtauris.com

Distributed in the United States and Canada Exclusively by Palgrave Macmillan
175 Fifth Avenue, New York NY 10010

First published in 2003 by I.B.Tauris & Co Ltd

ISBN: 978 1 84885 090 3

A full CIP record for this book is available from the British Library
A full CIP record is available from the Library of Congress

Library of Congress Catalog Card Number: available

Project management by Steve Tribe, Andover
Printed and bound in India by Replika Press Pvt. Ltd.

To my parents

Contents

Maps, tables and figures

Acknowledgements

I owe a special debt to a great many people, but most of all to every member of my family, all of whom have provided emotional and financial support without reservation, especially my parents David and Patricia Cocks. I would also like to thank James Vernon and Conrad Leyser who supervised this project when it was a Ph.D dissertation. Their good humour, patience and imagination were central to the formation of this book.

Thanks also to colleagues and fellow students at the University of Manchester and elsewhere who have read sections of this work, and offered commentary and encouragement, in particular Morris Kaplan, Lesley Hall, Patrick Joyce, Frank Mort, Mark Micale, Leif Jerram, Helen Pussard, Aris Sarafianos-Bogiatzis, Sally Huxtable, Chris Otter, Francis Dodsworth, Nathan Roberts and Matthew McCormack. For their encouragement and supportive comments at various times I would also like to thank Randolph Trumbach, Jeffrey Weeks and Glyn Redworth.

Warm thanks to the librarians and staff at the Public Record Office in Kew, Bolton Library Local Studies section, Trinity College Cambridge, John Rylands Deansgate, Corporation of London Record Office and the British Library. Thanks to both Manchester University which funded the Ph.D on which this book is based, and the Leverhulme Trust for providing post-doctoral funding which enabled me to revise the manuscript. Thanks also to Lester Crook and all the staff at I.B.Tauris and to Steve Tribe.

Part of chapter five has appeared as 'Calamus in Bolton: Spirituality and Homosexual Desire in Late Victorian England', in *Gender and History* 13, 2 (August 2001), pp. 191–223. I am grateful to Basil Blackwell for permission to reproduce part of that article here. I would also like to thank the editors and readers of *Gender and History*.

Parts of the 2009 introduction first appeared as 'Safeguarding Civility: Sodomy, Class and Moral Reform in Early Nineteenth-Century England', *Past and Present*, 190 (February 2006): pp. 121–146, by permission of Oxford University Press, and as 'Modernity and the Self in the History of Sexuality', *Historical Journal* 49, 4 (2006), pp. 1211–1227.

Finally, Philippa Grand deserves the most credit, for providing intellectual companionship, discussing important parts of this project with me, occasionally laughing at my jokes and generally humouring me beyond the call of duty.

Introduction to the Paperback Edition

This book observes a paradox: why and how, in an age when homosexuality was increasingly visible via the operations of the criminal law and through the development of the press and print, did it become identified as secret, unknowable and even indescribable? Why, at the end of the nineteenth century, did those who wished to redeem same sex desire have to invent their own terms to describe it? How did British culture come to deny its existence and reality, while at the same time clearing the ground for a much broader discussion of its nature? Although homosexuality was unnameable in British religious and legal traditions dating back to the Bible, the other reason why it took on this dual character was that silence equalled discretion and above all safety. To say that homosexuality was marginal, unimportant and unknown was to defend the sexual privileges of masculinity and class in a much broader sense than resulted from merely denying 'unnatural desire', and acted to insulate a masculine public realm from its unruly presence.

Taking this line of argument perhaps helps to explain why male homosexuality, above all other sexual sins involving consent, continued to be punished by the state in modern Europe – and more severely than ever – while adultery, fornication and other sexual infractions were gradually relegated to the realm of private morality over the course of the three centuries preceding 1800.[1] Clearly, for most of Western history, sodomy was disdained by civil and religious authorities, and subject to severe penalties, but these were also very infrequently enforced. Moreover, many other sexual sins, including adultery, incest and other types of fornication, shared a very similar status, a fact which histories of homosexuality, in their willingness to dwell on the severe punishments and moral condemnation of sodomy – in any case a 'confused category' of sins and crimes, not all of which were homosexual – have tended to obscure.[2] So why was homosexuality singled out, to be separated from this complex of sin, and effectively divorced from common life, placed into a separate domain of knowledge and distanced from the 'normal' psyche, a process which culminated in the creation of a sexual identity defined by its fundamental separateness. *Nameless Offences* tries to question the self-evidence of that process, to show, how, in its initial stages, it happened.

This process of isolating and distancing can be seen at work in the operations of the criminal law and repeatedly viewed in the many trials and scandals described below. Perhaps its moment of origin, though – or the moment when the problem of sodomy became obvious to the point of intolerability – can be found in one case for which documentation emerged only in 2005 after the British Library had catalogued the papers concerned. In May 1805 24 men were arrested in Warrington in the north east of England, of whom five were later found guilty of sodomy at the Lancaster Assizes of August 1806 and hanged.[3] It was discovered that the men belonged to a loose network of association centred on Warrington, Manchester, Liverpool and the towns in between. The men met regularly in a village called Great Sankey to the north west of Warrington, where, as the local press put it, they pretended 'to hold a kind of Masonic lodge'. They had, it was reported, even 'taken a house to carry on their diabolical purposes…where they met on Monday and Friday evenings', when they 'accosted each other with the title "Brother"!'.[4] The most alarming thing about these men was that their networks of association seemed to mimic more legitimate forms of civil society and masculine sociability. When it was discovered that they had not only copied the cross-class nature of Masonic civility but that some of those involved with the house at Great Sankey were also members of the local militia, and even connected with gentry families in the area, the idea that these legitimate social and political networks might be contaminated by sodomy caused widespread panic. Persistent rumours began that at least eight members of the local ruling elite – a mixture of former Sheriffs of the county, senior clergymen, relations of the major local landowner the Earl of Derby, local gentry and politicians – were all said to have met for 'infamous purposes' at the house in Great Sankey.[5]

The problem was that these rumours, though seemingly without solid foundation, would not go away. Even after the executions of the main suspects in September 1806, the inquiries of two Lancashire magistrates continued, much to the discomfort of the local elite, some of whom protested in the strongest terms to the Home Office. One of the men under suspicion, a former Whig MP named Joseph Birch, also complained to his patron, the locally powerful Earl of Sefton, who weighed in against the zealous magistrates and the Home Office to which they answered. Sefton feared not only for Birch's good name, but also for the safety of the local landed class as a whole. He was, he said, 'impressed with a conviction that no man's character could for a moment be safe while he was exposed to the operations of an inquisition, as mysterious in its principles and more baneful in its effects than that which existed in the most furious times of Bigotry.' His first impression of the magistrates' 'mysterious' conduct, that it threatened the peace of many more men than those directly implicated, had been fully confirmed by more thorough scrutiny. It was, Sefton continued, his 'duty to awaken the feelings of the Gentlemen of this neighbourhood to a sense of the danger to which they are exposed'.[6]

The unpredictable effects of sodomy trials, which ended up disturbing the peace of Lancashire's local elite just as it unsettled powerful men throughout the nineteenth century, resulted in part from the fact that it was – unlike most other crimes – an offence which was not confined to a particular class of offenders. The house in Great Sankey demonstrated that fact, showing as it did that artisans, labourers, lawyers and wealthy merchants could be part of a regional sodomite network which crossed social boundaries. At Warrington, two disturbing facts came to the fore. On the one hand, the case showed that regulating 'sodomites' was in many ways to regulate the conduct of men in a much wider sense, or at least to unleash dangerous ideas, rumours and assertions that might easily backfire on members of an elevated class. It was then universally agreed by those in power, at least until the development of the popular press in the 1880s, that silence was the best way of dealing with this problem. That, I argue here, is one of the key reasons why homosexuality was repeatedly understood as secret, as hidden, surprising in its very existence, not something often encountered, distant from common life, and belonging, ultimately to a 'minority'. In spite of evidence which contradicted this view, this was the way of thinking to which the nineteenth century gave significance and power.

The problem was that homosexuality was not distant and unknowable, and in the Warrington case and others was also described with surprise as an everyday, casual and widespread phenomenon. The key source of evidence for the investigation, a 47-year-old artisan named Thomas

Rix who had been a regular visitor to the Great Sankey house, told the magistrates that he had entered this world easily in 1786. Then, a friend had told him of the many men who met at the Exchange in the centre of Manchester. 'These sort of persons,' Rix recalled in 1806, had their own code and way of behaving. They 'generally stood in the night as if they were making water...in the corner in the inside, and...if any person wanted to be connected with people of that sort they might go and stand near them and put their hands behind them.' If they 'were of this description of people they would put their yards into their hands'. Rix, intrigued by this story, then for the next ten days went to the 'Change to see if it was true. He took his place in the corner of the building, beneath the portico, and was accosted by two men who invited him to a nearby street where 'they all applied friction to their yards till they spent.' Subsequently, Rix 'often repeated this experiment at the 'Change...but never with any person that he knew'. Most of them refused to tell him their names, or gave made up ones. In about 1790, Rix moved to Liverpool, living there for four years and found that again, 'there were several persons who followed the same practices' in that town who met in the Rope Walk in the centre of the city. Most of Rix's sexual partners were other artisans but some were from other classes and petit-bourgeois milieus. They included three gentleman's servants, a man named Simister who was a fustian cutter and who was said to 'make a practice of inveigling all the young men he can into these wicked practices', a broker, a publican, a joiner, and a weaver.[7] Fifteen years later, when Rix recounted all this to two magistrates at Lancaster Castle in an attempt to save himself from the gallows after being convicted of sodomy, those who took his statement anxiously calculated that 'hundreds' had to have been involved in Manchester alone.

One of the most troubling features of Rix's testimony, then, was the apparent extent and casual character of plebeian sodomy, along with the way it was woven into the fabric of everyday life. Even though those at the Exchange might be regarded as 'a sort of people', the lesson the authorities took from the affair was that sodomites were more or less ubiquitous. Lord Ellenborough, the Lord Chief Justice, commented anxiously that the cases threatened to spread 'the knowledge that so widely extended a conspiracy against nature exists in point of fact'. Worse still, the cases promoted public awareness of the 'generality and notoriety of the crime'. Investigating the affair still further, Ellenborough judged, would show how common and even acceptable homosexuality actually was in some circles, and threatened to 'diminish much of the abhorrence which it is to be wished should always belong to it'. The crime should remain as nameless as possible, Ellenborough argued, because, in addition to corrupting public morals, it posed a direct danger to individual men. 'A mischievous curiosity is by the very description of the subject excited in vicious and depraved minds,' the Lord Chief Justice argued, which had led, 'in some ascertained instances, to the commission of the crime by persons who otherwise would never have thought of it.'[8] In this view it is Thomas Rix, a man who had almost unintentionally fallen into the Warrington circle, and not any recognisable figure of flamboyant otherness such as Oscar Wilde, who should be regarded as the representative sodomite of the nineteenth century.

The consequence of the Warrington affair was the realisation that not speaking of what had occurred was the best way to deal with its unpredictable effects. As with many of the cases described below, magistrates and investigating policemen were enjoined to caution, circumspection and silence. The trial judge, Sir Robert Graham, had in fact advised the investigating magistrates to this effect. When one of the Warrington magistrates consulted Graham about the case after the assizes, the judge told him that with respect to the rumours about gentry involvement, his 'first duty was silence'. Neither should a magistrate pursue such charges on his own account, but instead, must 'wait any event that might bring this painful story officially before [him]'.[9]

The seeming ubiquity of same sex desire, as revealed in 1806, was a regular feature of commentary on nineteenth century trials, no doubt partly reflecting the assumption that it could not possibly exist in so widespread a form. Yet it is an impression given force by the archive of criminal cases. Although it was common for a while for historians to insist that the most significant element of homosexual life was its tendency to arrange itself into separate subcultures not unlike those which developed in Britain and America after 1945, what I have tried to show in *Nameless Offences* is how dispersed and everyday the presence of same sex desire actually was. Reading the accounts of how cases occurred and came to court, the impression is that homosexuality was far from confined to any self-defined subculture or minority, but, as in Georgian Warrington and Manchester, a feature of common life which might occur anywhere and perhaps to anyone, like Thomas Rix, for instance. The same is true of the records of blackmail and extortion, which give the impression that it was encountered regularly, even frequently, in the everyday disputes of ordinary people.

In a way, then, *Nameless Offences* participates – but without really announcing it – in the major trend in the history of homosexuality which has developed since the 1990s, in short, a determined reluctance to dwell in Sodom. In the Sodom and Gomorrah sections of *In Search of Lost Time*,

Marcel Proust suggests that, partly out of necessity, inverts prefer to swim in the sea of 'normality' rather than mark themselves out as a separate species. If anyone actually rebuilt the city of Sodom, he says, no self-respecting homosexual would ever want to live in it. No sooner had they arrived there, 'than the Sodomites would leave the town so as not to have the appearance of belonging to it'.[10] Historians of homosexuality have shown a similar disinclination to live in the city of their own creation, undermining the very idea that homosexuality can have a unitary history or be a single phenomenon represented by a single subject. Their principal contention in recent times is that homosexuality is not necessarily apart from common experience, is not a matter of sole interest or significance to those who identify as homosexual, and is not comprised only by those who do identify themselves according to their sexuality. This is an idea associated with queer theory, but is particularly marked in books like Matt Houlbrook's *Queer London*, or George Chauncey's *Gay New York*, both of which describe a world in which gender roles, and not sexual object choice, define the way homosexuality was understood.[11] In *Queer London* and *Gay New York*, men could retain their masculine status as long as they ostensibly retained the active role in sex, and projected a tough, working class identity. 'Trade' such as this could participate in queer assignations as an aspect of the life cycle, and this did not make them part of a gay minority, a pattern which seems to have been common in the many European and American cities up to the Second World War.[12] This way of being, perhaps, is not so far from the world of Thomas Rix in Georgian Manchester, or that of the many men who appeared in the police columns of the nineteenth century press.

The problem with this new queer subject of history is that he is in danger of being installed as the central and representative figure in histories of homosexuality, just as his predecessor, the effeminate 'modern homosexual' was before him.[13] However, this change of focus, while it threatens to once again obscure the varied character of homosexuality, was a necessary reaction against the dominance of Michel Foucault and his more literal interpreters. In his *History of Sexuality*, Foucault suggested that the idea of the homosexual as a type of person whose anatomy and psychology was defined by his sexual preferences was essentially an invention of the nineteenth century. Before then, the sodomite was understood not as a being with an identity but only as the perpetrator of forbidden acts. Many of those who followed Foucault argued that this idea of homosexual identity and being ousted all others, leading to the domain of modern sexual identity, in which the self is most clearly understood by its desires, its manifold mysteries best articulated by its sexual object choice, and in which every aspect of anatomy and personality is colonised by the sexual instinct. Foucault's history is a world of rupture, in which one idea gives way to another in temporal sequence, but recent histories of homosexuality, including *Nameless Offences*, tend to think instead in terms of continuities. Instead of assuming that one 'model' of homosexuality completely obscures another, we should, David Halperin argues, see sexuality as a kind of palimpsest which contains elements of earlier forms of understanding. In Halperin's terms, the modern idea of homosexuality as an 'identity' is a necessary fiction which obscures its own history, and the variety of same sex experience. As an alternative he proposes that same sex behaviour has been structured historically by five different models of desire and selfhood. These are age-differentiated, for example the institutionalised pederasty of ancient Greece; role-specific, in which the 'effeminate' sexual partner is the one penetrated and in which the active partner retains his masculinity (as in *Queer London*); the friendship tradition of sworn brotherhood and religiously-sanctioned same sex intimacy; gender crossing, that is effeminacy and all forms of gender deviance; and homosexual, or the modern assumption that sexual acts and inner psychology always align and within the 'specious unity' of which all these other ideas shelter.[14] Each of these ideas, Halperin says, has come to the fore at various times in Western history but without fully displacing the others.

Same sex desire, in this view, is an everyday phenomenon which is not, and has never been wholly subsumed by the idea of an exclusive sexual identity set apart from 'normality' in the terms which became common in Europe and America after 1968. Neither is it just one thing. These by now fairly obvious ideas seem to undermine a Foucaultian chronology which posits the 'invention' of homosexuality-as-species and the subsequent twentieth-century dominance of that notion. Should we then discard Foucault, and read *Nameless Offences* as an anti-Foucault text? The answer is no, for two reasons: firstly that *Nameless Offences* doesn't necessarily assume that there is such a thing as sexual identity in the nineteenth century, merely that there were many different ways of understanding homosexual behaviour. It could be the object of a 'minoritising' discourse which stated that it belonged to a 'detestable race' of men ('margeries,' 'poofs' and 'Mary Annes'), but it could also be the final stage of a long process of moral degradation, and therefore within the compass of anyone, including 32-year-old men such as Thomas Rix who had seemingly never thought of it before. A same sex relationship might even be a spiritual experience for ordinary men, or a quasi-familial 'marriage', widely tolerated and even encouraged.[15] It could be situational, and associated with toughness and masculinity, or inherent and a sign of weakness and effeminacy.[16]

The other reason for not abandoning Foucault is that his account of the emergence of homosexuality is in the service of a larger story, namely the rise of bio-power. For Foucault, the specification of the homosexual as a type of person, rather than the perpetrator of acts, is not simply the discovery of some kind of essence. Instead, it is an effect of a particular way of thinking, what he calls bio-power, defined as the various ways in which states and their agencies have, since the eighteenth century, tried to govern the entirety of natural processes within any population. In the modern period, birth and death, health and mortality, reproduction and the family, work and productivity have all become objects of rule in new ways, Foucault says. From the eighteenth century onwards, statistics exploring these phenomena were compiled, subjects examined, and problematic groups addressed by a series of social interventions from legal punishment to welfare schemes. It was through the rise of this kind of bio-power in its various forms, Foucault suggests, that sexual behaviour came to have a new significance. In particular, during their search for patterns in society which could be understood, mapped and anticipated by policy, experts of all kinds began to generate ideas about the nature of physical and psychological normality. Some of these experts, notably criminologists and psychologists, began to inquire into the case histories of individual 'perverts' and sex offenders, and gradually produced the idea that these people were not aberrant, but represented one aspect of sexual behaviour that could be mapped, measured and understood using scientific techniques. The principal sign of this process, Foucault implies, was the alignment of inner psychology or physiology with sexual acts in a new way, one aspect of which was the 'invention' of the homosexual as a type of person.

Bio-power in this sense not only led to the specification of various perversions, understood now as the result of an individual's physical or psychological development, but also the placing of heterosexuality along a spectrum of various types of behaviour. The perverse, therefore, was 'implanted' within normality, whereas before it was merely a deviation from the natural. What was truly different about modern sexuality, however, was neither the way it exploded the idea of normality, or its delineation of types – this had been done before on a lesser scale – but the fact that it was surrounded by an array of scientific and sociological disciplines that generated pervasive ideas about what were the normal attributes of individuality, psychology and sexual behaviour. In turn, these forms of knowledge produced powerful regimes of expertise and inspection, ranging from eugenics to criminology, psychiatry and the welfare state, all of which were devoted to eternally calibrating the modern subject.

How does my account of the nineteenth century, in which homosexuality is a constant, everyday presence, albeit mainly in the courtroom, police office, and newspaper, align with this story? As Foucault and others have pointed out, the criminal law provided the raw material for the earliest sexologists – in Britain 'medical jurists' such as Alfred Swaine Taylor, writing in the 1850s, and in Austria Wilhelm von Kraft-Ebing, the latter harvesting case studies in his work with the Viennese police in the 1880s. Although silence was regarded by most as the best policy, *Nameless Offences* shows various forces in British life, namely the criminal law, the state, and more significantly the press, gradually overcoming their own reluctance to engage in a protracted discussion of homosexuality's significance. This, I suggest, was a necessary stage in the emergence of bio-power, that is, through scandal and press sensation. As Foucault suggests in his later work, bio-power is not the creation of the state, but begins with civil society. Thomas Laqueur has pointed out that it often emerges first in the most disreputable locations, in the alarming but scientifically dubious claims of quack doctors, the shocking revelations of low-life journalists, in the disorderly corners of print culture, and not in the consulting rooms or studies of doctors, writers and theorists.[17] In that sense, *Nameless Offences* does not try to bury Foucault, but broadens his account of bio-power's difficult birth.

Although defending Foucault might seem deliberately nostalgic, or even superfluous, it does point us in an old-new direction. It suggests again that histories of sexuality should tell us about more than their immediate details, than about how this or that identity worked, who went where, and did what to whom. They should be about wider formations of power, they should align with other histories, of the state, the self, religion, politics, ideas and beliefs. I hope readers will find *Nameless Offences* useful in that respect.

Introduction

Histories of the Closet?

The 'unspeakable' quality of homosexual desire in nineteenth-century England has become a familiar presence in historical writing and literary criticism. A body of work has emerged which interrogates late Victorian judgements about the impossibility of describing the 'unnameable vice'. The most famous of these statements are contained in the resonant phrases of some of the most celebrated Victorian homosexuals. Lord Alfred Douglas' clichéd description of the 'love that dare not speak its name' normally takes first place, along with E.M. Forster's *Maurice* and *A problem in modern ethics* by John Addington Symonds. Just as Maurice described himself as 'an unspeakable of the Oscar Wilde sort', Symonds, considering how to approach the subject, could 'hardly find a name which will not seem to soil this paper'.[1] This book is devoted to two main questions. Firstly it asks how this particular form of namelessness, what later came to be called 'the closet', was intensified, institutionalised, policed and used at a time when homosexuality was increasingly visible in English culture. Secondly it examines the varied and subtle languages that were available to describe directly and publicly that which was assumed to be indescribable.

Since Michel Foucault's *History of Sexuality*, it has almost become a truism to say that questions of naming and disclosure – which are still vibrant and applicable – have positioned sexuality in modern western culture. Although dismantling Foucault's intellectual legacy has become one of the favourite pastimes of some historians of sexuality, his presence

presence still looms over the field.[2] Much of the work in literary studies that has been done on nineteenth-century sexuality in the last 15 years, for instance, responds in some way to Foucault's analysis of the repressive hypothesis. Instead of asking whether sex actually is censored and repressed, Foucault posed the question of how we have come to think of it as a taboo, a secret which must be uncovered. 'By what spiral,' he asked, 'did we come to affirm that sex is negated? What led us to show that sex is something we hide, to say that it is something we silence?'[3] Answering, or re-posing this question is the principal theme of this book.

As well as providing the key question on which queer theory and the recent historiography of homosexuality has turned, Foucault also focused attention on the forms which this peculiar negation has taken. In particular, his suggestion that power which seeks to identify objects for investigation and control does not repress or censor, but instead incites forms of representation, is the origin of recent critical endeavour. While the law, and its language, has been the focus of historians, queer theorists and literary scholars have devoted themselves to disinterring the hidden meanings and evasions of Victorian literature. Queer theory in particular has encouraged practices of reading which seek to draw out the homosexual undercurrent in texts which, because of their historical location, could not explicitly identify or name their desire. Therefore, this body of work adopts the suggestion that silence about sex does not produce an absence, but merely incites other, richer languages of description. William Cohen has also pointed out that secrecy enabled, rather than prevented, certain forms of speaking. Following on from Foucault, Cohen argues that the 'secrecy' of sex for the Victorians was the very condition of its articulation. Talk about sex went on under a form of erasure, so that silence about sexuality composed 'a strategic form, not an absence of representation'. Instead of seeing secrecy or unspeakability as repressing the truth of sex which would otherwise be fully present to us, we should see silence as 'the very condition for its modern discursive formation'. Neither did such repression function as a set of prohibitions, but instead afforded 'abundant opportunities to develop an elaborate discourse – richly ambiguous, subtly coded, prolix and polyvalent'.[4] Indeed, attempts to theorise secrecy itself have suggested that it should be seen as one of the modes in which power operates.

Critical work which has sought to describe the connection between subjectivity and secrecy dates back to D.A. Miller's 1988 dissection of Victorian literature, *The Novel and the Police*. Miller argued, like Cohen later, that secrecy was one of the characteristic modes of modern power. As he suggested, 'instead of the question "What does secrecy cover?" we had better ask "What covers secrecy?"' In other words, what is it that 'takes secrecy for its field of operations'? From a theoretical perspective, the book which set the tone for writing on nineteenth-century homosexuality and its relationship to secrecy and disclosure was Eve Kosofsky Sedgwick's *Epistemology of the Closet* (1990). As well as setting out a contemporary theoretical agenda, Sedgwick examined the way in which the homosexual became a figure who was uniquely associated with secrecy, and whose sexuality belonged in a secret place, known to us as 'the closet'. This formation came about not simply because of the illegality of homosexual acts or the fact that individuals hid their criminal desires, but was the product of a certain historical and discursive formation. As Foucault pointed out, the assumption that sex in general and homosexuality in particular were actually silenced is simply inaccurate when one looks at the diverse and voluble range of sources which, since 1700, have identified and described sexual matters in a ceaseless and lengthy manner. In addition, homosexuality was far from absent from modern life, especially in cities. So, Sedgwick implies, following this Foucauldian line, 'repressing' same-sex desire was a habit of mind, a tendency to try and hide homosexuality in every context in which it might appear.

By the end of the nineteenth century, Sedgwick argues, sexual knowledge was, at the very least, marked by difficulties of representation and disclosure. The homosexual came to embody the problematic nature of this kind of representation. By 1900, Sedgwick says, the continual refusal to acknowledge the existence or legitimacy of same-sex desire had turned it into *the* sexual secret. By then, she argues, 'there had in fact developed one particular sexuality that was distinctively constituted as secrecy: the perfect object for the by now insatiably exacerbated epistemological/sexual anxiety of the turn of the century subject'.[5] There was, therefore, a tremendous cultural imperative to make homosexuality into a secret vice.

Epistemology of the Closet, then, directs attention to the fact that a series of regulatory practices were devoted to ensuring that homosexuality remained unknowable. The closet, the repository of a supposedly hidden desire and invisible social phenomenon, was protected, enforced and maintained in particular ways. What I intend to do here is to examine the specific practices which led to the historical formation, institutionalisation and exploitation of this 'namelessness'. My aim is twofold. Firstly, I examine the practices of law which encouraged both the naming of the crime and its erasure. Secondly, I show how those very practices of legal regulation and discursive constraint encouraged a paradoxical public discourse about a nameless crime.

Studies of the literary and historical relationship of homosexuality and secrecy have not been lacking since Sedgwick's *Epistemology* appeared. These have tended to treat the nineteenth century as a long prelude to the trial of Wilde and the emergence of sexual science, which, a number of historians have argued, established the terms on which a homosexual identity could be made. Ed Cohen's *Talk on the Wilde Side* (1993) sought, in the manner of Foucault, to map the emergence of a discourse which defined the homosexual as a type of person rather than the perpetrator of forbidden acts.[6] Alan Sinfield's similar 1994 study of Oscar Wilde also traced the emergence of a queer identity that dominated the twentieth century and justified his description of it as *The Wilde Century*. Sinfield's project, like the more recent efforts of Christopher Lane, was not to point out that a 'real' homosexuality was lurking beneath the Victorian condemnations which were the principal means of understanding homosexual behaviour before the 1890s.[7] Instead, he suggests that we should see a gay identity being gradually formed from diverse elements as the century progressed. Part of this process of emergence was the constitution of a semi-public discourse about same-sex desire. Sinfield agreed with Miller that the Victorian secret of sex was always an open one. It did not conceal knowledge, but concealed 'knowledge of the knowledge'.[8] That is, it prevented a more general investigation and public discourse which would have had disturbing consequences for class privileges and social boundaries. Secrecy, then, acted as a warning to keep private matters in their proper place. As such it helped to constitute the boundary of public and private. The secret of homosexuality, then, is not kept, but remains on the edge of public isibility as a reminder that it must remain there. The historiography of nineteenth-century homosexuality has a similarly divided and contradictory nature. On the one hand, literary studies has tended to concentrate on the coded language of sexuality present in the rich emotional vocabulary of the Victorian novel. On the other, legal studies and cultural histories have explored those moments when the nameless crime was identified and described. This book takes the latter path, suggesting that homosexuality was not always coded or secretive, but that it was named openly, publicly and repeatedly. It explores the consequences of such naming and the consequent anxious attempts to replace the boundaries around closeted desire. The 'secret' of sexuality was clearly one aspect of a wider pathology of concealment. James Eli Adams has pointed out that secrecy was not always sexual and that the secret vices which could be lurking in individual psyches, cities and societies might not be (homo)sexual ones.[9] Instead secrecy was distrusted on a wide front as the cloak of multifarious evil influences, partly because a belief in the benefits of transparency in government and public affairs was a central part of an increasingly dominant liberal politics and philosophy. However, the virtues of publicity produced corresponding anxieties about what it might be proper to hide. The simultaneous negation and incitement of sexuality then, resulted in part from a paradox at the heart of liberalism which formed around the contradictory need to represent public affairs and at the same time control the nature of knowledge.

The qualified secrecy which created the repressive hypothesis, then, performed particular and discernible functions. Secrets might not only work as a means of concealment, or as a field for the operation of power. If, as Foucault suggested, modern methods of power revolve around getting the self to confess its 'truths' through diverse processes of scrutiny, then secrecy might also be a resource for resistance or even self-making. John Kucich has argued that social, medical, and legal discourses which demanded 'compulsory confession' of sensibilities, pathologies and propensities automatically generated 'reflexive forms of evasion'. In his 1994 study, *The Power of Lies*, Kucich suggests that sincerity was a distinctly Victorian form of subjectivity. Candour and truth functioned as socially necessary indicators of integrity in an industrial society based on commercial credit and became the corresponding cornerstones of Victorian masculinity. The feminine vices of deceit and even mendacity were the negative of the masculine and counterpointed the frank openness of the manly ideal. Yet, Kucich argues, lying, theatricality and artifice had an insidious appeal even to those who upheld the value of sincerity. In particular, the ability to play with theatricality and deceit, and to demonstrate what Kucich calls 'dexterity with the truth', became crucial markers of class distinction.[10] The paradox of incitement and negation which structures modern knowledge of sex therefore resulted in part from the confused status of secrecy. Secrecy, as Kucich demonstrates, had its uses and therefore, when employed in certain ways, was not uniquely malign.

The uses of secrecy, censorship, repression and concealment were many. The most prominent of these was the protection of public morals without the politically awkward necessity of direct intervention in the private sphere on the part of legal or state authority. Where the actual powers and will of the police and the state ended, injunctions to morality, silence and circumspection were employed with the greatest force. Secondly, making discussion of sexuality illegitimate in certain specified public arenas protected masculine privilege and maintained the order and civility of the public sphere. Clearly, secrets and silence often operated as more than simple and instrumental methods of concealment. However, when combined with an ethos of spiritual comradeship the unspeakable nature of homosexual desire might also generate a perverse form of subjectivity that was not only a response to repression, but which might allow nameless and ineffable desires to be experienced without the taint of pathology.

The criminal law was obviously central to this paradoxical process of negation and naming. Studies of the relationship between homosexuality and the law began in the 1960s with the comprehensive work of H. Montgomery Hyde. His pioneering books provided the first reference point for the study of homosexuality and law in British history. Hyde's account of the Wilde trial, his later synoptic study, *The Other Love* (1970), and his account of the *Cleveland Street Scandal* (1976) still retain their authority. In the 1970s and 1980s, pioneering historians such as A.D. Harvey, Arthur Gilbert and Louis Crompton moved the focus back from Hyde's emphasis on the late nineteenth century to its beginning. Harvey and Gilbert both established that the eighteenth-century emergence of a homosexual identity or role described by Mary McIntosh and Randolph Trumbach had produced a corresponding increase in sodomy trials.[11] Gilbert's examination of the early Regency showed that the period was marked by a series of scandals surrounding the discovery of homosexual behaviour in the navy and the nation's capital. Gilbert, Harvey and others also examined the sensation which resulted from the punishment of sodomites, especially that which surrounded the prosecution in 1810 of the 'Vere Street Coterie', a group of men who met at a tavern in Clerkenwell. The accounts of Gilbert and Harvey presented these brutal punishments as the outcome of a temporary 'moral panic' produced by war, anxieties about divine punishment and the consequent search for socially marginal scapegoats. Similarly groundbreaking work by Jeffrey Weeks, in particular his two books *Coming Out* (1977) and *Sex, Politics and Society* (1981), placed the punishment of homosexuality in a context of social change, urbanisation, the restructuring of the family and the emergence of homosexual identity. Legal matters have been fundamental to more specific studies such as Cohen's *Talk on the Wilde Side* and Michael Foldy's *Trials of Oscar Wilde* (1997). More recently, the paradoxical naming and negation of specific forms of legal language has been addressed in Leslie Moran's *The Homosexual(ity) of Law* (1996).

In spite of the growing volume of this work, it nevertheless presents particular problems. Specifically, the concentration of historians on scandals such as Vere Street, Wilde or Cleveland Street has tended to produce a detailed but relatively decontextualised picture of exceptional cases and individuals. This work tends to present a picture of the legal process that is episodic, spectacular and sensational. I suggest here that the relationship of law and homosexuality worked in an entirely different fashion. From the late eighteenth century onwards, the workings of justice were sustained, unspectacular, insidious, everyday and even familiar. Moreover, in spite of recent work which presents substantial evidence on the matter, it is still the case that confusion abounds as to what exactly was an offence and when.[12] In some quarters, the easy assumption is still made that forms of homosexuality other than sodomy were only made illegal at the end of the nineteenth century. This persistent assumption has meant that historians' attention has been overwhelmingly directed at the *fin de siècle*. However, as I show in the first part of this book, it is the first half of the century which deserves greater attention.

Studies of the law also perform an opposite function to that of literary theory. They direct attention away from the codes and evasions of literary sources and towards the detailed attempts to satisfy legal evidence and hence name the crime in specific and detailed ways. Therefore, any account of the criminal law will emphasise the ways in which the crime is specifically named and described. In my account, I suggest, perhaps unsurprisingly, that in spite of the many warnings against naming homosexual acts, a public discourse about 'unnatural crimes' that resulted from legal investigation and sanction did in fact emerge.

I suggest that the problem of naming the crime of sodomy and other 'unnatural offences', which was part of a long Christian tradition, became especially acute at the beginning of the nineteenth century because of the unprecedented number of prosecutions and the gradual expansion of police jurisdiction. Regulatory practices like the law were themselves held to be responsible for bringing same-sex desire to public attention, and perhaps even advertising its appeal. The relationship between the law, the press, the act and an emerging mass readership was therefore presumed to be an incestuous one. Judith Walkowitz has pointed out that journalists looking for a language with which to describe urban sexual depravity in the 1880s used many of the melodramatic conventions associated with popular literature.[13] A similar process of borrowing from narratives of shocking facts and mysterious locations was used to define the urban sodomite. Through a complex process of interaction between the two forms, the figure of the sodomite was marked out as an especially urban and even modern type because of his association with both secrecy and the supposedly deceptive surfaces of the city. I then look at the function performed by these forms of representation, and suggest that they acted in a paradoxical fashion to both recognise and distance homosexual desire from common life. However, the sodomite and his nemesis, the blackmailer, did bridge the gap between the world of the street and the orderly world of public life. Finally, I say that in spite of these repressive circumstances, the namelessness of the crime did provide certain paradoxical opportunities for homoerotic expression.

Starting in about 1780, increasing numbers of men were prosecuted for homosexual offences. This was a sustained increase that lasted throughout the nineteenth century, although the largest expansion in prosecutions took place between about 1780 and 1850. This transformation in criminal justice produced a corresponding shift in the status and representation of homosexual desire. The law also provided the terms and the forms by which a legitimate public discourse could be made. Recent writing by Peter Barlett and Leslie Moran has argued that the criminal law is not a simple reflection of social change but can provide an important structuring context for public knowledge. For Moran, the significance of the law 'lies in the fact that it is an important social space, a particular set of cultural practices through which meaning and order are generated and enforced'.[14] It determined what could and could not be said legitimately about homosexuality and its authority took on a legitimising force.

The law, then, produced an influential form of words to describe same-sex desire. It also functioned as a public theatre, as well as generating a response from the press. In particular, newspapers sought to legitimise the naming of unnatural desire by imitating the style of the court, and thereby presenting an apparent 'transcript' of what had been said. In this function the public press went along with the intention of the law, which, Moran argues, seeks to limit and specify as well as generate meaning.[15] The press not only used legal forms to gain authority by mimicking official and hence authorised forms of speech, but also used these forms to present powerful claims to truth. In addition to the reports of the press, varied sources of popular knowledge were also generated. Yet the knowledge of the street and of a subculture which occasionally expressed itself through handbills, broadsides and songs was kept at arm's length from legitimate forms of public knowledge and the authorised, official discourse produced by the legal process.

This book, then, is also about the clash of worlds. It explores the characteristic nineteenth-century dilemma of how to keep the urban world of the street, the realm of the criminal, the prostitute and the blackmailer, at arm's length from the sphere of the respectable. As Sinfield has pointed out, that respectable world was partly constituted by structures, laws and forms of representation which defined and policed the distinction between public and private. One of the principal methods employed to distance these two worlds was to control knowledge and speech. Far from being an obsession of postmodern critics, questions of representation and speech were very real expressions of a public policy in an area where the state, for much of the century, feared to tread too heavily for fear of compromising the liberty of the subject. Controls on speech were also seen as a means to prevent the further proliferation of the crime by bringing it to public attention. In many ways, controlling public knowledge was the easiest way of masking the intimate connection between the legitimate public world of men and the 'city of dreadful delight'.

These worlds collided far more frequently than has been assumed. The boundary between them required continual and anxious policing.[16] It was not the case that sodomites were only occasionally encountered in the courts during famous trials and then forgotten. The policing of language and the moral necessity of silence were anxiously and continuously maintained. However, threats to this *cordon sanitaire* were generated, paradoxically, by the legal process itself. The blackmailer in particular represented a serious threat to this policing of privacy and secrecy. It was recognised that on the street the blackmailer held sway, and that he could make indiscriminate accusations against any man and generate promiscuous speech about a nameless offence. Policing the crime of extortion therefore also functioned as a way of separating the legitimate public world from the threat of the street criminal.

There were, then, two forms of knowledge and speech about same-sex desire: that of the street and the criminal sodomite, and that of the press and the law. As long as these two worlds and separate forms of knowledge were kept apart, a public world of masculine privilege could function as normal. During the 1880s it was realised that confining public discourse to an authorised and limited form of words had actually protected the privileges of all public men from slander, scandal and accusation. Restricting knowledge had its advantages for the respectable in more ways than one though. Keeping sodomy unspeakable in polite society could, paradoxically, facilitate the creation of a homosexual subjectivity. This could be done in two ways. Firstly by simple closeted concealment, but also by making sure homoerotic desire remained literally unspeakable. If desire remained ineffable, it could be thought of as something outside the personality, as a transcendent quality which belonged to another, often spiritual, realm. Hence, to be unspeakable was not only a sign of repression, but could be a valuable resource for those who experienced homoerotic feelings.

This book is divided into three parts and makes use of the two different approaches outlined above. Legal history and literary theory are both employed here, in what may seem to some like a shotgun marriage. However, this interdisciplinary meeting is, I hope, both productive and necessary. To make the union work, the first part of the book examines how the problem of homosexuality for nineteenth-century society was established through the expansion of the criminal law. The second part looks at the ways in which the 'sodomite' was, as a result, placed in a cycle of description and negation. It then examines how the promiscuous speech of the blackmailer competed with the authorised language of the courts and in doing so threatened the civility of the public world. The final part investigates the way in which secrecy and the unspeakable nature of homosexual desire in certain contexts could be used as a resource for homosexual self-making.

Chapters one and two, then, utilise some of the methods of legal and police history to demonstrate the extent to which the law punished homosexual acts between men. Chapter one examines the numbers of prosecutions, what counted as a crime and the way in which the law defined public and private in this context. I also look at the way in which cases reached court, and present available data about offenders, 'victims'/partners and prosecutors. In Chapter two, I look at the influence of the new police forces on the prosecution of sodomy, especially in London, with a brief detour to late Victorian Manchester. These chapters explore the terms of a legal discourse which had an enormous influence on the production of knowledge about the sodomite. In Chapter three I move on to questions of representation. In particular, I examine the role of the press in building a public discourse about sodomy trials, and the paradox that the 'respectable' press were the papers that publicised these matters most fully. Terms to describe the sodomite were available, I argue, and these tended to place him at the heart of modern urban culture. Chapter four also considers the metropolitan street culture of sex and the way it impinged on the world of the respectable through the unpredictable accusations of the blackmailer. The blackmailer here is considered as an unauthorised source of public speech and knowledge. He is also a seen as a cause of considerable anxiety not only through his ability to accuse, but also because he generated uncontrolled speech and unauthorised knowledge. I also explore the history of blackmail, and show that it moved from having quasi-legitimate public status to being a crime and back again during the course of the century. I argue that the investigative methods of the 'new journalism' of the 1880s were frequently equated with those of the blackmailer, and that in some famous cases, blackmailers and new journalists worked together in the investigation of sexual scandal. Chapter four also highlights the realisation during the 1880s that secrecy about sex performed a valuable function for public men: that of protecting them from slander.

Part three represents a movement away from the consideration of legal matters and metropolitan subcultures towards the investigation of literary sources and provincial culture. In Chapter five, I look at the way in which the unsayable nature of homoerotic desire in respectable circles worked in a perverse fashion to enable the expression of homosexuality. I look at the lives of a group of men in the circle of Edward Carpenter and use their letters and diaries to show how homosexual desire could be experienced as a form of ineffable, spiritual communion. I also present this evidence as an alternative to the story of the 'modern homosexual' set out in some of the work mentioned above. Some of this Foucauldian work tended to imply that Wildean aestheticism and decadence was the only source of homosexual identity in the twentieth century. I suggest in Part three that there were other sources which have not received similar attention, and which belong in the tradition of namelessness which I outline here. It will be clear from this summary that I am not going to explore the more canonical figures and texts of gay and lesbian history. Wilde, the sexologists and other famous men and women of the *fin de siècle* have been extensively explored elsewhere. What I intend to do here is to provide evidence which provides both a more extensive context and a suitable counterpoint to that historiography. The 'closet', then, was the result of particular practices of enforcement that were not simply confined to the law. Instead, the simultaneous negation and description of homosexuality was generated by a conflict between the necessity of guarding morality and the needs of a liberal polity.

Part I

1

Prosecuting the 'Unnatural Crime'

In September 1858, a 20-year-old agricultural labourer named Fred Larner received a series of letters at his home in Sevenhampton in rural Wiltshire. They were addressed to 'My Dear Fred', and appeared to be from a gentleman in nearby Cheltenham who called himself Mr Smith. The unexpected correspondent claimed that they had met before in a train and that he would like to meet his young friend again. 'I had a great liking for you,' the writer recalled, promising to visit in the near future. 'I shall want to be put up near there,' he continued, 'and if so I'll look you up and very likely you'll let me share your bed or else tell me of some young man that will do so.'[1] Two more letters arrived that September, one of which informed Fred of its author's genuine affection. When they had met initially, its sender declared, 'I thought what a nice fellow you were and how I should like to know you intimately… I think I should be so fond of you if we knew one another well.'[2] Fred Larner's response, if there was one, went unrecorded, but he and his mother Rebecca did entertain the mysterious James Smith on 10 September that year. Smith, who appears to have turned up unannounced, insisted on staying with the Larners and on sleeping with Fred, a wish that his mother was only too happy to accommodate. Her only qualm was that 'the room was not so nice as I should like for a gentleman like him', although 'he seemed to think it would do'. They had, she said, 'parted good friends'.[3]

Fred's night was not a tranquil one, however. After drinking some beer with Smith at the local pub, Fred got into bed with his visitor. He later told the police that he had been in bed for a matter of two minutes when Smith 'began muddling me about'. Fred claimed that he had resisted but his guest 'began again... and said it would be better than any girl'. Then, on seeing Fred's reluctance, Smith asked him if he 'would tell him of any young man or young girl'. The same thing happened at about 4am, whereupon Fred got up and left for his work. In spite of this relatively unsuccessful encounter, Smith turned up again on 25 October, whereupon he was arrested for indecently assaulting his host. However, it was not Fred who had complained to the police, but one Richard Allmond, a valet on the nearby Brockhampton estate, who had taken it on himself to investigate the mysterious visitor. According to Fred, Allmond 'kept asking and asking me, what the prisoner was and what he had done'. Allmond informed the police, who were waiting for Smith on his next visit. Smith's ignominy was not complete, as the police discovered on further inquiry that he was in fact a Cheltenham clergyman named Wallace Olive.

Can this singular case tell us anything beyond the fact that it was possible to impose on the goodwill of agricultural labourers? Since Olive does not appear to have been tried, the incident clearly throws up more questions than the brief pre-trial legal documents and collection of letters can answer. Did Fred Larner really meet Olive on a train, and why do Smith/Olive's letters have such a speculative character? Did he make a habit of befriending labourers? For all its impenetrability, the extraordinary meeting of Larner and Olive is representative in some ways. I suggest that in spite of its exceptional features it does tell us a few key facts about the way homosexual behaviour was policed in nineteenth-century England. Firstly, the alleged offences took place in private, and secondly, their private nature did not place these supposed crimes beyond the reach of the law. They were, in fact, brought to the attention of the police not by diligent detection on their part, but by an interested third party, on whose motives we can only speculate. In 1658, and perhaps even in 1758, Rev Olive might have got away with his indiscretions, but by 1858 this kind of impunity was no longer possible. It was clear that even the bedrooms of agricultural labourers, far from urban subcultures and associated modern forms of policing, could be the arena of legal investigation when 'certain crimes' were involved. Olive's case, and thousands like it before and since, ensured that the punishment of 'unnatural crimes' became a troubling and inescapable part of English society. In the nineteenth century, homosexual behaviour was punished on a scale never before witnessed in English law. Although homosexual offences were a tiny proportion of total crimes, they were nevertheless regarded as some of the most loathsome and serious. And although 'sodomites' represented a small percentage of the total number of convictions, it was still the case that thousands of men went to prison and hundreds were sentenced to death for no more than having consenting sex. This chapter is devoted to explaining how this came to be the case. What exactly was a homosexual offence, and how were these cases prosecuted? Why did so many of them reach the courts in the nineteenth century? Who prosecuted the cases, and what was the attitude of the authorities? These questions can only be answered using the fragmentary evidence which remains, but an overall impression of the nature of 'unnatural offences' can be gained.

Although historians have described homosexual offences before, the question of what forms of behaviour actually constituted a crime at the beginning of the nineteenth century is still relatively unclear. This lack of clarity is partly the consequence of the retrospective interpretations of those, like the Liberal MP Henry Labouchere, who took it upon themselves to change the law and thereby reinvigorate public morals. On 6 August 1885, Labouchere moved his now notorious amendment outlawing acts of 'gross indecency' between men both in private and in public. He justified his clause by arguing that before 1885, 'the law was insufficient to deal with it, because the offence had to proved by an accessory, and many other offences very much of the same nature were not regarded as crimes at all'. He had therefore provided the means by which 'Parliament armed the guardians of public morality with full powers to deal with this offence'.[4]

In spite of Labouchere's claims, it is now clear that his efforts did not change the law in a dramatic fashion. As the case of the Rev Olive shows, it was possible to prosecute all kinds of homosexual behaviour, consenting or otherwise, in public as well as in private, long before 1885. This was possible because homosexual offences could be prosecuted under a law which predated Labouchere's amendment by three centuries. This law, which outlawed all forms of sodomy, dated back to the reign of Henry VIII. His statute, passed in 1533, was adapted, probably during the eighteenth century, to outlaw all homosexual acts. Labouchere's amendment, therefore, was not a radical break with the past, but part of a process which had begun a century before. It was the settled practice of the common law to treat any attempt to commit a crime as an offence in itself. Therefore any homosexual act came to be regarded in law as an attempt to commit sodomy, and hence fell under the jurisdiction of the 1533 law.

It is also clear that during the eighteenth century the common law had made it possible to prosecute a number of relatively new offences, which from then on were grouped together as 'unnatural crimes'. This term covered sodomy, bestiality and any homosexual act or invitation to the act, usually described as indecent assault or 'assault with intent to commit sodomy'. These offences were applied in two ways, which affected both public and private expressions of homosexual desire. Sexual commerce on the streets of major cities began to be increasingly circumscribed, while private and consenting acts, which had hitherto passed largely without the intervention of the courts, were also more likely to be prosecuted. At that date, the development of case law and the application of the sodomy statute to cover all kinds of homosexual acts amounted to the most sustained assault on homosexual behaviour ever carried out in England.

Why did this happen? Historians have interpreted the increasing stigmatisation of homosexual behaviour in a number of ways. An apparent consensus among historians suggests that the eighteenth century was a key period for the formation of modern categories of gender. Randolph Trumbach has suggested that the emergence of a doctrine of human rights, which at the very least promoted theoretical equality of individuals, necessitated new justifications for gender inequality.[5] Therefore, new rules for gendered conduct based on the supposed 'natural' differences of the sexes emerged. In particular, Trumbach suggests that a greater investment in heterosexual relations and marriage led to increasing stigmatisation of same-sex acts and the emergence of identifiable 'homosexual' men and women, defined by the inversion of their gender. These men and women, 'mollies' and 'tommies', were then subject to persecution by vice societies and moralising churchmen. Dror Wahrman and Katherine Binhammer similarly detect a 'gender panic' at the end of the eighteenth century, in which stricter rules of male and female behaviour emerged in response to anxieties about emergent discourses of human rights, foreign revolution, internal security and the social order. Thomas Laqueur's famous contention is that anatomical and scientific descriptions of the male and female body reflected these cultural imperatives. In particular, he has suggested that the homologous and functionally similar gendered bodies of early modern anatomy were replaced in the late eighteenth century by the description of fundamentally distinct genders differentiated on the basis of their reproductive organs.[6]

However, the answer to this question emerging from the legal sources is that it took place partly by what might be called a process of accident rather than by coherent design. Rising numbers of homosexual offences were a by-product of other changes to the structure of criminal justice, which acted to increase the level of prosecution for all other offences. Sodomy trials increased in number at the end of the eighteenth century along with prosecutions for crimes against property and other crimes against the person. However, there was no single intention on the part of police, state or reforming moralists to persecute an identifiable group of men who might be 'addicted' to unnatural lust and who had gathered in urban subcultures. During the period of expansion in homosexual offences, roughly between 1780 and 1850, the majority of cases seem to have come to court in a manner that might be expected given the nature of criminal justice at the time, that is via unrelated, individual decisions to prosecute. The campaigns of moral reformers do not appear to have been the principal reason for the institutionalisation of sodomy prosecutions. That is not to say that changes to the structure and practice of the criminal law did not have a moral intention. Evangelicals and reforming magistrates hoped to increase the level of prosecution, and thereby both restore morals and revive a flagging social order. But this intention frequently took the form of attempting to empower the prosecutor, rather than directly intervening in individual cases of immorality. Cultural change and moral ideas, then, acted at one remove from the structure of criminal justice.

Therefore, in spite of the seismic nature of cultural change at the end of the eighteenth century, it is difficult to make a direct connection between the majority of decisions to prosecute and wider religious, moral or cultural changes. The available evidence suggests that in only a few cases did moral reformers or zealous magistrates play a part in the investigation or prosecution of sexual offences. Those who proposed new moral codes and accepted what Louise Jackson has called a 'Christian moral economy', which linked personal sin and social disorder, did not necessarily involve themselves in the prosecution of sex offences.[7] Neither did they take what we now call sexual offences as their primary goal. Morality could simply be more easily enforced by encouraging the observance of the sabbath and discouraging overt signs of public disorder. Changes in the structure of justice instead produced a framework by which private disputes could be placed within the jurisdiction of the courts. Clearly, these cases might have been motivated by a surrounding culture of moral reform or evangelical Christianity, but prosecutors, in the few recorded instances of motivation, rarely indicate that this was the case. Personal disputes over moral infractions were, as a result, increasingly settled not using folk remedies like 'rough music' or informal violence, but by recourse to legal means. In the early nineteenth century at least, ordinary people were not the victims of upper-class moral codes and instead appear to have increasingly prosecuted each other rather than being prosecuted by their social superiors. What happened at the end of the eighteenth century, then, was that it became easier than ever for individual prosecutors to take the initiative in solving legal disputes and in bringing cases to court.

Therefore, the most sustained legal assault on homosexual behaviour in English legal history, which set a pattern of prosecution and punishment that lasted at least until 1967, was made up of countless individual and separate decisions. As we shall see, some localised efforts by moral reformers and the state did produce small clusters of prosecutions, but these were not very common. That is not to say that the history of homosexuality should not be part of a history of moral governance, or that it can be isolated from cultural change. Instead the evidence presented here merely complicates this picture. In particular, this chapter locates the regulation of sexuality not necessarily in the decisions of those in authority, and not in elite texts of anatomy and sexual science, but primarily at a local and familiar level.

The state was also reluctant to intervene directly in these cases before the 1850s. As is the case with other crimes, the police do not appear to have become involved in prosecuting sex offences on a large scale until the end of the 1840s. New policing systems simply did not have the manpower, resources or the political will to punish sexual offences on a large scale in the first years of their existence. As a result, they were usually dependent on individuals bringing homosexual offences to their attention. As in other types of offence, the private individual assumed a large measure of responsibility for initiating the early stages of investigation and prosecution. In this way, the private individual and the prosecutor unwittingly assisted in the extension of surveillance and policing not only to the public world but also to the private sphere.

METHOD

The difficulty of this research was compounded by the English legal tradition of trying not to name the crime of sodomy. Although records which historians have relied on for nineteenth-century legal history, such as the Old Bailey Sessions Papers, record most criminal trials in exhaustive detail, the same cannot be said for transcripts of sodomy trials. Nineteenth-century sessions papers list only the offence and the verdict in these cases. In contrast to the relatively scrupulous recording of eighteenth-century trials, the evidence in subsequent cases of 'unnatural crime' was simply not recorded and, even when it was, it has been destroyed. High-profile cases, such as the trial of Boulton and Park and the Cleveland Street scandal, both dealt with below, were considered worthy of record, but most of the trials of ordinary men were not. Therefore, I have had to rely on the fortuitous survival of some documents and case papers, legal briefs and the occasional police report. Fragmentary records such as indictments exist in large numbers, but tell us little.

In these circumstances, newspaper reports are a vital, if problematic resource. The press reported trials and committal hearings at length, often over several days, and included a large amount of the evidence and other information. However, the content of newspaper reports clearly reflects editorial decisions about what was both significant and decent. Much of the evidence in cases of unnatural crime consisted of determining who did what to whom, most of which was deemed unfit for publication. I have nevertheless included information from a sample of 332 newspaper reports in the statistics presented below, especially when the age and occupation of offenders, prosecutors and 'victims' is recorded. Newspaper evidence may not be representative, in that it is usually biased towards London and would deal with the crimes of gentlemen in more detail than others, but even with these limitations it has value. In particular, it can show us how a public image of the 'sodomite' was produced by dwelling on certain characteristic features of the crime, in particular the secretive nature of offenders, or more strongly, the association of sodomy with the city.

Using this variety of sources, I have collected information on 750 cases out of the 8,000 or so committals which took place in the nineteenth century. Some of these cases are trials, others are indictments, threatening letters, extortion cases, proceedings and Home Office papers. This represents an unsystematic sample. For example, sodomy/indecent assault indictments present a particular problem. Owing to their relative scarcity and the fact that they are hidden inside a mass of documentation for other crimes, I have tended to choose years in which there were a large number of indictments, so as to facilitate the ease of research. In using the indictments, I have also tended to concentrate on evidence that can tell me how prosecutions proceeded before 1850. Therefore, my research into indictments is concentrated in the period 1790–1850. I have also followed the assumption of most legal historians that the police assumed prosecutorial duties in most cases by 1850. This method, and the difficulties of finding indictments, means that my sample of 185 indictments from London courts and 85 from outside London is concentrated in particular years, namely 1798, 1825, 1828, 1835, 1836, 1840, 1841 and 1844.

The other principal sources used here are the 105 surviving petitions written by those convicted of homosexual offences before 1870. It might be assumed that these were written only by the literate or those able to afford to have the documents transcribed. However, although this is true of some of them, a large proportion relate to ordinary offenders and even illiterate labourers who had been condemned to death. It was not uncommon for the associates of an 'ignorant' labourer, even including magistrates and gentlemen, to organise and sign petitions which attempted to save the life of the unfortunate offender. The petitions contain invaluable information and also present the voice of the offender, which is not otherwise heard.

The statistical evidence presented below is therefore far from systematic. I present it here as a digest of the available information, and as a guide to an overall impression of the law in this area. Some of the statistics, which are based on newspaper reports, tell us more about the public perception of offenders than they do about the majority of offenders. This information is nevertheless important in demonstrating how the image of the offender was made. Where conclusions have been drawn from the data, they are backed up by anecdotal evidence from other sources, and tend to confirm what is assumed about general nineteenth-century patterns of prosecution.

Trends in the Prosecution of Sodomy, 1750–1900

As we have seen, legal and cultural changes in the status of homosexual behaviour have usually been interpreted as the combination of two main factors. The first is a conscious intention on the part of social elites to stigmatise or eradicate immorality in response to major shifts in the understanding of gender, religion, subjectivity and culture. The second 'agent' in these explanations is usually the progress of statute law, again interpreted as a conscious attempt by governments to establish a moral standard by specifying the illegality of same-sex acts. Yet statute was usually a long way behind the common law and simply confirmed patterns of policing, sentencing and prosecution which had grown up in response to local necessity. Moreover, the greatest periods of expansion in the numbers of prosecutions occurred independently of changes in statute law. Economic and social change was also distantly related to the progress of justice in this area. Instead, the most reliable speculations are those which explain trends in criminal justice by reference to changes internal to the justice system.

As can be seen in Figure 1, there was an uneven increase in the numbers of committals for sodomy, assault with intent to commit, incitement to and soliciting the offence and all other 'unnatural misdemeanours',[8] during the first half of the nineteenth century. Committals for all 'unnatural offences' rose in the first half of the century before levelling off to a relatively constant proportion of population.[9] However, absolute numbers of committals for indecent assault continued to increase throughout the century. These figures testify to a qualitative as well as a quantitative change in the nature of prosecution. In particular, the figures, as well as other evidence which I discuss below, point towards the increasingly routine character of prosecutions for sexual misbehaviour. Arrests in the nineteenth century would no longer result from sustained campaigns against a 'molly' minority, as appeared to be the case in the previous century, but would stem mainly from the location of these offences at the heart of common life, in every-day encounters, casual accusations, rejected advances and forced proximity.

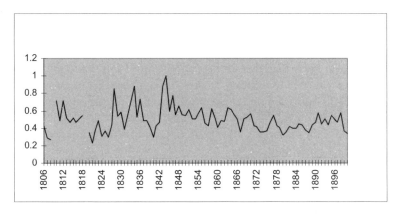

Figure 1. Committals for Sodomy and Related Misdemeanours per 100,000 population, 1806–1900. [10]

Figure 1 indicates that committals for homosexual offences represented a very small part of the total number of prosecutions, and scarcely reached one per 100,000 of population at any time during the nineteenth century. However, it has to be borne in mind that sodomy was one of the few capital crimes to survive Peel's reform of the death penalty during the 1820s, and that other 'unnatural crimes' were regarded as some of the most serious which could be committed.[11] These crimes were commonly pronounced beyond nature and understanding and therefore crossed the boundary of common humanity. In addition, homosexual acts always appeared to have come from nowhere, to be permanently on the increase, and therefore to have a kind of unseen, menacing ubiquity.

It should also be remembered that official statistics of committals for trial represent only the tip of an iceberg. When we look at cases dealt with in magistrate's courts, we find that the numbers of arrests were as much as one third higher than the level of committal.[12] Also, the statistical category 'offences known to the police', representing crimes which were not always prosecuted, was frequently twice as large as the official figure for committals. In addition, other categories of offence covering crimes against public decency, indecent exposure, loitering, vagrancy and disorderly behaviour were also used to regulate homosexual behaviour, further obscuring the actual volume of formal and informal policing.

The most noticeable statistical trend is the difference in the volume of committals between the eighteenth and nineteenth centuries. This sustained increase, as opposed to intermittent clusters of cases, was a genuinely new phenomenon. The law had been occasionally used against sodomites throughout the eighteenth century, mainly in the 1720s by vice societies keen to destroy the culture of London's mollies. Yet the level of yearly committals for sodomy and related offences before about 1780 was far lower than that for the period 1780–1850. The latter period saw a gradual, steady increase in the absolute numbers of committals per head of population and the establishment of 'unnatural crimes' as a permanent and regular feature of criminal justice.

Studies of the operation of the law in eighteenth-century London, where the number of committals for same-sex acts was usually greatest in any year, shows that trials for sodomy and related offences usually occurred in groups at widely-spaced intervals. Looking at Old Bailey trials in the period between 1752 and 1795, Anthony Simpson discovered only 22 indictments, the vast majority at the end of that period.[13] As Figure 2 illustrates, the 1780s seem to mark a turning point, in that the pattern of indictments presented at the Old Bailey shows a sudden acceleration in the numbers of committals after this date. In a 23-year period between 1756 and 1779, only 24 indictments were presented, whereas, in the ten years between 1779 and 1789, 35 similar bills were put before the Grand Jury. Fourteen indictments were presented in 1798 alone.[14]

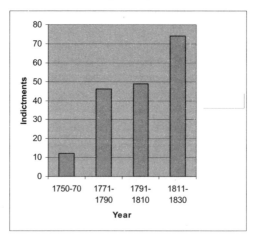

Figure 2. Indictments for Sodomy, Indecent Assault and other Homosexual Offences Presented at the Old Bailey, 1750–1830.[15]

Sodomy and indecent assault generally followed the same trends as other types of crime, especially between 1780 and 1850. Between 1806 (when reliable records begin) and 1900, over 8,000 men and one or two women were committed for trial in England and Wales. This total includes all the various descriptions of the crime: sodomy, assault with intent 'and other unnatural misdemeanours' and gross indecency between men. On average, 89 committals took place every year. However, in some years, especially during the 1840s, more than 150 men were committed.[16] In London, trials and committal hearings were more frequent than elsewhere partly because of the existence of police courts which were constantly in session. By the 1830s, at least one committal hearing per week was being heard in front of one or other of the capital's magistrates, and given the directly proportional relationship between numbers of committals and hearings before magistrates, there is little reason to suppose that the numbers declined as the century progressed. The national figures are made up of at least three different offences: bestiality, indecent assault (that is advances or acts where consent was ostensibly withheld) and consenting sex between men. Bestiality was more common outside London, while in the capital and surrounding counties like Kent and Surrey the majority of indictments were for same-sex acts.[17]

The majority of committals were for indecent assault or assault with intent to commit sodomy. These terms appear to have been synonymous, but were also used to describe consenting acts. In contrast, Simpson has pointed out that the majority of offences which reached the courts in mid-eighteenth-century London were for sexual assaults, principally on children and youths by older men. Louise Jackson, in an analysis of all kinds of sexual assaults prosecuted in nineteenth-century England, also concludes that most of these cases involved assaults on children.[18] Yet when we look at the age profile of the victims/sexual partners in homosexual offences reported in the press and in criminal petitions for the nineteenth century (Figure 3), we find that this is far from being the case.

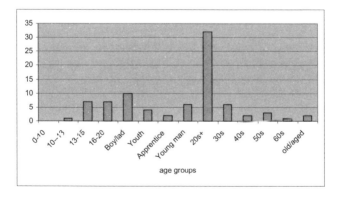

Figure 3: Age profile of Victims/Partners in homosexual offences reported in the press and criminal petitions (where stated), 1800–1900. Source: Newspapers, Criminal Petitions. Total: 83 cases.

This sample suggests that the largest group of victims/partners were adult men. This age group comprises a large number of assaults on soldiers, men in the street and policemen, whose age was either stated, or who can be expected to be at least in their twenties. The next largest groups were probably adolescent, given either their stated age or their description in press or case papers as 'boys,' 'lads' or 'youths' in the press. It also has to be borne in mind that the term lad or youth could describe a wide difference in age from early adolescence to early adulthood.

Adult men seem to have made up the largest group of reported victims, and were also the largest group of offenders. Figure 4 indicates that those between 16 and 30 made up 44 per cent of reported offenders. From these samples, it seems that the vast majority of reported offences took place between adults, rather than, as Jackson has intimated, on children by adults. A large proportion of offences also appear to have been consenting, a fact which I will return to below.

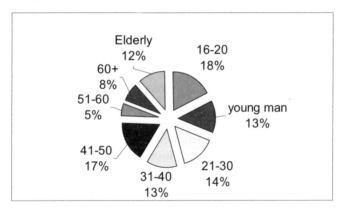

Figure 4: Age of Offenders (where stated), 1800–1900. Source: Newspapers, Criminal Petitions, Home Office Papers. Total: 77 cases where age stated.

What type of people were committing these offences? When this is stated in press reports and legal documents, it is clear that a wide variety of classes and occupations were involved. Figure 5, compiled from 128 cases reported in newspapers, home office papers and criminal petitions, shows that the largest single occupational/status groups represented in reported cases were artisans/skilled labourers and gentlemen. The preponderance of gentlemen and other professionals like clergymen and teachers in press reports clearly reflects editorial decisions about what was likely to be of interest to a public fascinated by the transgressions of the respectable. Also, the number of soldiers indicates that most press reports dealt with the concentration of cases in London. In spite of these limitations, this sample can provide at least some indication of the classes involved. The other major source used here, bills of indictment, tells a slightly different story. These list almost every offender as a 'labourer', although this may have represented formal legal language rather than an actual description of a prisoner's occupation. Artisans, labourers and those in service make up nearly 50 per cent of the sample of offenders in Figure 5, while gentlemen make up more than one fifth. The preponderance of artisans and gentlemen in this sample perhaps reflects the fact that many reported cases described assignations across class, especially when these took place on London streets.

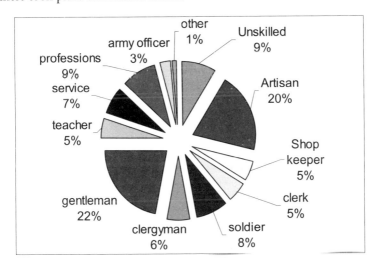

Figure 5: Occupation/social status of those arrested for homosexual offences (where stated), 1800–1900. Source: Criminal Petitions, Home Office Papers, Newspaper reports. Total: 100 cases.

The cases in the above samples often describe unwanted advances made in a public place with the clear expectation that they might be accepted. This fact indicates that consenting sex was readily available on the streets of London. If Simpson is correct in his analysis of eighteenth-century prosecutions, it was also the case that a higher proportion of consensual sex was prosecuted in the nineteenth century than ever before.[19] This is demonstrated by the sample of 212 cases from the press and criminal petitions shown in Figure 6. This sample is slightly skewed by the inclusion of a raid on a fancy dress ball in 1880, with the 47 men arrested there included as participating in what the law would describe as consenting acts, indecent conduct or incitement to the offence. In spite of the apparent preponderance of consenting sex in the sample presented in Figure 6, bills of indictment again complicate this picture somewhat. The majority of indictments presented in London in the 1830s and 1840s specified that the offence was an indecent assault which was defined by an absence of consent. For example, of 31 indictments presented at the Central Criminal Court in 1836, only eight explicitly described consenting sex.[20]

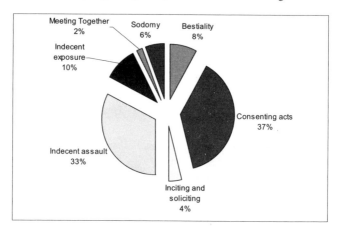

Figure 6: Types of offences reported in the press and criminal petitions (where specified), 1800–1900. Total: 212 cases.

These figures suggest that a large proportion of these cases were non-consenting. However, we should be wary of using indictments as a guide to the actual level of consenting sex. The charge of indecent assault was often used retrospectively as a means to ensure that one of the partners could testify against the other, since if both had given consent their evidence would have required further corroboration. In addition, the term 'indecent assault' was often used as a shorthand term in legal documents to connote consenting sex. This was particularly true of the Daily Reports from London's magistrate's courts, which I will discuss in more detail in chapter two. In 1836 for example, two men were arrested in a London street for the paradoxical offence of 'indecently assaulting each other'.[21] Similarly, 'suffering and permitting' a sexual act to take place on one's own body could itself be construed as part of an offence, or as one count in an indictment, but could be described on the bill and in official statistics as a 'misdemeanour' or an 'assault'.[22] Moreover, consent was often difficult to determine and was frequently a legal grey area. In addition, many of those cases in which it was claimed that an advance was made were frequently surrounded by suggestions of extortion and conspiracy. Therefore, estimating the actual number of consenting homosexual acts which were prosecuted is problematic. Official statistics and press reports probably underestimate the proportion of consenting acts.

Where did these offences take place? Most of those cases reported in the press happened in London, and when it can be determined, were the result of public encounters and advances. A significant proportion of these cases were also the result of private assignations, deliberately or unwittingly witnessed by others. The location is only specified in a small number of cases, yet some indication of their distribution between public and private space can be made. The offences shown in Figure 7 would seem to indicate that the most heavily policed area of homosexual contact was the 'cruise', the public quest for a sexual partner, which in these cases took men to certain streets and metropolitan parks. Public places including urinals and theatres made up just more than half of the offences prosecuted in this admittedly metropolitan sample, whereas private places such as rooms, lodgings or private rooms in pubs or hotels made up 42.8 per cent. Cases reported in the press should clearly be treated with some caution, as they refer primarily to London and its subcultures. Yet this sample nevertheless gives us an indication of the nature and location of a metropolitan public culture of assignation which was increasingly subject to the surveillance of the police as the century wore on.

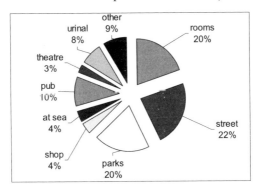

Figure 7: Location of offences reported in the press and criminal petitions (where stated), 1800–1900. Source: Newspapers and Criminal Petitions. Total: 105 cases.

Although most of the samples shown above deal with London, the national picture shown in parliamentary judicial statistics shows a similar intensification of prosecution and punishment. In particular, these figures show that homosexual offences followed the same statistical trends as other types of crime. The number of trials per head of population follows the same pattern recently outlined by Howard Taylor for crime in general in England and Wales.23 During the period c.1780–1850, the numbers of trials for all crimes outpaced growth in the population by seven times. This period of expansion coincided with the rise of moral reform, the emergence of prosecution societies which sought to raise funds for private prosecutions and the increasing tendency of the courts to pay the costs of the prosecutor. Taylor argues that the absolute numbers of committals after 1850 are remarkably stable, with almost exactly the same amount being sent to trial every year until about 1925. However, although homosexual offences per head of population conform to this trend, in absolute terms they tend to contradict Taylor's picture. As Figure 8 shows, the total number of committals for indecent assault tended to keep rising against a stable background of committal for other crimes, especially in the 1890s, when 'indecency with males' was added to the official statistical record of homosexual crimes. Sodomy, on the other hand, went into gradual decline as a criminal offence after 1850, reflecting the increasing use of the more flexible charge of indecent assault.

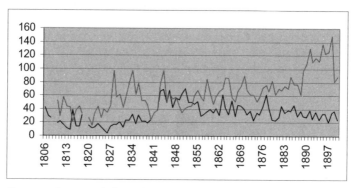

Figure 8: Committals for Sodomy (dark line), Indecent Assault and 'other Unnatural Misdemeanours' (light line) in England and Wales, 1806–1892.

Given the pattern of offences, direct changes in statute law relating to offences against the person cannot be said to have had a very marked effect on the national level of prosecution. The major legislative changes were in 1828, 1861, 1885 and 1898. The first of these changed the requirements of evidence in sodomy trials from penetration and emission in the body to penetration only.[24] The 1861 Offences Against the Person Act formally abolished the death penalty for sodomy and introduced instead life sentences of penal servitude. It also formalised maximum and minimum sentences for indecent assault by introducing a prison term of between two and ten years as the standard sentence.[25] In 1885, Labouchere's amendment ostensibly introduced the new offence of 'gross indecency', but did not enlarge the scope of the law any further. Neither did it affect sentencing practice in a noticeable fashion. The law regarding soliciting was changed in 1898, making it possible to prosecute someone for 'importuning' a homosexual offence. However, as I will show in chapter two, this legislation also formalised the existing practice of prosecuting the offences of incitement to sodomy and of vagrancy. Although homosexual offences were increasingly specified as separate crimes worthy of specific treatment, changes in statute were mainly confirmations of existing common law practice. The practice of the courts anticipated all the legislative changes in this area. Therefore, changes in the law were not a conscious effort by successive governments to enforce an abstract 'bourgeois' moral standard, as some recent work has suggested, but an attempt to catch up with practice determined at a local level in response to the daily needs of court, prosecutor and police.[26]

As we have seen, Labouchere's amendment of 1885 did not revolutionise the law or move its focus from sexual acts to particular 'homosexual' types of people, as has been frequently claimed. If it had any effect, it was the delayed one shown in Figure 8, which shows an apparent increase in committals following the 1892 addition of 'gross indecency' to national statistics. In relation to population, the level of committal remained substantially the same after 1885. Neither did Labouchere change much in legal terms. Although his clause specified a new description of offence by outlawing 'gross indecency', this term was increasingly used to define consenting acts, which, as we have seen, were illegal anyway. In addition, it is often argued that Labouchere's amendment represented a move away from the harsh penalties of an earlier legal regime in which sodomy had been punishable by death, and towards a more modern, graduated and more easily applied set of offences. Sentencing regimes did become more regular towards the end of the century, and sodomy was increasingly punished by ten-year terms of penal servitude rather than death. However, sentencing in indecent assault did not become more lenient, as a comparison of pre and post-1885 sentences will suggest. In 1844 the average sentence for indecent assault was 16.05 months, while in 1887 it was 25 months.[27] This trend probably reflected the regularisation of sentencing which followed changes in statute law, as well as the difficulty juries seem to have experienced in deciding guilt before 1850. Yet the fact remains that local practice was more important than legislation in changing the law. The nature of the law, as well as any decision to prosecute, was overwhelmingly determined by local pressures and individual necessity.

The criminal law, then, was employed most frequently at a local level. In the period of the greatest expansion of homosexual offences, it threatened to intervene in almost any circumstance and could be applied to any acts anywhere. By 1800, at the very latest, it had developed the pervasive reach which enabled the arrest of the Rev Olive. It is clearly the case that both public and private sexual acts or advances were increasingly subject to criminal prosecution after about 1780. Also consenting acts were more likely to be subject to legal intervention. These developments, along with sporadic assaults on public indecency, can only have had the effect of policing same-sex desire to a much greater extent than the statistics of actual committals might suggest. The casual indulgence of homosexual desire, which Alan Bray and Tim Hitchcock see as characteristic of everyday living arrangements in the seventeenth and eighteenth centuries, was, if not rendered impossible, then hedged about with far greater dangers than ever before.[28] Fred Larner and his gentlemanly suitor, and thousands like them, were no longer beyond the reach of the courts in theory or in practice.

WHAT COUNTED AS AN OFFENCE?

As we have seen, sodomy had been made a civil offence in 1533 by Henry VIII, a law confirmed during the reign of Elizabeth I. Although the 1533 Act did not attempt to define what was meant by 'buggery', later jurists attempted to specify what the act of sodomy actually described in law. Sir Edward Coke's *Institutes of the Laws of England* (1642) defined it as anal penetration of a man by a man, or a woman by a man. With animals, penetration by a man was required, but any act between a woman and an animal appears to have been defined as sodomy.[29] In 1781, a judicial ruling specified that the emission of sperm in the body was required for the offence to be complete, but in 1828 this was reversed and the older rule (requiring penetration only) reinstated.[30] For a charge of sodomy to be made, there had to have been an act of *anal* penetration, whether emission was necessary or not.[31] Oral penetration was not actual sodomy, but still counted as a crime, usually an assault.[32] While sodomy itself appears to have had a very precise definition, other related charges like assault with intent to commit sodomy, inciting someone to the act, or conspiring or soliciting the act could be extended to cover all sorts of sexual acts or words. One of the earliest recorded prosecutions for attempted buggery took place in 1699, when a clergyman was fined £100 for his offence.[33] By 1700 at the latest, and certainly by 1800, almost any advance or suggestion of intimacy could, it seems, be interpreted as an attempt to commit the felony (sodomy) and was therefore a criminal act. A great variety of sexual acts, overtures and invitations were criminalised by the interpretation of the 1533 Act. However, as we have seen, the law was not applied in the widespread manner that later became customary until the late eighteenth century. Most of the case law which defined sodomy and indecent assault relates to a formative period between 1780 and about 1840. Clearly, new interpretations of existing laws were demanded by the increasing ability of the courts to punish homosexual behaviour.

The legal meaning of indecent assault and other offences which fell short of the actual felony was therefore determined in response to the questions raised by individual cases after 1780. Indecent assault and other charges which came into the general category of unnatural crimes could also describe a variety of circumstances. As we have seen, indecent assault could be used in an imprecise way in some forms of legal documentation. Although sexual assault is by definition a case in which consent to any sexual acts is withheld, it could also have certain specific meanings. Sometimes the felony could not be proved, so therefore the charge was reduced to indecent assault which was a misdemeanour. When this happened, it could mean two things. It could have been that the offence was not 'completed' in the eyes of the law (that is penetration, or emission before 1828, did not take place or was not witnessed satisfactorily) or that a prosecutor, magistrate or jury did not wish to press the capital charge. This seems to have been the case in a large proportion of bestiality trials where the indictment is marked 'guilty of the attempt only'.[34]

An unnatural crime of any kind, including an indecent assault, could include consenting sexual acts such as oral sex, kissing, touching or mutual masturbation, plus attempts to force someone to have sex or to engage in any homosexual acts.[35] The crime of a gentleman named Henry Arundel, for instance, was merely embracing and kissing a youth in Berkeley Square, for which he was charged with an indecent assault.[36] Although fellatio was not actual sodomy, it could still be grounds for a charge either of indecent assault, or of 'suffering and permitting' this to take place. Thomas Buttle, for instance, was indicted at the Old Bailey in 1823 for 'unlawfully receiving the naked private parts of a person in his mouth'. In a similar way, other kinds of touching were also criminalised. The crime of John Day was 'permitting a person to handle [his] private parts naked'.[37] In addition, acts and words could also be subject to the law. Charges which were subsidiary to sodomy or indecent assault included soliciting the offence and conspiracy or incitement to the act, both of which covered words, letters or gestures. The laws used to police public space such as those covering the crimes of indecent exposure, vagrancy and arrest on suspicion were also employed to control public sex, but because they were subject to summary jurisdiction in magistrates' courts, carried far more lenient punishments than charge of assault with intent to commit sodomy.

It was also possible to charge offenders with 'meeting together' for the purpose of committing sodomy, or with making indecent overtures to each other. The latter was regarded as 'inciting and soliciting' someone to the offence and seems to have been a crime as long as it could be fixed to particular words or phrases. Meeting was the offence of Thomas Powell and George Murray who were tried in September 1839. The indictment said that they 'unlawfully did meet… in a certain privy… with intent and for the purpose of committing divers filthy, wicked nasty lewd and beastly unnatural and sodomitical acts and practices'.[38] Similarly, Edward Harrison and James Neil were tried in May 1841 for laying hands on each other in the street and in a second count were charged with simply meeting in the street for the purpose of committing 'sodomitical acts and practices'.[39]

The charge of 'conspiracy to commit sodomy' could also be employed 'after the fact' but was notoriously difficult to prove. Conspiracy was used when a *prima facie* case was suggested by the existence of letters, photographs or other incriminating circumstances, but when the evidence to the sexual acts was unavailable or unreliable. In the trials following the Dublin Castle scandals in 1883–4, the charges against the principal defendants were 'incitement to commit the offence', 'conspiring to incite the commission' and 'conspiracy to procure the commission of sodomy', based on the evidence of letters and witnesses.[40] Yet most of the trials which followed the Dublin scandal ended in acquittal or disagreement of the jury over the charge. The charge of incitement to or solicitation of sodomy was equally difficult to prove, since it seems to have required that specific invitations to the acts be both heard by a witness and attributed to particular individuals.[41]

The only factor preventing the prosecution of homosexual acts was the difficulty of finding competent witnesses, which itself depended on definitions of consent, and whether the offence could be described as sufficiently public. Public in this sense did not refer to a physical location, but merely to the presence of competent witnesses, that is, those who were not involved in the sexual acts themselves, or those who were involved, but had not consented. Therefore, in order to prosecute homosexual behaviour, it was imperative that any consent to the acts be denied or later proved not to have been given.

INTERPRETING CONSENT AND CORROBORATION

The criminal law had a considerable reach, but the possibility of prosecution depended on the law of evidence and in particular on the interpretation of consent. In general, the evidence of a sexual partner or 'victim' was crucial and was often the only evidence available. In such a situation, this evidence could only be used to convict if the victim/partner had not consented to the acts in question. By 1807, English law required that the evidence of an accomplice be corroborated.[42] Anyone over the age of 14 who consented to sodomy or indecency was a principal in the acts themselves, and therefore regarded in law as such an accomplice. If both parties stated that they had given their consent, then they were both accomplices to the act and as such their evidence would require corroboration. Therefore, if the acts were consenting, and there were no other witnesses, the offence was sufficiently 'private' to prevent the possibility of prosecution. A 'public' offence was one which was seen by a competent witness, that is, someone who was not willingly participating in the acts. This meant that public and private were defined according to the rules of evidence and the number of competent witnesses, that is those who were not accomplices – and not by any reference to the location of the offence.

The requirements of evidence also complicate the question of consent and whether it was given in a number of cases. As I will show below when discussing the Finsbury Square prosecutions of 1798, the absence of consent might be retrospectively construed or insisted upon. Also, a witness who might have given his consent at the time could not be relied upon to preserve his alliance with a defendant and therefore render him immune to prosecution. If a sexual partner could be persuaded to retrospectively withdraw his consent, his evidence could be used to convict without corroboration.

The rule requiring corroboration also appears to be have been selectively employed. In one example at least, it appears to have been the case that the evidence of only one *consenting* partner was enough to convict. In 1877, a gentleman named James Smith, who claimed connection to the aristocracy and the upper ranks of the Conservative party, was sentenced to life imprisonment for sodomy with a 16-year-old telegraph messenger called George Wright. He was convicted in spite of the fact that the offence had taken place in private – in Smith's home – with no other person present, and that Wright's evidence was unsupported. Wright had given his consent, in that he had, like many other Victorian Telegraph boys, been paid for services not covered in his job description.

After being pressured by the police to give evidence for the prosecution, Wright pleaded guilty at the trial to participating in sodomy with Smith, but his evidence still went uncorroborated. Smith protested to the Home Secretary, complaining that legal rules had been flouted. He was sure, he told the authorities, 'that the evidences of at least two independent witnesses of the actual perpetration of the alleged crime were indispensably necessary before the case could be legally left to the Jury'. He claimed that the arresting detective, realising the limits of the prosecution's case, had gone to see Wright's mother and told her that since, 'the Government were prosecuting and as he [Wright] was in their employ "it would be better for him to plead 'guilty' and turn Queen's evidence"'.[43] This fact, along with unsubstantiated charges by other telegraph boys, had ensured his conviction.

Smith also argued that the rules of evidence had been suspended in order to make an example of him. He claimed that he had been informed by his solicitor that:

> the crime for which I am sentenced has been very prevalent amongst the Telegraph lads and that many have been found out and dismissed in consequence and that the authorities were determined to prosecute me... as a warning to others, but I most respectfully submit that the Treasury ought to have obtained some *independent* testimony before pressing for a conviction instead of relying on the unsupported testimony of lads who admitted having allowed themselves to be defiled for five shillings.[44]

It would appear from this case that corroboration of the acts themselves was not always necessary.

The use of a single witness was not without its critics, who saw it as a threat to the liberty of men generally. In 1842, another gentleman, John Ellis Churchill, was accused of an indecent assault in Hyde Park and the case went before the magistrate at Marlborough Street. Soon afterwards, a letter appeared in *The Times* from 'A Solicitor' arguing that the case had proceeded, and Churchill been committed for trial (on bail of £2,000), despite the fact that there was only one thoroughly unreliable witness, the man who had given Churchill in charge to a policeman. If this were to be the law, the Solicitor asked, 'what security is there for any man's reputation?' According to the magistrate's decision:

> it appears that a gentleman cannot walk through Hyde Park unless he be strong enough to knock down any blackguard who may find it more convenient to lay his betters under contribution in this legal and authorised manner, than to subject himself to the penalties due to highway robberies.[45]

Although rules requiring the corroboration of evidence when given by a sexual partner were in place, they appear to have been imperfectly respected. In addition, in the case of Smith it appears that only one witness was necessary to secure a conviction. Therefore the legal protection of private acts afforded by the rules of evidence appears to have offered only a minimal degree of assurance that a prosecution could not take place.

Defining Public and Private

As we have seen, private offences were partly made so by the rules of evidence. In this context, public sex meant acts which had taken place in the presence of a witness who could testify. Therefore, acts taking place 'in private', that is in private rooms or similar locations, were on the same legal footing as those taking place in the street or park. It has often been assumed that the law before 1885 did not punish homosexual acts which took place in private. There are two reasons for this. The first is section 11 of the Criminal Law Amendment Act of 1885 (Labouchere's amendment), which specified that acts of gross indecency were illegal 'in public and in private'. This has led to the misleading assumption that hitherto, private acts had been legal. The eminent advocate Sir Travers Humphreys, who was junior counsel for the defence at the trial of Oscar Wilde, argued that few in the Commons at the time Labouchere proposed his amendment 'realised that the insertion of the words "in public or private" completely altered the basis of the law'.[46] Yet the rules of evidence which dictated that there must be competent witnesses to the act, and whose evidence required corroboration, remained in place. Theoretically at least, it remained unsafe for someone to be convicted on the unsupported evidence of an accomplice.

The second reason for this misconception is the fact that because of the rules of evidence, the law tended to *operate* against sex which took place in public. As we have seen, the majority of arrests reported in the press resulted from sexual encounters in the streets, parks, theatres, urinals or other 'public' places. In addition, the prosecution of homosexual behaviour using laws against public indecency has further confused matters. In some cases, a charge of indecent exposure was used against public sex. To prove this charge it had to be shown that the offence had taken place in public and in some cases convictions were challenged on this basis. This has given the impression that same-sex acts were only illegal in public, when in fact they were being contested on the grounds that indecent exposure had not been proved.

In 1857 Henry Jarvis and Frederick Scott, were charged with being in Bride Lane 'for the purpose of then and there openly publicly and indecently committing and perpetrating with each other divers filthy... and unnatural acts and practices'. It was charged in the indictment that Jarvis did 'indecently exhibit and expose' himself to Scott. The judge, however, decided that the offence was not public enough to prove indecent exposure, since, 'upon the authority of two cases decided by the Court of Criminal Appeal, there was no case against the prisoners, there being only one person present'.[47] Similarly, in *R v Bunyan and Morgan*, both of whom were charged with indecent exposure in August 1844, the conviction was challenged not on the issue of whether they had committed the acts in question, but whether they had done so in a public place. As Mr Prendergast for the prisoners put it, 'since publicity constituted the very essence of this offence at common law, it should be proved... that the parties had committed these acts in a public place, such that the natural consequence would be that they would be seen by others'.[48]

Some rulings as to publicity or privacy seem to have resulted from a particular reading of the rules of evidence. In practice, private acts seem to have counted as private when only the consenting parties were present, which in turn meant that insufficient evidence could be put in against them. When Henry Lee and Alex Thompson were charged in 1852 with indecent conduct in a public room, their barrister, Mr Wilkins protested that the indictment could not be supported 'as it was not such a public exposure as the law required; it was a private room and the two prisoners alone were present'.[49] They were instantly acquitted. In another case, publicity is explicitly defined as the presence of at least two witnesses. In 1870, Henry Cocks and Samuel Harris were acquitted on a charge of indecency in a Hyde Park urinal. Mr Justice Wills concluded that to be an offence, it 'must be so publicly done as to affect two or more of Her Majesty's subjects'.[50] In most cases, then, arguments over publicity meant either that indecent exposure was at issue or that there were insufficient witnesses to the act concerned.

Having sex in a place which could be thought of as 'private' by a commonsense definition was no protection against the law. As we have seen from the cases outlined above, privacy and secrecy were virtually impossible even for those, like James Smith, who could afford it. However, wealth did confer at least a degree of impunity as long as sexual partners could be chosen with greater care than Smith had employed. In contrast, communal living arrangements made sure that poor lodging houses were very dangerous places for such encounters. One London magistrate, Hesney Wedgwood, argued that sodomy was 'the only capital crime that is committed by rich men' but they were usually able to avoid capture. He had committed two men, John Smith and James Pratt, who later were the last men to be hanged for sodomy in Britain. They had, Wedgwood argued, been in a room in a lodging house and 'The detection of these degraded creatures was owing entirely to their poverty, [for] they were unable to pay for privacy, and the room was so poor that what was going on inside was easily visible from without'.[51]

These opinions were borne out by the fact that sometimes witnesses to private sex between men went to great lengths to ensure that the guilt of the participants could be proved. In November 1851, John Harris and Peter Wack were arrested after the efforts of one of their neighbours in a lodging house in Soho. A man named Barwell, had, 'in consequence of suspicions that were entertained... pierced holes so as to give him a view of the interior of... Wack's bedroom'. He then told a policeman who, along with two others 'stationed themselves in such a position as to obtain the fullest evidence of the offence of the prisoners'.[52]

Indecent assault, then, described a wide range of behaviour which might sometimes have been consenting. The criminal law was also applied both to indecent assaults and consenting acts, but was dependent on detection and reporting in the private sphere. This decentralised structure, combined with the rules of consent and corroboration, ensured that the crime of indecent assault reached far beyond the courtroom and any street subculture of sex. At least theoretically, and sometimes in practice, it was possible to police the private sphere in a new way.

WHO WERE THE PROSECUTORS?

So far, we have established that the law could apply to any acts, anywhere, depending on the status of witnesses. But can we tell who brought these cases? Available evidence indicates that the majority of homosexual offences which came to court before the involvement of the police on a large scale in the late 1840s were brought by private individuals initially acting apart from organised structures of law enforcement. This evidence suggests that although some magistrates sought to enforce the law with vigour, most prosecutors were not in such exalted positions. Instead they were workmates, acquaintances, casual pick-ups of the accused.

Prosecutions came from three main sources. Firstly, there were the efforts of reforming magistrates who occasionally clamped down on molly houses or other haunts of sodomites. Secondly, groups of gentlemen who probably made up a local vice or prosecution society mounted some short-lived campaigns against similar 'sodomites' walks'. The third and largest group of prosecutors before the police took on the role, appear to have been ordinary people with no apparent connection to vice societies or moral reformers.

The Home Office did occasionally intervene to organise and pay for the prosecution of military and high profile cases, but this does not appear to have been a common practice. When Percy Jocelyn, the Irish clergyman known to anti-clerical and radical printers as the 'Arse Bishop', was caught with a soldier in a tavern in 1822, Peel forwarded the documents to the Solicitor General with the instruction that he 'take this subject into your earliest consideration'.[53] Another prosecution of three men for frequenting the Bull Inn molly house in 1825 was paid for by the government to the tune of £21.[54]

Yet this course of action does not seem to have been very common. Also, as M.J.D. Roberts has pointed out, extra-governmental moral groups were similarly reluctant to prosecute sexual offences.[55] Societies for the suppression of vice and the prosecution of felons proliferated at

the end of the eighteenth century, but most of these sought to improve
the quality of policing and to share the cost of bringing prosecutions for
crimes against property. Adding to the prosecutorial activities of these
societies were religious and moral reform groups which had sponsored
the various societies for the reformation of manners or the suppression
of vice throughout the previous century. These began to receive the
backing of influential magistrates and important public figures after
George III's influential Proclamation Against Vice (1787). Together, these
two movements contributed to the increasing numbers of committals
for all offences in the late eighteenth century, especially against property,
violent crime and public order.[56]

Although the principal objective of the prosecution societies was the
defence of property, the aim of the religious and moral reformers was the
inculcation of religious repentance and moral order through the use of the
criminal law. To this end, they devoted their energies principally to the
prosecution of public indecency, prostitution, obscene publications and
Sabbath-breaking. The influence of evangelicals and orthodox churchmen
on the two most important moral societies, the Proclamation Society
(founded 1787) and the Society for the Suppression of Vice (founded
1802) meant that it was through the activities of these organisations that
religious influence on the operation of the law was at its most direct.

It might be expected that religious and moral reformers would take
the prosecution of sex offences as one of their principal aims, but in
practice this was often not the case. Although there was substantial
unanimity within these groups on the necessary objectives of moral
reform and national repentance, evangelical groups and moral reformers
did not always agree with regard to the necessary methods. The use of
informers and paid agents, and the necessity of entrapment to police
sexuality and obscenity, seemed, in the eyes of critics, to encourage a
form of criminal complicity. Roberts has established that metropolitan
evangelicals in particular objected to the use of these methods.[57]
Therefore, it is a mistake to simply interpret the detestation of 'the sin
of Sodom' amongst evangelicals or a campaign against public indecency
as necessarily leading to the prosecution of individuals or groups. The
difficulty of collecting enough evidence to prove a sodomy or indecent
assault case, plus the scruples of their own members, meant that there
were significant limits to the effect of evangelical and religious moralism
on the actual policing of sexuality.

However, it was the case that some groups of influential people, who
probably formed small prosecution societies, did undertake prosecutions,
as a selection of indictments presented at the Old Bailey in 1798 shows.
In July of that year, a number of cases were brought to the Guildhall

magistrates' court in the City of London, apparently at the instigation of a group of gentlemen living in and around Finsbury Square near Moorgate, just to the north of the City. John Mason, John Eley, William Foskett, George Osborn and Charles Farnsworth, all described in court documents as 'gentlemen', had probably formed a local prosecution or vice society to curb the notorious immorality of nearby Moorfields. In all, they were involved as prosecutors or witnesses in 12 of the 14 cases which came to the Old Bailey in that year. Thomas Bullen, who was clerk to Foskett, appeared as a witness to prosecute no fewer than 11 times and was the 'victim' of one assault. Mason himself solicited three indecent assaults and appeared as a witness four times, while between them Osborn, Foskett and Farnsworth appeared as witnesses 11 times.

The sequence of events can easily be imagined. Bullen would probably have solicited an advance which was seen by his employer watching from the shadows. The transaction would have been allowed to continue until enough evidence was collected. These cases also highlight the problematic nature of consent. Clearly, Bullen invited sexual advances and went along with them as long as was necessary. Yet in legal terms it was still possible for these acts to be interpreted as an indecent assault and written into the indictment as such.

These local efforts could be astonishingly successful, but the infamy of such cases often rubbed off even on prosecutors and witnesses, with the result that their efforts were short lived. All of the indictments sponsored by the Finsbury Square gentlemen resulted from arrests made in one month – July 1798 – and the campaign was not repeated. Only two indictments for indecent assault were presented at the Old Bailey in the following year.[58]

Other reformers were, at the very least, aware of male prostitution. Joseph Sadler Thomas, the reforming constable of St. Paul's Covent Garden, a parish which included the notorious area around Drury Lane, told the 1828 Select Committee on the Police that the streets were not only 'thronged with every description of nuisances' but were also walked by 'a number of the worst characters, which scarcely deserve the name of men, that I have every reason to believe were of the most infamous description'.[59] Magistrates in the early part of the century were also prepared to act against molly houses or disorderly houses within their jurisdiction. This was especially true when a complaint was made by respectable citizens. These matters will be dealt with in more detail in the next chapter where I will also show that the limitations of this kind of action were immediately apparent to those who carried it out. In addition, the Metropolitan Police appear to have developed a circumspect, not to say pragmatic, attitude to private gatherings during the course of the nineteenth century.

There is reason to believe that some witnesses were threatened by magistrates or constables into giving evidence. Yet this was a dangerous course of action, since it could make a case dependent on a single witness of bad character, whose evidence might be tainted. Such witnesses could easily bring prosecutions into disrepute and thereby tarnish the reputations of those who had sponsored such inquiries. This kind of evidence was sometimes used, however, and did form the basis of an inquiry into 19 men, some of whom were tried and executed at the Lancaster Assizes of 1806. Unfortunately for the defendants, these trials took place one year before the rule requiring corroboration of accomplice evidence had emerged, with a number of them sent to the gallows on the evidence of one witness. John Knight, a Warrington publican, gave evidence against four men, despite having consented to sex with one of them, while another key prosecution witness was shown to have been 'in the habit of committing this horrid crime for a great number of years'.[60] Thomas Taylor, a shopkeeper also of Warrington, gave evidence against three men, but admitted that 'promises of pardon' had been made to him provided he gave evidence. On behalf of the defendants, James Scarlett asked if it had not been suggested by the magistrates that, 'if you would tell all you knew, and make good your story against the Prisoner, you should not be prosecuted'. Taylor replied, 'I was told if I spoke the truth I should not.'[61] Even in the face of this evidence, the prosecution denied that such promises had been made.

In spite of the rules of corroboration which were in place after 1807, sexual partners were a useful source of evidence, and many trials turned on testimony which may have been obtained under duress. In one case, a man calling himself Captain Beauclerk, who was part of a group of three men (the others were John Goode and Captain Henry Nicoll of the 14th Infantry)[62] who were all finally imprisoned or executed between 1832 and 1834, was prosecuted on the evidence of John Steyne Veres, 'who had been living with him in the ostensible capacity of a servant, for the last three months'. Veres, described as a 'lad', proved that he had 'seen Captain Nicoll, Beauclerk and Mr Goode at his master's cottage, concerting together as to the best means of ensuring the escape of the former'. He also testified that 'a capital offence had been committed upon him' by his employer.[63]

As is clear from these examples, some magistrates clearly intervened to force a witness to prosecute a case. They also felt pressure to commit sodomy and bestiality cases for trial. When Jesse Gibson was sentenced to death for sodomy at the Leicester Assizes in March 1834, the prosecutor argued that pressure had been brought to make him bring the case. Richard Hardy had employed Gibson as a labourer and had witnessed the offence. But, he maintained, 'Tho' I was the prosecutor in this case I did not wish the prosecution to be proceeded in, on account of Jesse's weakness of intellect:- it was the parish officers of Saxby who forced me to it as witness'.[64] According to one of the petitioners trying to save George Lane from the gallows for a similar offence in Somerset, there was considerable reluctance on the part of the magistrates to send the case for trial. The only 'shadow of an apology that can be offered' for his crime, was 'his extreme ignorance', which was so great 'that the committing magistrate (whose name is appended to the memorial) told me that if he could have avoided committing him he would have done so'. The other three magistrates had agreed, but had sent the case for trial in spite of their reservations.[65]

The action of magistrates was supplemented by that of the private prosecutor, whose role was magnified by the structural changes to the funding of criminal justice. At the turn of the century, and until the early 1840s, prosecutions were still, as far as can be determined, initiated by individual men and women who were parties to the acts, or who claimed to be their inadvertent witness or unwilling 'victim'. Similarly, if we take the numbers of indictments witnessed by constables as a guide to their involvement in actual cases, we can see that their influence was often absent. Hardly any indictments presented at metropolitan courts list constables or policemen as witnesses before the 1840s. Police officers may have taken over the running of some of these cases, but in the first half of the century they did not take much part in detection or prosecution.[66]

In the absence of the state, the private prosecutor was obliged to act. He or she was assisted in this duty by a body of legislation designed to lessen the financial burden of prosecution. Between 1752 and 1826, six statutes governing prosecutorial expenses were passed. The first of these covered cases in London, and recognised the principle of granting costs in certain cases, especially to poor witnesses and prosecutors. Subsequent acts extended the provision of costs to other expenses associated with bringing a case such as the reproduction of documents and the cost of attending committal hearings. However, these provisions applied only to cases of felony until 1826 when some misdemeanour prosecutions were granted expenses including any assaults with intent to commit a felony. Yet, even before 1826, it was possible for poor prosecutors to bring cases. J.M. Beattie suggests that as many as 20 per cent of prosecutors at quarter sessions in the late eighteenth century were poor.[67] Peter King reached similar conclusions in his study of property crime prosecuted in Essex courts in the last half of the eighteenth century and has argued that it was the courts themselves, rather than prosecution societies, which provided prosecutorial expenses.[68] So although expenses were initially confined to sodomy trials, which qualified as felonies rather than misdemeanours, it was possible for the poorest prosecutors to cover at least some of the costs of these prosecutions. There is also some evidence to show that the granting of expenses to misdemeanours after 1826 had an effect on the ability and will of prosecutors to proceed in cases of homosexual offences. As I will show, expenses appear to have been routinely promised by the police to witnesses and expected by prosecutors. In London at least, the numbers of prosecutions for homosexual misdemeanours began to increase significantly after the 1826 Act allowed expenses to be granted for certain kinds of assault (see Figure 9), really gathering pace in the 1830s and 1840s.

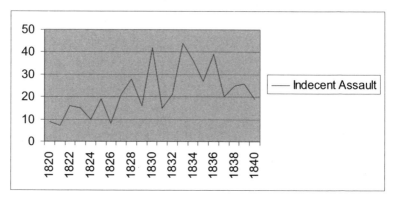

Figure 9: Prosecutions for indecent assault and other 'unnatural misdemeanours' in London, 1820–1840. Source: Parliamentary Papers.

At the beginning of the nineteenth century, the prosecutor was given more assistance than ever. His or her role was crucial, since prosecutors were frequently the 'victim' of an assault or a sexual partner, judging by the evidence of indictments. As late as 1844, the first witness listed on the indictments presented to the Central Criminal Court was the apparent 'victim' of the assault in 23 out of 31 cases, although in many of these they were assisted by police officers, also listed as witnesses.[69] Such lists of witnesses note those testifying before the grand jury and probably list the prosecutor first. In addition, the small amount of evidence which can be gained from the 105 criminal petitions and those cases reported in the press in which the prosecutor is explicitly identified indicates that prosecutors were usually of relatively low social status, as Figure 10 suggests. Although this is a small sample – 48 cases mainly from London courts – it does give an indication of the occupation of prosecutors and those bound over to give evidence before the large-scale assumption of prosecutorial duties by the post-1829 Metropolitan police.

Some of these indictments list all those bound over to give evidence, and those from the Old Bailey in the 1820s often list a constable as one such witness. In such circumstances it is difficult to tell who the actual prosecutor is, so all those listed as being bound over have been included here. Policemen or constables are therefore included here as one of those bound over in each case. Even though police are listed as major witnesses or prosecutors in a nearly a third of these cases, unskilled or skilled labourers still make up over half of the sample.

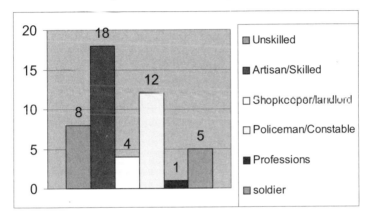

Figure 10: The Occupation of Prosecutors (where stated), 1800–1850. Source: Criminal Petitions, Newspapers, Old Bailey indictments. Total: 48 cases.

The cases presented here show that the prosecutor was frequently of low status and in one example was even unemployed, a fact that did not prevent the case going ahead and the accused being convicted. In fact, over half the cases in this sample were prosecuted by artisans or unskilled workers. While artisans or labourers might have been connected to evangelical religion in some way that is not evident from the available legal records or press reports, they were unlikely to have been members of moral reform groups like the Vice or the Proclamation Society, both of which appealed to and recruited from higher social classes. Rewards for the arrest and conviction of felons, which might have featured in the motivation of some prosecutors, had been abolished by Parliament in 1818 and, according to one magistrate, did not apply to cases of unnatural crime.[70] In spite of this obscurity about motives, it is clearly the case that people of low status appeared as prosecutors, a fact which suggests either that they were able to obtain expenses by themselves after 1826, or that another agency – probably the police – were willing to arrange the provision of costs. As Douglas Hay has shown, the police were increasingly blamed in the 1840s and 1850s for the inflation of costs, perhaps indicating that they were catering for witnesses as well as themselves.[71] The prevalence of soldiers as prosecutors also reflects the fact that cases reported in the press tended to have occurred in London, where the sentries in the various Royal parks operated a sideline in prostitution and extortion which required frequent court attendance.

In spite of the mainly humble origins of these prosecutors, cases sometimes required a person of status to be bound over in order to ensure the respectability or perhaps success of the proceedings. A master or police officer was apparently necessary in order to guide the case through the legal thicket or to prevent accusations of conspiracy. In the Finsbury Square indictments from 1798, only 'gentlemen' could be bound over to prosecute, and in other cases similar guarantees of status were sought. In 1833 a man named Arthur Garton was accused of an indecent assault by a group of men after he had spent an evening drinking with them in a tavern at Steyning in Sussex. They visited him a few days afterwards and told him that 'unless he paid them they would accuse him of Being in a Disgusting Situation' with another man. The master of one of the accusers had been bound over to prosecute.[72] Similarly, when a shop-boy tried to complain of an assault in London in 1841, the policeman who heard his story told him to 'apply to his... master'.[73]

Although respectability was clearly important, it is also clear that prosecutions were initiated by those in lowly social stations. In 1834, an ostensibly respectable man named John Goode was convicted of indecent assault on the evidence of one Elizabeth Taylor, daughter of a lodging-house keeper. Taylor was, according to the judge, 'a poor untutored person', who was, she said, merely convinced that 'all was not going on right' at the house.[74] The man who prosecuted messenger John Avis in London in 1829 was also in a lowly position. Avis complained that his accuser was nothing more than a waiter out of place and was living in 'a coffee shop of the lowest description' which was also 'the resort of low characters'.[75]

Outside London, a lack of respectability appears to have been even less of an obstacle to prosecutorial status. Also the new possibility of obtaining the expenses available to prosecutors did begin to influence those in a position to advance evidence in these cases. James Yeo, whose evidence had contributed to the capital conviction of John Andrews in Devon in 1844, was a failed merchant and a known liar. Yeo and another witness with whom he had colluded, were, according to the local constable, 'given to drink', in the habit of 'following Beershops and are dissipated men boath'. A judge who had had experience of the litigious Yeo at the Plymouth Court of Requests also asserted that he was 'a very dishonest man, and not worthy to be trusted... whose testimony I should receive with great suspicion'. Yeo's obviously dubious status was easily established after Andrews' conviction and subsequent petition for mercy. Simple inquiries of the arresting officer, in particular his opinion of Yeo, elicited the most damning remarks. Nevertheless, these doubts were initially ignored and the case went ahead, with the result that John Andrews was sentenced to death.

The provision of expenses was clearly an important issue for prosecutors and witnesses. Yeo was supposed to have said that he intended to make money out the prosecution of John Andrews. He was said to have boasted that he would make £3 in total out of the case, partly from being 'entitled to five shillings the day before the magistrate and ten shillings a day at Exeter [assizes] as Master Merchant'.[76] Elizabeth Taylor was also obliged to deny that her evidence was motivated by money. She told the court that 'the Police man never gave me any money', while her mother also protested that her daughter had never said that 'she... would have her expenses'.[77] Witnesses were, at the very least, *suspected* of taking money from the police or authorities as a way of making sure that their evidence was presented. One Warwickshire policeman was supposed to have told a reluctant witness that he would 'see that you are all right', in order to ensure his appearance at the local petty sessions.[78]

These cases illustrate that, as in other forms of crime, before 1850 prosecutions were chiefly the business of private individuals who were not necessarily wealthy or middle class, and who were sometimes but not always, assisted by the police. If indictments are a reliable guide, police involvement in sodomy cases gradually began to increase and to become customary in the 1840s. Prosecutions also tended to rely on the evidence of victims of assaults or sexual partners. Although vice societies may have involved themselves in individual cases, moral reform did not always lead directly to the prosecution of 'sodomites'. The early nineteenth century, then, saw the development of homosexual offences as an increasingly routine part of everyday life.

Popular opinion, then, might be assumed to be violently antipathetic to homosexual behaviour. This factor, and the attraction of expenses, might explain the willingness of those of relatively low social status to risk the time, trouble and potential expense of a court case in order to obtain some kind of redress for what they clearly felt was a moral injury. If we read public opinion in this way, we could conclude either that moral and religious reform had done its work with spectacular success, or that popular attitudes were resolutely and historically 'homophobic'. On the other hand, the relatively small numbers of prosecutions per head of population also might indicate the contrary: that only a minute proportion of all homosexual behaviour was being prosecuted. However, there are other signs of popular detestation of the 'crime not to be named'. In addition to the violent and implacable crowds which gathered at the pillory before 1818, or those which met outside courts to hiss at convicted sodomites after that date, some judges also appear to have noted the violence of public opinion on this subject. In 1835, Mr Justice Patterson found himself in sympathy with a man named William Booth who had been sentenced to death for sodomy in August of that year. The judge argued that the death penalty should normally proceed where specified, and the Crown should be prepared to consider whether the law was too severe in any particular case. Yet the unfortunate Booth should, he felt, be saved from the gallows, and the judge recommended a punishment other than death. He recognised, however, that in cases of sodomy the public as a body were more likely to demand the full penalty than the courts. According to Patterson, a popular climate of intolerance should be taken into account. 'Public opinion,' he told the Home Office, 'should doubtless in these cases be much regarded, and I believe it now contrary to my own.'[79]

The criminal law, then, had an extensive reach, at least in theory. It could be employed in a number of contexts, to police both public and private behaviour, and its extent was only limited by the question of corroboration and consent. The operation of the law also reflected its decentralised status and increasingly routine character. Sexual misbehaviour could be punished even when it was encountered by those of relatively humble origins. The impression of the criminal law that this data – albeit limited – gives, is one of pervasiveness. In nineteenth-century England, homosexual acts were more likely than ever before to be subject to criminal penalties.

The greatest expansion in prosecutions for homosexual offences appears to have been driven by the private prosecutor, who was frequently of low social status. These facts suggest that the provision of costs and expenses must have had a major impact on the prosecution of these cases. The prosecution of unnatural crimes also appears to have depended on a popular antipathy to homosexual behaviour. The examples presented here are clearly not an exhaustive sample, but are indicative of the various ways in which the law could work, and the various ways in which prosecutors could act. These sources therefore show that it was the sporadic efforts of reforming magistrates and local anti-vice initiatives, combined with the activities of private prosecutors whose motives have not survived in any clear form, which combined to make homosexual offences a routine aspect of criminal justice. This development was the inadvertent result of changes to the structure of justice and therefore was the outcome of a series of largely unrelated individual decisions. In the period which witnessed the greatest expansion of homosexual offences, between 1780 and 1850, it was the actions of men like Allmond, the prosecutor of the Rev Olive, that were the most typical. Individual decisions were more representative of the regulation of sexuality than the organised forces of moral reform or of the police. That is not to discount the acts of individuals or of certain magistrates or policemen, but to suggest that they acted within a framework of legal practice which had grown up in response to local and individual necessity. The developments in legal practice and policy which emerged between 1780 and 1850 determined the ways in which homosexual behaviour was talked about in public, and also set up the structure of punishment which was to endure until 1967. The effect of this means of proceeding was, I suggest, to decentralise the policing of sexual deviance. This situation ensured that in spite of the fact that homosexual offences made up a relatively small part of the total number of trials, the influence of the criminal law could extend far beyond the limited sphere of the courtroom and police house. The private sphere and the street transaction were, as we have seen, the prime locations of homosexual 'offending' and were the principal source of witnesses and prosecutions. Consenting or private sex was also clearly within the scope of the law. The development of the law in this respect meant that even though the criminal process established boundaries of public and private, it also breached these barriers and invaded the intimate sphere when it was deemed to be necessary. Privacy was both sanctified and violated. As the anonymous homophile poem *Don Leon* (*c*. 1835) put it:

> Now no couple can in safety lie
> Between the sheets salacious lawyers pry.[80]

2

Policing Sodomy in the Nineteenth-Century City

The state, in the form of the police, does not appear to have become directly involved in the investigation and prosecution of homosexual offences in a routine manner until the 1840s. In this chapter, I will explain that, although the police and certain magistrates had moments of enthusiasm for prosecuting unnatural crimes, this initial attitude turned into circumspection as the century progressed. The police and their superiors in the Home Office and other branches of government appeared to become increasingly conscious of the difficulties involved in pursuing moral offences and ever more aware of the limits of their powers in this respect. Law officers and those in authority came to regard the prosecution of homosexual offences as a very unfortunate duty, likely to cause public scandal and thereby alert the unsuspecting to the existence of unnatural lust. What were the reasons for this lack of enthusiasm? Firstly, the thinly spread nature of Metropolitan Police manpower in the first few decades of its existence limited the amount of time and trouble that could be taken over detecting immorality. In addition, the initial function of the police was not to detect, but to deter. Secondly, I suggest that it soon became evident to the police that sodomy prosecutions were particularly dangerous. The requirements of evidence were stringent and specific and contributed in no small way to the likelihood of failure and embarrassment at the hands of a respectable defendant and his barrister. Thirdly, those in authority, such as Home Office officials, directors of public prosecutions and Treasury solicitors were painfully aware that convictions in these cases were not easily obtained. Such prosecutions therefore risked scandal, threatening to bring sodomy to public attention without the certainty that a moral lesson might be transmitted. As I will show, the state and the police were more conscious of the limits of their authority than anything else when dealing with 'sodomitic' crime.

That is not to say that the police did not become increasingly involved in these cases. It seems that they tended to assume the role of prosecutor rather than devoting themselves to detection in the systematic ways that developed in the twentieth century. The 'pretty policeman' and the *agent provocateur* only became acceptable and routine practices in the twentieth century. Policing the unnatural crime in the nineteenth century was hedged about with questions of disclosure and complicity. It was also limited by matters of class and respectability and by the necessity of maintaining the sanctity of public and private. New urban police forces developed an attitude of supervision and control towards homosexual behaviour, rather than one of direct intervention. The same attitude developed towards public heterosexual indecency and female prostitution. Since public offences of immorality and indecency were much easier to prosecute, these were the principal kinds of offences prosecuted by the new police.

The overall effect of these police practices, I suggest, was a policy of *de facto* toleration of private offences by the police. They would, of course, still prosecute private offences if discovered by individual officers or prosecutors, but generally would not pursue these offences themselves. Anxieties about publicity and privacy and about disclosing the existence of unnatural crimes spread in this way to the very practice of the police. Therefore, jurisprudence, the workings of the committal process and the actual practice of the police themselves institutionalised and encouraged certain discursive and practical boundaries in relation to homosexual desire.

POLICING LONDON AND MIDDLESEX

By 1829, London had a centralised police force under the authority of the Home Office and directed by commissioners appointed by the government. The 1829 Act which established the Metropolitan Police divided London into 17 police districts, each of which was staffed by a superintendent, four inspectors and 16 sergeants (see Map 1). The old watch system remained in some places as a supplement to the new authority and in the case of the Bow Street Runners and Horse Patrol, was eventually incorporated into the new police itself. The process by which Peel's police replaced the old watch system used to be presented by historians as the replacement of an inefficient, wretched, corrupt and undermanned system of overlapping local jurisdictions by a rational, modern efficient force. However, it is now generally accepted that the watch system at the parish level was valued by many of its defenders as an organisation that was responsive to local needs and had itself undergone a process of reform and invigoration in the decades leading up to 1829. Elaine Reynolds has shown that most London parishes employed a paid watch to prevent crime and public disorder even before 1790.[1] There was, therefore, a gradual movement away from the system of unpaid local constables towards the establishment of paid watchmen which grew in pace and scope in the last half of the eighteenth century. Ruth Paley has noted that by the 1820s most central London parishes were increasingly concerned about rising crime and took steps to improve the quality of the watch and its recruits.[2]

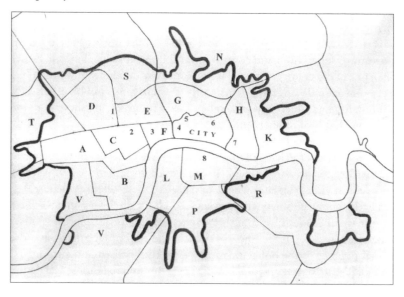

Map 1: Metropolitan Police Districts and Magistrates' Courts, 1837.
1. Marylebone (est. 1821); 2. Marlborough Street; 3. Bow Street; 4. Hatton Garden; 5. Queen Square; 6. Worship Street; 7. Lambeth Street; 8. Union Hall.

Recent work, then, has stressed the continuity between the functions of the pre and post-1829 police. However, reforms to the watch, Reynolds suggests, were accomplished mainly for the purpose of protecting property and guarding against political extremism. Although crime was intimately connected with the social order and linked to personal sin by most police reformers, in Reynolds' account sexual offences were not one of the main practical objectives of the reformed watch.[3] The parishes were clearly concerned with public order, but the protection of property was the principal objective of reform at the local level.

The historiography of the police seems to confirm the view that its functions both before and after 1829 did not extend to the sustained prosecution of sexual assaults. As we have seen, the policing of same-sex desire was a diffuse process involving interaction between prosecutors and witnesses rather than diligent detection or surveillance on the part of police agencies. I suggest that this was partly because of the difficulties of evidence and also because of the political problems surrounding the methods necessary to get it, particularly the complicity encouraged by 'spying' and plain clothes. Before 1829, the watch could be employed in a private capacity by those who wanted an end to molly houses or soliciting in the streets, but this was often prohibitively expensive. Magistrates sometimes sent the watch on raids against molly houses, but these expeditions seem to have been relatively rare. By the 1850s, the majority of all criminal cases were brought by the police, and the suspicion which had often fallen on private prosecutors that the trial was a conspiracy in pursuit of expenses or extortion, was attracted by officers acting as both prosecutor and chief witness. In addition, a poorly prepared police case would often attract criticism from magistrates for risking indecent publicity without the certainty of conviction. Therefore, although the police were increasingly involved in the prosecution of indecent assault, there were few sustained efforts on their part to raid the haunts of 'sodomites'.

As we have seen, the rise in the level of committal for unnatural crimes which took place in London and Middlesex was part of a much wider increase in the level of prosecution for all offences. Rising numbers of offences were not necessarily the result of any sustained campaigns against sodomites, or mollies then, but were incidental to other changes which altered the policing of public order. Neither did the arrival of the Metropolitan Police mark a break with the ways in which same-sex desire was policed. Levels of crime, which appeared to be rising during the 1820s, were frequently interpreted as the result of improvements to the watch system instituted at a local level by vice and prosecution societies and parish authorities.[4] The new police simply carried on this trend towards the control of public indecency and the implementation of new standards of public order. As we saw in Chapter 1, increasing numbers of indictments were presented at the Old Bailey after 1780, and this trend continued into the 1840s (see Figure 11). The new police also appear to have had an impact on absolute numbers of committals, as Figure 11 shows.

We have seen that there were two principal influences on the total level of prosecution in the first half of the century. The first was Peel's 1826 Criminal Justice Act, which allowed expenses to prosecutors in cases of misdemeanour. The second was the gradual impact of the police, especially on the policing of public space and decency. Although the combination of these two forces does seem to have had an effect on the statistical level of committal for indecent assault, these figures tell us only about successful arrests, and do not accurately illustrate the extent to which homosexual acts were policed during the first half of the century. The national statistics can be fleshed out, however, by the records of individual magistrates' courts.

These courts, or 'police offices', had been established by the 1792 Middlesex Justices Act. This legislation set up eight offices, at Marlborough Street, Bow Street, Hatton Garden, Queen Square, Worship Street, Lambeth Street, Union Hall (Southwark) and Thames (Wapping). Each office was staffed by three stipendiary magistrates and six constables with jurisdiction in the surrounding area (see Map 1). An office was added at Marylebone in 1821, when the Thames office was closed.

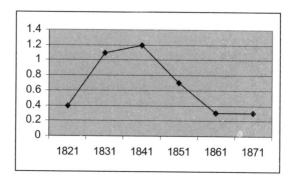

Figure 11: Committals for Homosexual Offences per 10,000 people in London and Middlesex, 1821–1871.[5]

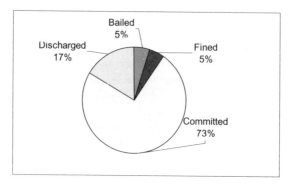

Figure 12: Results of Committal Hearings in London in cases of sodomy, indecent assault and other homosexual offences, 1828, 1830 and 1836. Source: Daily Reports from the Various Police Offices, PRO HO 62/1, 2, 5 and 6.

The statistics from individual magistrates' courts show that the level of arrest was considerably higher than the level of committal and that summary justice was sometimes employed in dealing with these crimes. In some cases a charge of indecent assault was reduced to one of common assault to enable the case to proceed summarily. In this sample, over 20 per cent of the total number of those arrested were either discharged or fined for common rather than indecent assault. The frequent complaints about bail jumping and tampering with witnesses made throughout the century might suggest that bail was frequently equivalent to releasing an offender for good. A significant minority of those arrested, therefore, were set at liberty. This means that those discharged by magistrates or fined for common assault rather than committed for trial did not appear in the official, centrally-produced statistics of committals for homosexual offences and that the real level of arrest and surveillance is only hinted at by these figures.[6] In addition, the use of summary justice and arrest on suspicion under the Vagrancy Acts further conceals the way in which London's street culture of 'cruising' the streets and parks was policed.

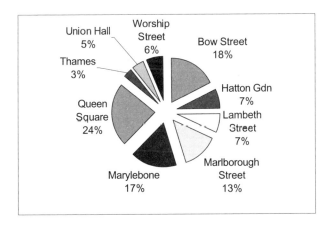

Figure 13: Proportion of committal hearings held at respective magistrates' courts in London, 1828, 1830 and 1836 Source: Daily Reports From the Various Police Offices, PRO HO 62/1, 2, 5 and 6.

Prosecutions for vagrancy had the advantage of being susceptible to summary jurisdiction and therefore avoided some of the problems associated with sending homosexual offences to higher courts. Robert Storch has suggested that the police controlled female prostitution by restricting its physical locations, and something similar seems to have happened with regard to unnatural offences. The use of the vagrancy laws allowed the police to control public space rather than to raid brothels or private premises.[7] Summary prosecutions against those who violated the Vagrancy Acts also required a far lower standard of proof than either soliciting, keeping a bawdy house or any of the charges against same-sex behaviour, and were likely to attract far less publicity.

Public order and decency had been subject to increasing scrutiny from the end of the eighteenth century onwards, as reformers tried to clean up city streets. Equally, the first third of the nineteenth century saw greater powers given to watchmen and police to arrest those they suspected of being idle and disorderly, culminating in the 1824 Vagrancy Act. The offence of loitering with intent to commit a felony had been introduced in 1783 with reference to private property and was extended to streets and public places by the Act of 1802. By 1830, this was used regularly against a variety of street offenders, from gamblers and con artists to pickpockets and suspected housebreakers. But the major impact of these laws on the way in which sodomitic crime was policed was in the laws directed against prostitution and streetwalking.

The Vagrancy Act of 1822 empowered police to arrest prostitutes and nightwalkers who were wandering about and 'not giving a satisfactory account of themselves' as 'idle and disorderly persons' liable for up to one month's hard labour. This legislation was consolidated in the 1824 Vagrancy Act, which named the offence as 'wandering in the Public streets or Public Highways, or in any Place of public Resort, and behaving in a riotous or indecent Manner'.[8] These laws were undoubtedly used against male streetwalkers, professional or otherwise, and were universally employed against other suspicious characters.[9] Henry James Smith, for example, was arrested in April 1869 after being found in women's clothes in Lambeth, and charged with assuming his attire for 'an unlawful purpose'. He was also charged under the Vagrancy Act with being an idle and disorderly person.[10] However, the use of the vagrancy laws and summary justice in the magistrates' court meant that prostitutes were less likely to be subject to the heavier penalties inflicted through a criminal trial.

The use of these various legal instruments ensured that, even in the 1820s, magistrates' courts were investigating increasing numbers of unnatural crimes. In 1825, *The Times* was complaining that, 'scarcely a week passes but the magistrates of this office have individuals brought before them... charged with indecent assaults on the sentries in the park'.[11] Again, in September, the Union Hall office was 'occupied for a considerable time in the investigation of one of those revolting and unnatural cases, so many of which have recently been heard at the different police offices in town'.[12] By 1830, an indecent assault in Brick Lane was 'as usual, of the most disgusting description'.[13]

The busiest courts were those covering the north-western edge of the City (Queen Square), Covent Garden (Bow Street) and Marylebone, although these figures might represent different degrees of efficiency of the respective officers stationed in each office and (before 1829) the relative enthusiasm of parish officers for police reform. Other sources are less ambivalent about the location of offences and their relation to police activity. Reports of cases in the press give some indication of the remarkable concentration of these offences in London. Of these reported cases, the majority were overwhelmingly located in three areas of central London: the City, Covent Garden and Hyde Park. In the City, most cases in this sample of 80 arrests were reported as having occurred in a small area bounded by St Paul's to the West and Bishopsgate to the East. The River and the area around Finsbury Square provide the respective southern and northern boundaries of this locale.

In the West End, the majority of offences were reported in Hyde Park, often in connection with soldiers stationed there. In addition, Green Park and Piccadilly were areas of high concentration. An area encompassing Covent Garden, Charing Cross and the Strand also witnessed a large number of offences. In addition to these areas of high concentration, a number of offences occurred in other locations such as Regent's Park, Regent Street, Berkeley Square and Marylebone High Street.

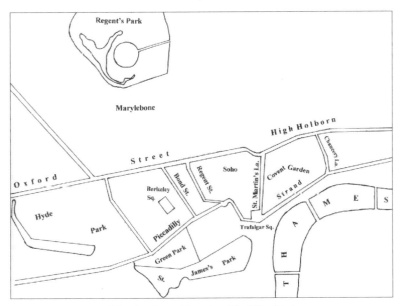

Map 2: Central London: The West End.

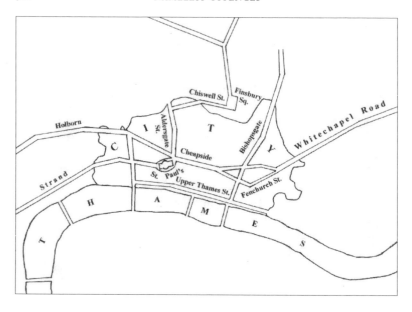

Map 3: Central London: The City and East End.

Many of these central London locations were historic 'cruising grounds', notorious for being 'sodomites' walks' in the eighteenth century and perhaps before. Moorfields and the area north of the City around Finsbury Square were frequently mentioned in eighteenth-century accounts, as was Lincolns Inn Fields and Covent Garden. At that time, the Strand and Marylebone were famous for their molly houses, as was Marylebone.[14] Covent Garden clearly maintained its historic notoriety. One letter to the Home Office in 1827 complained that around Drury Lane 'swarms of lads who carry on the infamous occupation of *catamites* infest the streets at night', while the police looked on and did nothing.[15] By the mid nineteenth century, the Quadrant at the lower end of Regent Street, as well as Fleet Street, Holborn, the Strand and Charing Cross were all said to be the habitual haunts of 'Margeries' and 'Pooffs'.[16]

By the 1820s, the Royal Parks offered a particular temptation in the form of soldiers stationed on sentry duty at various points. They were famously open to all manner of solicitation and not above extortion and blackmail. The parks at night were also the resort of rough-sleepers, criminals, civilian blackmailers and the homeless, and as such became places of license and danger. Complaints about the parks were a frequent occurrence throughout the nineteenth century, apparently exacerbated by confusion about where responsibility for policing them rested. In the 1860s, for example, St James's and Hyde Park became the focus of concern. John Laurie, a resident of the neighbouring Hyde Park Terrace, called the attention of *The Times* to the condition of the park, where may be seen 'hordes of half-dressed, filthy men and women lying about in parties, and, no doubt, concocting midnight robberies'. The police and park-keepers appeared to be plentiful enough, Laurie said, but 'they state they have no orders to remove them'.[17] Again, in 1866, 'Carthusianus' complained that the state of St James's Park at night was 'disgraceful'. It had, he complained, 'become a source of danger to walk alone from the Duke of York's Column [on Constitution Hill] to the Horse Guards or to Storey's Gate'. The police were at fault again, since they 'seem to look upon the park as charmed ground, on which they may not enter, and as nobody takes their place, the consequences are what might be expected'.[18] Complaints about the parks were publicised again in the early 1880s, and continued to be made in the early twentieth century. In 1912, a deputation to the Home Office from the South London Free Church Council complained that 'indecency, sexual intercourse and sodomy are being constantly carried on in various parts of [Hyde] Park especially after dark'.[19]

From this evidence it appears that, in the 1860s at least, the police did not include the open areas of the parks in their jurisdiction and that the parks went largely unpoliced at night. A police report on the state of the parks written in 1864, probably in response to the complaints made above, stated that those who frequented the parks knew how to escape the police, 'whose duty it is to confine themselves to the roads or paths'.[20] This policy was reiterated by the Commissioner of Police, Sir Richard Mayne, who wrote to an MP in the same year on the subject of robberies committed in Hyde Park. He affirmed that the police had never 'since their first establishment been employed within any Park or grounds during the time they are closed to the admission of the Public'. These areas were the responsibility of Park constables, who, however, were withdrawn at night, usually at 9pm.[21]

The West End, Parks and the City were central to the public culture of homosexuality. However, this picture is complicated somewhat by the evidence from bills of indictment presented at the Old Bailey and Central Criminal Court between 1825 and 1844. These sources list the location of the offence and residence of offender by parish. An unsystematic sample from the first half of the century also locates the majority of homosexual offences in the West End, but in parishes slightly further to the west and north than Covent Garden and the City. This source complicates the picture offered by newspaper reports by showing that of the 169 indictments considered, the offences are fairly evenly spread across central London. Only St Marylebone, with 18, has more than ten offenders in the period between 1825 and 1844, although this may reflect a more zealous attitude to the reform of the watch, at least in the 1820s. Most parishes in London had between five and ten offenders in the years covered by the sample.

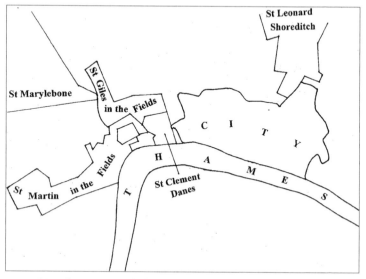

Map 4: Homosexual offences by parish, London, 1825–1844.

The parishes in which most offences took place in these years, in addition to St Marylebone, were St Giles in the Fields on the east side of Oxford Street and north of Covent Garden (10 offenders), St Clement Danes on the west side of the City and bordering St Giles to the south (9), St Martin in the Fields, stretching from Westminster in the west to Covent Garden and the Strand in the east (7), and St Leonard, Shoreditch at the north-east corner of the city (6).[22] Although most of these parishes are in the West End of London and cover the areas in which homosexual offences were concentrated, the remaining 119 indictments were spread evenly across the city.

Two tentative conclusions might be reached from the mapping of homosexual offences. Firstly, that in the mind of the Victorian public and press the historic sites of 'sodomitic' assignation narrowed to two or three circumscribed areas of central London as the century progressed. Also, we might speculate that these areas became the places in which the police sought to contain and control the market for homosexual sex, just as they controlled the market for female prostitution. Secondly, the mapping produced by indictments might suggest that at least in the first half of the century, the policing of sodomy was perhaps a more diffuse and less geographically concentrated business than would appear from newspaper reports. The containment rather than the eradication of homosexual behaviour might also be assumed from these figures to be the principal object of the Metropolitan Police. As we have seen, the police were keenly aware of the limitations of their jurisdiction and powers in relation to the parks and open spaces of London. I suggest below that this situation was indicative of a more general caution.

THE POLITICS OF POLICING

1. Scandal and Authority

The limitations to police action against public immorality were partly dictated by the nature of the force as a whole. The delicate status of police authority, at least before 1850, ensured that large numbers of arrests were not necessarily welcomed by judges, magistrates or law officers. The use of methods like plain clothes, which was the most reliable way of obtaining evidence against sodomites on the street, were widely seen as 'continental' methods associated with secret police, despotism and systems of spying. They also encouraged complicity in the crime. Therefore the initial enthusiasm of the new police for these tactics tended to bring their authority into disrepute. In the 1830s and 1840s the police were by no means universally regarded as an improvement to law enforcement and complaints against their brutality and corruption were numerous. Their quasi-military uniforms and systems of rank also appeared to many critics to be a real or implied threat to the liberty of the subject. In cases of sodomy and indecent assault it became common for barristers to impugn the motives of the police, especially when they began to act as the principal witness, arresting officer and prosecutor.

In addition, it appears that the government officials who were ultimately responsible for the actions of the police were reluctant to encourage the public scandal that resulted from inflated numbers of sodomy prosecutions. Law officers always sought to take the possible scandalous effects of prosecution into account. In the case of James Smith, charged with committing sodomy with a number of Telegraph boys in 1877, the probable effects on public morals were carefully weighed by the officials involved in the decision to prosecute.[23] Augustus Stephenson, at that time the solicitor to the Treasury, argued that 'The public scandal which a prosecution on such a charge whether it failed or succeeded – would be very great – and such scandal is much to be deprecated.' These reservations would play themselves out in a more dramatic fashion during the Cleveland Street scandal of 1889, to which I will return in Chapter 4. At this earlier stage in his career, Stephenson's opinion on unnatural offences was typical of his fellow law officers. He argued that it was only the aggravated nature of Smith's case which meant that it should be organised and financed by the Treasury. The corruption of public employees of the Post Office clearly made it a public matter and the ensuing scandal should be risked in this case. Some scandal, he wrote, should 'be risked for the protection of children – and to show that persons like Smith cannot indulge their passions without complete impunity'.[24]

The avoidance of scandal was probably why law officers developed a particular distaste for direct involvement in sodomy prosecutions. On at least one occasion before 1889, something like a policy was sketched out. When Robert King, Earl of Kingston was arrested in 1848 for an alleged indecent assault on a young man in Oxford Street, the government refused to fund the prosecution on the grounds that such cases were best left in the hands of private prosecutors. Correspondence between the committing magistrate and various Home Office officials shows a conflicting set of attitudes, but also highlights the fact that even in this high-profile case it was not deemed either wise or necessary for the Treasury to direct and fund the prosecution. The magistrate in the case noted that the prosecutor, George Cull, was a painter and unable to afford counsel. He therefore requested that the case be undertaken by the government.[25] Legal advice from Home Office officials suggested that 'the magistrate's recommendation [was] ill-judged' and argued that the government 'should not take up *such a charge*. The party who brings it, should defend it'.[26] The official response of the Home Office was that even though the Attorney General 'was disposed to prosecute, this being a moment when any apparent indifference pertaining to the trial of a peer will be jealously scanned', in this case 'considering the nature of this charge, I think the government should *not* prosecute'.[27]

Grand Juries showed similar circumspection in allowing cases to go forward to higher courts. Jurors appear to have been more scrupulous about the evidence of unnatural crimes than they were about other types of crime. In London at least, a larger proportion of indictments for sodomy and indecent assault were rejected at the Grand Jury stage than were refused for other kinds of offence. In the years used for this sample, between 1828 and 1844, 29 per cent of bills were rejected at the Old Bailey and Central Criminal Court, a figure which compares with much lower rates of rejection – around seven per cent – for crimes against property and the person prosecuted in other parts of England.[28]

In spite of the caution of law officers and the difficulty of bringing prosecutions for sodomy and indecent assault, other evidence shows that the police gradually became involved in the prosecution of homosexual offences as a matter of routine. A rough guide to the involvement of the

Metropolitan Police can be found in the number of times police officers are listed as witnesses on bills of indictment presented at the Central Criminal Court. Although this is not an infallible indicator of who prosecuted the case, and the police witness may have simply taken the charge without being involved in the arrest, it does at least show the increasing willingness of the police to be involved. It is possible to see a gradual increase in the number of police witnesses in indecent assault and sodomy trials in London. In the cases presented at the Old Bailey in 1798 only one of 14 indictments listed a constable as witness, while in 1825 three out of nine were witnessed by constables.[29] Although these pre-1829 figures may have been complicated by the fact that, as notionally private citizens, the constables may not have been listed in an official capacity, they do provide a rough indication of how deeply involved parish officials were in prosecutions.[30] By the 1830s, increasing numbers of indictments list the division and number of a police witness. At the Central Criminal Court in 1836, ten out of 31 indecent assaults had the benefit of police patronage whereas by 1844 this proportion had increased to 82 per cent of the total (28 police witnesses out of 34 indictments).[31]

However, the efforts of the Metropolitan Police as witnesses and prosecutors were by no means universally appreciated. Their new role raised a number of objections from judges and politicians who were concerned that the discretion allowed to individual officers represented a temptation to corruption and a threat to liberty. Douglas Hay and Francis Snyder have shown that by the 1850s it was common for police officers to assume prosecutorial responsibilities in most criminal cases. As such, the police took control not only of the process of arrest, charge and detention, but also of the provision of expenses and costs.[32] By 1837, the Royal Commission on the Criminal Law had concluded that the individual officer was the prosecutor in 'many cases', while in 1855 the police were said to manage 'vast numbers' and the 'great majority' of prosecutions.[33]

This situation not only gave the individual officer enormous discretion over what crimes to arrest and bring to trial, but also laid their motives in doing so open to question. The police, no less than the private prosecutor before them, were frequently suspected of bringing cases in order to collect the expenses given to witnesses and prosecutors at the trial. John Hughes Preston, a solicitor who had been appointed by Parliament to look into the claiming of expenses in trials on the Oxford Circuit, told the Select Committee on Public Prosecutors, 'I find on the part of the police an anxiety to get up cases, and to put themselves in communication with attorneys and different parties, and I am afraid that in their hands there is often not only a failure of justice, but that also corrupt influences are at work.'[34]

Hay and Snyder suggest that the primacy of individual officers in bringing cases to court, and the danger of partiality on their part, caused considerable anxiety among judges and jurists and became one of the principal arguments for the establishment of a public prosecutor. The architect of legislation designed to establish such an office in the 1850s, the MP John Phillimore, argued that the present system:

> gave to policemen, to a class amongst whom were to be found some of the most hardened and profligate of mankind, and over whom the most incessant vigilance was requisite to prevent flagrant and cruel abuses of their authority... an unlimited power of pardon and connivance.[35]

Similarly, in 1855, the Attorney General Sir Alexander Cockburn, who later became Lord Chief Justice, argued that the predominance of the police in bringing prosecutions was a 'great scandal', which had the effect of making policemen 'over-zealous in the conduct of prosecutions'. The reason for this was that 'the promotion of policemen is made to depend upon the prosecutions which they successfully conduct'.[36]

Part of the early bad reputation of the police for corruption and excessive, arbitrary authority came from their conduct in cases involving homosexual offences. Although at least one magistrate expressed confidence that the new police would repress 'so enormous an offence', suspicion of the police was much more common.[37] Some of the tensions resulting from the rise of the policeman as prosecutor, and the apparently excessive authority he enjoyed, were fully demonstrated in a number of indecent assault cases which came to court in 1830. In the spring of that year Michael Cannon and Edward Nugent, officers of 'S' Division in north London, mounted a campaign against those men who met in Hyde Park which netted them 19 arrests in two months. When some of the cases went before the Westminster Sessions, the tactics of the officers were criticised and their motives held up to inspection. The additional fact that Hyde Park was not even in 'S' division, and was actually in 'A' division, some way to the south and west of the officers' official jurisdiction, might have caused some comment, but it was their plain clothes which attracted the most opprobrium. At the first trial, Charles Phillips for the defence and 'the other barristers present expressed the utmost indignation against the demoralising system of policemen disguising themselves to ensnare to crime'.[38]

In the second trial, Phillips returned to this theme. Cross-examining the police officers, he discovered that Nugent and Cannon had brought six similar cases between them. He made good use of the prevalent suspicion surrounding the new police to ensure the acquittal of his client.

Very little credit was due, he said, 'to the testimony of witnesses, who acknowledged that they went into the Park in disguise for the avowed purpose of soliciting the commission of abominable crimes'. Such a mode of employing police officers was, he continued, 'most degrading, and was calculated to bring the present system into public odium'. It was well known that 'the police constables had motives for trumping up such charges', chief among which was 'obtaining the expenses attending prosecutions'. No man, he stated, 'who had observed the conduct of the new police in courts of justice could doubt this fact' and he referred to 'the circumstance to show the sort of reliance which ought to be placed upon the testimony of such men in giving evidence where the character and liberty of the subject were at stake'.[39]

Bringing prosecutions for homosexual offences often reflected badly on the arresting officer and laid him open to the ridicule of barristers and the suspicions of juries. Such a situation was clearly in the mind of the Tory MP William Bankes when he was arrested in 1841. Shortly after being surprised with a soldier in a secluded part of the Green Park, he told the officers that making the arrest and exposing his name would 'do you no good nor the others'.[40] Anxieties over police evidence were easily raised, and were intended to encourage courts in their willingness to protect both respectability and the freedoms of gentlemen from the accusations of their social inferiors. In 1833, Charles Baring Wall, an MP and nephew of the banker Sir Thomas Baring, was accused of soliciting a policeman in the street. Sir James Scarlett argued that if such a charge, based as it was on the most 'improbable' evidence, could be brought to court, 'no man who walked the streets at 12 o'clock at night could secure himself from the designs of a policeman'. He himself, he went on, had walked abroad in the fresh night air, 'and how many others had done the same[?]'. He told the jury that his client had to be acquitted, for the sake of 'the safety of their fellow subjects, [and] for [your] own security'.[41]

That the police frequently acted as a lightning conductor for the fears of the respectable about the expansion of the state and the sanctity of privacy did not mean that sometimes these fears were without foundation. The discretion of police officers over arrest, prosecution and costs could clearly provide a set of powerful temptations. One of these was complicity in the crime itself. As we have seen, the police clearly were not above soliciting homosexual advances in order to make an arrest, a practice which had been prevalent in the eighteenth century and which was still the most reliable way to make such an arrest in the twentieth. A small minority of indictments presented at the Central Criminal Court suggest that this was the case before 1850 as well. In three cases out of 28 indictments presented in 1836 and three out of

31 in 1844, a police officer was both the 'victim' of an indecent assault and the principal witness for the prosecution.[42]

The suspicion of complicity which attached to police prosecutions of sodomites encouraged a particular focus on the character of the arresting officer. Estimations of good character were particularly important in deciding whether a prosecution should go forward. When a gentleman like William Bankes was arrested, it was the police and not the defendant who had to prove their moral rectitude. The man who had arrested Bankes, PC William Bennett, was, according to the brief for the prosecution, a safe pair of hands whose evidence would probably be unshakable. He had 'been years a police constable' and 'owns an excellent character in the force, and Inspector Pearce will be in court to prove it'.[43]

Bribery could also make the police complicit in the crime. Other evidence given in this case demonstrates the nature of temptations available to those arresting gentlemen of means. One of the officers in the Bankes case, William Hard, claimed that a man named Tidmarsh, whom he assumed was one of Bankes's associates, had offered him some lavish bribes. Mistaking Hard for the arresting officer, Tidmarsh had told him that he was 'foolish I did not accept of Bankes's offer' but that 'I had now an opportunity of doing some good for myself'. After inquiring 'how I was situated in the force' and how he was off for clothes, Tidmarsh offered Hard £50 with a further £500 to follow, plus a trip to Doncaster Races if he went before the Grand Jury 'and said something to get the bill thrown out'.[44] This offer was refused, and Bankes was forced to escape by jumping bail.

The tendency of offenders to 'compound' in this way not only put considerable amounts of money in the way of punishment, but also facilitated extortion on a much larger scale. Extortionists sometimes disguised themselves as, or pretended to be, policemen in order to make use of the willingness of those accused to pay off arresting officers. In 1884, the trial of Edward Glynn, Walter Lusty and Alice Nelson for extortion exposed a system of threats which the three had been using for a number of years. Lusty would invite an advance from a stranger, whereupon Glynn, who 'had previously been in the police force and knew the ways of the courts and police', would appear in police uniform and demand money to forestall an arrest.[45] The result of this combination of disguise, extortion and bribery was that police evidence of an indecent assault was often insufficient to convict. By the 1860s it could be confidently asserted that accusations of this kind were 'very frequently made by soldiers and a bad class of policeman'.[46] Suspicion of the motives of the police and the legitimacy of their authority were important factors in reducing their enthusiasm for the prosecution of sodomy and sex offences in general.

Stefan Petrow has shown that by the 1880s difficulties of the kind listed above had ensured that a *laissez-faire* attitude to most forms of prostitution was firmly in place. Petrow suggests that, as a matter of policy, the police disliked the amount of time taken up by the policing of prostitution.[47] Convictions were difficult to obtain against brothels and the people involved in their management, often involving considerable expenditure of manpower for an uncertain result. Most policemen, Petrow argues, 'regarded policing street prostitution as an unwelcome chore, diverting them from more important work'.[48] Charles Warren, who was Commissioner of the Metropolitan Police in the 1880s, even directed that the police were no longer to be used to watch brothels at the request of local authorities, although the Home Office disagreed. Warren's successor, James Munro, wrote in February 1889 that the discretion over the policing of prostitution operated by the individual police officer was an understandable result of the complexities of the law and the demands on manpower. 'I cannot feel any surprise,' he wrote, 'at the system of laissez faire adopted, as on the whole under the circumstances, the safest.'[49] As Petrow demonstrates, the Home Office was in full agreement. Its stated policy was to be 'entirely against' clamping down on prostitutes. However, it was conceded that the police may have to act in individual cases as 'public opinion will not allow the matter to be left entirely alone' and 'decency requires the most glaring cases to be suppressed'.[50] The policy of the Home Office and the police, then, was to act only when it became unavoidable. The Cleveland Street scandal of 1889 showed that the same attitude prevailed towards homosexual prostitution. During cross-examination of John Saul, who was a self-confessed 'mary anne', it was claimed that the police in the West End had 'deliberately shut their eyes' to his 'infamous practices'. They had, Saul added, 'shut their eyes to more than me'.[51]

2. Evidence

The police, both before and after 1829, not only faced considerable temptations resulting from the discretion which they enjoyed over whether or not to prosecute, but, as we have seen, also faced strong objections to the supposed threat they posed to individual liberty. An even greater obstacle to the policing of same-sex desire was the severe practical difficulty in collecting the appropriate evidence, a problem which appears to have encouraged the temporary use of 'disguise' and entrapment. These difficulties, I suggest, appear to have encouraged the police to act mainly against public offences which could be easily prosecuted. Private offences, although equally illegal, were a different matter.

Some problems of evidence related to the nature of investigation. In 1826, the high Tory evangelical Duke of Newcastle, who had sent his valet and two others to the gallows in 1823 after discovering a love letter to them from a gentleman, initiated his own inquiries against 'certain persons supposed to be guilty of unnatural practices' in London. However, his agent, the Bow Street officer Samuel Taunton, was unsuccessful in obtaining 'information amounting to proof'. The Duke expressed surprise that 'men so skilled in gaining information should have been able to obtain so very little on the subject'.[52] Employed in this way, Runners could be an expensive luxury for amateur policemen like the Duke. Even in 1806 each officer employed by a vice/prosecution society in Shoreditch cost half a guinea per day, plus 6s per day for two assistants.[53]

Another case from 1825 highlights the lengths that Bow Street officers had to go in raiding or infiltrating private premises. In July, the magistrate at that office, Sir Richard Birnie, had been warned 'by some respectable persons living in the Strand… that there was strong reasons to believe that a gang of fellows were in the habit of meeting at the Barley-Mow public house, in the Strand, for purposes that cannot be named in a public journal'. Sir Richard ordered two of his patrol to visit the house, mix with the company and investigate. However, as *The Times* reported:

> The patrols, on first going to the house in the characters, of course, of mere casual customers, were unable to gain admission to the room upstairs, where it was said the meetings of the filthy gang were held, and they were under the necessity of spending a great deal of time and money, and of making themselves very friendly and familiar with the landlord and his customers before they were permitted to join the company upstairs.

When they did gain access, they discovered that their suspicions were well founded: every Sunday and Monday a musical evening known as a 'free and easy' was held and 'It was on these nights that scenes of the most horrible kind took place'. The patrol 'were obliged for some time to be patient witnesses of them, in order to get a sufficient knowledge of the principal actors to enable them to support a case against them' but 'at length it was thought that sufficient evidence was obtained' and 25 men were arrested.[54] However, only seven were eventually convicted of indecent assault, a result which could hardly be said to justify similar action elsewhere.[55]

As a result of the difficulties of evidence, compounded by the general sensitivity of the subject, the Metropolitan Police began to draw a distinction between homosexual offences committed in public and private. The fragmentary archive evidence suggests that they were unwilling to raid private premises, probably because of the difficulty of obtaining reliable evidence. Neither was publicity to be risked without the certainty of conviction. It is difficult to find any evidence of official attitudes to the policing of sodomy and male prostitution in official records before the Cleveland Street affair of 1889 revealed the shocking extent of governmental inaction. However, one fragment from the files of the Metropolitan Police might be taken as an indication that the authorities took a supervisory attitude towards prostitution as long as it remained in private. One 1875 letter from Sir Edmund Henderson, Commissioner of the Metropolitan Police, to Sir Richard Airey, Adjutant-General of the Horse Guards, refers to police action with regard to a house of ill-fame in the Regent's Park area. At the house, soldiers and gentlemen were seen coming and going, circumstances which call to mind John Addington Symonds' own erotic adventures in the area in 1877.[56] The letter encloses a series of reports, which have not survived, and draws attention to the house in Park Place, 'in which you will see some additional soldiers are implicated'. However, the Commissioner continued:

> We think we have now carried the investigation as far as we can with advantage and I have instructed the superintendent to have any civilians leaving the house to-night 'interviewed' by the Police and requested to state their business etc. which as we do not propose to undertake a prosecution is all I can do to make them I hope uncomfortable. On Monday I shall post a constable in uniform to take note of persons entering, but the house will probably be closed for those practices after to-night.[57]

It was often the case that the police tolerated other illegal gatherings because they felt they could not present a watertight case. This aspect of policing was illustrated by attitudes to one of the characteristic institutions of urban culture in mid-Victorian England, the fancy dress, or drag ball. These gatherings were not only part of a 'sodomite' subculture but were regular features of popular entertainment in the mid-century and after. They provided justification and cover for all kinds of indecency from cross-dressing and prostitution to homosexual desire, while preserving at the same time the image of semi-legitimate entertainment.

The constraints on the action of the City of London police were exposed by one case in 1854, which revealed that a blind eye had been turned to a drag ball for nearly two years. In August 1854, the police arrested two men who had been at a fancy dress ball in the Druids' Hall, an unlicensed dancing place in Turnagain Lane in the City of

London. John Challis, aged 60, who was 'dressed in the pastoral garb of a shepherdess of the golden age', and George Campbell, 'completely equipped in female attire of the present day',[58] were placed at the bar of the Guildhall magistrates' court before Sir Robert Carden and charged with incitement, or, as the papers put it, 'conducting themselves in a manner to excite others to commit an unnatural offence'.[59]

At the committal hearing, the testimony of former City policeman Joseph Brundell that he had known of the existence of the drag balls for eighteen months, and done nothing about them, was received with incredulity by the magistrate. 'Do you mean to say,' Sir Robert Carden asked him, 'that you saw these things going on for eighteen months and reported them to your sergeant?' Brundell replied that he had, but the sergeant 'told me not to interfere unless I saw such conduct take place in the public street'. This, according to Carden, was a very serious charge to make, 'and one that ought to be investigated by the Commissioner, for it is monstrous that a house of this character should be allowed to exist in the City of London for two years and no steps taken to suppress it'. In an attempt to justify his inaction, Inspector Teague told the court, 'It is very difficult to catch them in the act, as they had men placed at every outlet to keep a look out' and that it was 'not safe' to mount a raid without proof. Carden was unimpressed, telling the police that:

> It seems to me very extraordinary if these immoral practices have been going on for some time, as the inspector and sergeant intimated, that they should not have taken greater precautions to apprehend the parties before; or, at all events, to have come prepared with a clearer case.

In the face of these problems, in particular the lack of clear evidence that it had been Campbell who had been seen committing certain acts while wearing a white muslin dress and veil, the case collapsed and the defendants were discharged.[60]

A similar sequence of events followed a fancy dress ball in Manchester in 1880. This episode shows how the wish to avoid scandal motivated the decisions of the bench and led to them to doubt the applicability of what appeared to be the clearest evidence. In the early morning of 25 September 1880, detective Jerome Caminada and a force of policemen raided the Temperance Hall in the working-class district of Hulme, having received a tip-off that a drag ball was taking place. Caminada had observed another ball four years previously without mounting a raid and had learned the means of entrance. He knocked on the door, which was answered by a man dressed as a nun, and gave the password 'Sister', imitating a female voice. The raiders, assisted by local men, then burst into the hall, and there they saw 47 men, half of whom were dressed as women, while the others were in fancy dress.

They were all arrested and appeared at Manchester magistrates' court the following day, charged with having 'solicited and incited each other to commit an unnameable offence' and with conspiring to assemble at a certain place and there soliciting and inciting each other to commit that offence.[61] The masqueraders were a mixed group, 'Their stations in life were evidently very different, some being well-dressed, while others were not only shabby and unkempt, but evidently belonged to the lower classes of society'.[62] They were not all from Manchester, but apparently formed 'a sort of private society and hold balls regularly in different parts of the country'. One of these had been held 'a short time ago' in a building near Waterloo Road in the city and although 'the police watched the proceedings on that occasion... no action was taken, though sufficient was seen to justify the suspicions which had been entertained'.[63] The masqueraders in this case, as in the Druids' Hall hearing, were well aware that no criminal charges could be brought if no acts were witnessed and went to some lengths to keep the proceedings private. Not only did they use a password, and had covered the windows with black paper, but had even employed a blind accordionist to provide the music.

Caminada and his fellow officers had got up on the roof of a nearby building in an attempt to see what was going on in the Hall. There he had seen over the black crepe paper which the masqueraders had put up against the windows and had witnessed a 'sort of dance to very quick time, which my experience has taught me is called the "can-can"' and in which 'the men in female attire took a prominent part'.[64] Richard Cobbett, putting the case for the prosecution at the committal hearings, also suggested that this was a gathering of professional sodomites and their clients and that the dancing could be interpreted as inciting the commission of an unnatural offence. The police, he said, had seen that 'From time to time persons left the public room and passed through the yard into an ante-room' and promised with grim relish that during the course of the prosecution's case the officers who had seen this, 'would describe the cries they heard and what they saw'.[65] This evidence was enough to proceed with a criminal trial, according to Cobbett, since it was 'settled law' that where one or more persons solicited to commit a felony, the fact of the soliciting was a misdemeanour in law punishable with no less than three years penal servitude. He quoted a recent case in which a surgeon at a public institution in Liverpool had been convicted of an offence exactly similar to the present one and in which the defendant had received a four-year prison sentence. It would also be possible, he argued, to charge them with conspiring to assemble with the intention of soliciting and inciting each other to the commission of unnatural offences.

However, the defence maintained that not only could the police see nothing from their vantage point on the neighbouring roof, but that there was no evidence to proceed on criminal charges of inciting or conspiracy. The defence also played on the uncertainties of the magistrates as to the evidence, and their obvious wish to avoid scandal. One of the barristers defending the masqueraders, Mr Nash, said that the police would have deserved the thanks of the community if they had been content to bring these men before the court for the offence which they had really committed: assembling in a manner calculated to be a nuisance to the people residing in York Street and taking part in an indecent exhibition.

> But when the police went beyond that and asked them to say that in this city – not in Turkey or Bulgaria or some places where these odious practices were common – but in Manchester this vice – a vice so hateful that it was unnameable among Christians – was practised or solicited, he submitted that the charge was wholly exaggerated and baseless, and one which it would require overwhelming evidence to prove.

The defence played skilfully on the magistrates' doubts about both the evidence and the probability of scandal. Mr Nash reminded the court of the difficulties of such evidence in similar cases, in particular one of six years previously in which two men had been arrested for inciting and soliciting at the Mayfield Baths in the city. Although the evidence was clear in that case, the judge, Mr Justice Bramwell, had ordered a *nolle prosequi* to be entered since, he argued, 'the words "inciting and soliciting" must be construed into an express invitation to, and naming of, the crime'. Granted, there were acts of indecency here and there in the Hall, but the police had not fixed them to any individual and as for the charge of conspiracy there was not a scrap of evidence that would connect any of them at any period previous to the night in question, and therefore it could not be said that they had conspired. The defence would be glad to put an end to this 'miserable matter' and Nash argued that 'this dirt should not be stirred up any longer'.[66]

The prosecution also recognised the reluctance of the magistrates and colluded in sending the masqueraders back to obscurity. Accordingly they suggested other ways of dealing with the case which were far more congenial to magistrates anxious to avoid further publicity. Cobbett proposed 'another way of dealing with the matter, if the bench felt that they would like such a case to be dismissed at once from public notice', which was that the defendants could be bound over to keep the peace.

He was, he said:

> aware that it was sometimes thought to be a proper thing, as a matter
> of public policy, to dispose of these kind of proceedings as quickly
> as possible, and it was his duty to call attention to the fact that the
> bench had the power, where people assembled to carry on indecent,
> disorderly, noisy and filthy proceedings of this kind, to bind the
> offenders over, and impose such sureties as they might think fit.[67]

As a result, all the prisoners were obliged to find two sureties of £25 each
and to be of good behaviour for a year. Defaulters were to be imprisoned
for three months.

Even when an apparent *prima facie* case like this could be assembled,
there was considerable reluctance to proceed. The avoidance of fruitless
prosecution, humiliation of police witnesses by counsel and the prevention
of scandal were the chief preoccupations of police and magistrates when
considering homosexual offences. The evidence of private, consenting
acts also appears to have been problematic. Distinctions of public and
private were therefore central to police practice and appear to have been
the determining factor in deciding whether to act.

Public rather than private space was the central focus of urban police
forces in a way that made the division between such spaces a boundary
line of contestation and enforcement. The police, then, were effectively
acting to prevent certain kinds of public display and disclosure. Their
efforts, and the way they were reported in the press, went a long way to
reinforcing the impression that certain areas of London were the
geographical ghettos of sodomites. For the press and public, the habitual
locations of 'Sods' and 'Margeries' were the West End, the Parks and the
City, a geography partly dictated by the regulatory practices of the police.
The parks were apparent spaces of impunity, while private spaces such as
drag balls and houses were also apparently beyond the operational reach
and the will of the police.

Metropolitan Police practice was partly dictated by operational
difficulties and by questions of authority and jurisdiction posed in the
first few years of their existence. These questions sought to dictate the role
of the new urban police. In being warned of their apparently excessive
authority by barristers and courts, the new police were effectively being
told their place within the legal system. In turn, police officers who were
scarcely better than working men were being shown where they should
work in the social hierarchy. When their arrests of upper-class men 'did
them no good' as they often did, important operational lessons were
learned. That is not to say that the police never arrested or successfully

prosecuted men of standing, rather to suggest that their most important operational decisions were made in the light of the attitude of the courts.

Evidence also presented certain difficulties, which ensured that, more often than not, the new urban police worked to prevent *public* immorality as opposed to constituting themselves as a continental-style *police des moeurs*.

The attitudes of magistrates who sought to prevent public scandal, and of lawyers who were all too keen to remind an educated audience of the excessive discretion of lower-class policemen, tended to reinforce the idea that maintaining a supervisory role with regard to homosexual offences was the best policy available. Distinctions of public and private, of secrecy and disclosure in relation to homosexuality, were therefore extended, reinforced and institutionalised by police practice.

Part II

3

Reading the Sodomite

We have seen that definitions of the public and the private were partly made by case law and were enforced by police practice. Dilemmas about disclosure also structured the practice of policing and the policies of law officers. The avoidance of discussion and scandal, which was one of the principal objectives of the police and their superiors, performed an important function, as it was seen as one of the principal tools for preventing the spread of sodomy to those who were not properly armed against its possibly insidious appeal. Recent work in the history of sexuality has emphasised the way in which discussions of homosexuality tried to escape these prohibitions by employing rich yet indirect forms of language. I want to explore here some of the direct and *public* ways of encountering and discussing the unnameable, and to suggest that there were persistent popular discourses which escaped the broad prohibition on naming the crime.

This chapter, then, explores the resources that were available for such a description. As Morris Kaplan has observed, these descriptive vocabularies employed a complex mixture of class, effeminacy, character and status rather than that of sexual identity.[1] By the 1880s, the language of social purity had been adapted to describe the city as a 'Modern Babylon' populated by aristocratic seducers of women and youth. However, the language of social purity was not the only means of associating the city with unnatural desire. Other terms were employed which linked the sodomite to the deceptive surfaces, mysteries and low life of the modern city. In spite of the often flagrant and obvious nature of urban subcultures of homosexuality, magistrates, police and journalists all used an interpretive vocabulary which tended to identify sodomites as furtive and concealed, as invisible 'impersonators'. These terms were borrowed from two sources. Firstly, from common ways of seeing the city generated by press reports of isolated crime and sensational, 'hidden' facts; and, secondly, from the Victorian obsession with appearance and 'passing', which applied most forcefully to those men and women who assumed the dress of another gender or class. Sodomites, along with a variety of other equally deceptive urban 'types', were seen as adopting various tactics of disguise to escape the gaze of the law, one of which was dressing, in an 'authentic' fashion, as a woman. In this chapter, then, I want to try and reconstruct the resonance of the language of concealment, disguise and impersonation, rather than dismissing it as insufficient or inaccurate. The language of impersonation, which applied most forcefully in the famous case of cross-dressers Ernest Boulton and Frederick Park, was used to collapse older ideas about passing and authenticity into emerging notions of sexual deviance, theatricality and urban modernity. A striking affinity therefore existed between the language generated by the criminal law and a more literary and popular account of the city and its people.

The practices of the press were clearly fundamental to the articulation of a public discourse which described homosexual desire. Yet in making this discourse, the press faced the difficulty that to even mention the unnatural crime was seen as tantamount to corrupting public morals. The difficulties of the press were a direct consequence of two factors: the increasing volume of criminal justice and the expansion of print culture. The changing nature of the press, with its increasingly liberal self-image as the central plank of a reformed, modern polity, was supposed to ensure the transparency of public institutions. However, this role meant that its public function in reporting criminal trials became ever more important, especially in the eyes of journalists, editors, barristers and politicians. Therefore the press, especially its 'respectable' part, found it increasingly necessary to pursue this form of transparency by recording political, governmental and legal proceedings in great detail. Yet at the same time, editors were morally obliged not to corrupt public morals by referring to the crime of sodomy in an open fashion. The dilemma of the press was therefore crucial in creating a form of discourse which simultaneously referred to homosexual desire, and tried to cover all traces of its existence with circumlocution and evasion.

The attempt to prevent discussion of sodomy was an established part of English legal tradition.[2] Sir William Blackstone's observation that 'the delicacy of English law... treats [sodomy], in its very indictments, as a crime not to be named' was applied in a literal fashion to the records of nineteenth-century courts.[3] Indictments for sodomy were marked 'misdemeanour', 'b———y' or 'assault with intent etc', as though even the clerks could not bring themselves to refer to the acts by name. Proceedings in these trials were not recorded in the bound volumes produced by the Central Criminal Court which covered all other criminal trials in exhaustive detail. Verdicts and names were the only way in which those convicted of unnatural crimes were recorded in official legal documentation. The trial process was also affected by the necessity of silence. For many judges and legal officials the public ritual of a sodomy trial, its reports in the press and popular forms such as the handbill or broadside threatened to spread moral corruption and even to encourage the acts themselves. Sodomy was defined by its very unthinkability, as an 'offence so unnatural as even to appear incredible'.[4] To allow it to enter the minds of unsuspecting observers was regarded as dangerous in itself. Grand juries were therefore customarily enjoined to throw out sodomy cases if they could not agree on the evidence as 'it was as well that this sort of offence should not be put into the heads of people of low education and low lives'.[5]

Self-censorship did not maintain ignorance, however. Public discourse could not be prevented, given the rising tide of prosecutions. The attempt to avoid speaking directly of the crime did, however, point to the universal assumption that homosexual desire should not be talked about, even, some thought, at the cost of abolishing the law which provoked such discussion. These discursive prohibitions also prevented any authoritative investigation into those who 'suffered' from addiction to these immoral offences. If disclosing the fact of homosexual desire was unwise, then describing sodomites was even less advisable. Nevertheless, a qualified discourse did emerge, which made the sodomite an equivocal figure whose nature could not necessarily be determined. Within these terms of representation, the lives of sodomites became defined by secrecy, by the hiding of their intentions and by their calculated imposture. Here, then, I want to examine some of the ways in which this discourse of sodomy and sodomites emerged in the press.

The avoidance of knowledge, in particular the refusal to name a particular crime, was in stark contrast to the emerging politics of liberalism and publicity. As David Vincent has pointed out, the principal liberal thinkers of the nineteenth century propounded the idea that the transparency of public institutions was an unqualified benefit. Jeremy Bentham argued that secrecy was 'an instrument of conspiracy' which 'ought not... to be the system of a regular government'.[6] Similarly, magistrates often expressed their distaste for hearings *in camera*, and usually refused requests for sodomy trials or indecent assault cases to be heard in this way. As one put it, there was 'a strong feeling against secret inquiries in the present age'.[7] The legal system was of fundamental importance to the English constitution and hence formed part of the public world which the newspapers were bound by their own liberal and self-aggrandising mission to report. Therefore, the reporting of sodomy trials represented a particularly acute conflict between the needs of political transparency and the requirements of public morality.

Press reporting of sensational court cases helped to generate anxieties over the potentially obscene nature of the press and print culture as a whole. In spite of their explicit public function, and the important role they played in exposing the guilty, police reports had an equivocal status. The presence of indecent facts in the respectable press, 'which must be shocking to ladies', was bad enough, but the prevalence of this matter also meant that women and other vulnerable readers could 'fall into [reading] it without being aware of it'.[8] Recent histories of pornography and the novel have made the point that a general concern for the morality of readers was one of the principal effects of the expanding and increasingly dominant nature of print. The work of Robert Darnton and Jean-Marie Goulemot on practices of reading in late eighteenth-century France has also shown that anxieties about new forms of representation like the novel centred around the idea that the reader might respond physically to the narrative. The danger of any text was that it might encourage solitary repose, enervation or even the acting out of what was described.[9]

Similar fears surrounded the emerging genre of pornography. Walter Kendrick has argued, famously, that the very category of pornography was a creation of the late eighteenth and early nineteenth centuries. Whereas sexual imagery had always existed, it had usually formed part of an artistic, satirical or subversive form. By the end of the eighteenth century, however, sex was beginning to be separated from its wider context and, Kendrick argues, was being placed in a new genre of sexual representation later described by the newly-minted Victorian word, pornography. Part of this process was the delineation of sex as a discrete domain of activity and knowledge.[10] Kendrick argues that pornography was not defined by its content, but by the assumption that it might cause harm and should therefore be controlled. The origin of this complex was symbolised by the eighteenth-century discovery that the revered ancient world had employed widespread and promiscuous forms of erotic representation. To protect the image of high culture and prevent the legitimisation of obscenity, sexual imagery had to be placed in a literal or metaphorical 'secret museum' and locked in a 'private case' to prevent its dangerous and corrupting effects reaching the general population. Hence, the problem of pornography was primarily one of access. As Lynda Nead suggests, pornography was problematic because it was a form of mass consumption. Questions of obscenity were therefore primarily a matter of its volume and accessibility rather than its nature.[11]

As a consequence, strenuous efforts were made by early nineteenth-century moral reformers to clamp down on this burgeoning trade. Pornography also provided an easier target for the vice societies than sex offences or public indecency, and its suppression rapidly became their principal objective. Both the Proclamation Society and the Society for the Suppression of Vice sought to eliminate London's trade in obscene, irreligious and radical books through the use of the libel laws. The main aim of the Vice Society after 1810 was 'keeping in check the Trade in obscene and licentious books and Prints'. It had, according to George Pritchard, its secretary and founder-member, 'by means of numerous prosecutions at Sessions and Assizes, [and] in Her Majesty's Court of King's Bench, been enabled to restrain it within very narrow bounds'. In particular, the exertions of the society had been 'crowned with considerable success in repressing the sale of works of the more atrocious description'. Prichard reported to Robert Peel in 1828 that one raid had effected the seizure of 241 'grossly obscene prints, [and] 64 volumes of obscene books, some containing prints of an unnatural description'.[12] Efforts to clamp down on this mainly metropolitan trade culminated in Lord Campbell's Obscene Publications Act of 1857, which was later interpreted by the courts as outlawing any form of representation which might have a tendency to 'deprave and corrupt'. The potential equivalence between seeing, thinking and doing, especially when applied to children and the working class, became the basis of England's obscenity laws, and the same principle was used to curtail discussion of unnatural lust.

It is clear that it was the morals and minds of the young, the poor and the uneducated that were the principal object of concern for men like George Prichard. In this respect, the different forms of publicity which sodomy trials attracted, from broadside singers, handbill sellers and the more legitimate 'respectable' press like *The Times* or the *Morning Chronicle*, all contained an equal threat of moral corruption. Yet even before the arrival of the 'new journalism' in the 1880s transformed coverage of scandal, the press was able to generate discussion of same-sex desire by the extensive use of euphemism and by justifying the description of such things as one of the public duties of a free press. Newspaper reports began to develop a formulaic response to the coverage of indecent assaults, involving the liberal use of asterisks, ellipsis and euphemism. Homosexual offences were always referred to as an 'abominable crime', a 'nameless', 'infamous' or 'revolting' offence. The repetition of explicit testimony was avoided by the admission that 'the evidence was, of course, unfit for publication'. However, the accompanying detail and the remaining evidence which was published left little doubt as to what type of crime had been committed.

The 'respectable' press was able to report crimes in some detail, and in ways which might have been seen as harmful to public morals, because of two key factors. The first was the legal exemption from libel proceedings which covered the reporting of criminal cases. Christopher Kent has demonstrated that the right to publish legal proceedings without fear of penalty was won during the 1790s, when a series of decisions in libel cases established that although individual reputation might suffer because details of court cases were published, such matters were 'of vast importance to the public'.[13] The second important factor was a set of assumptions which were made about the presentation of facts. What Kent has called the 'visual sobriety' of the Victorian press, and especially the way it laid out column upon column of text, tended to suggest that public institutions could be transparently viewed through its minimal mediation. The aesthetics of the newspaper report, Kent says, encouraged the belief that it was a 'colourless medium'.[14]

Perhaps more importantly, the press also justified crime reporting by claiming that police and court reports fulfilled an important public duty. Not only were they ensuring that offenders were exposed to public view, but they could argue that they were producing an authoritative account that would actually protect rather than harm public morality. Ian Burney has noted how Bentham's followers in the legal profession saw the role of the press as integral to the functioning of a reformed, liberal polity. Burney points out that Thomas Denman, a leading Benthamite barrister, saw newspaper reports as a necessary component of legitimate legal and political authority. If criminal cases aroused public attention, Denman argued, it was common for those in attendance to propagate their own version of events. One result of this situation might be that rumours which were 'partial, garbled, exaggerated, full of error... and rash suspicion' would be spread. The press, however, could act as counterweight to such proceedings by 'being present at the examination, and recording every part of it with an accuracy beyond all dispute'. The authority of scrupulous reporting would ensure that 'gossip flies abroad neglected' and also that everyone would wait 'for the next journals, which correctly represent the truth, and instantly convey it with the rapidity of beacon-lights to the most distant corners of the land'.[15] In a similar fashion, the Irish judge Baron Dowse argued in 1884 that secret hearings were themselves injurious to public morals, since it is apprehended that if the proceedings are not reported by the local journals... imaginative reports will be furnished by unprincipled persons, which will find their way into papers of the lowest class, which feed on scandal, and... possibly greater mischief [will be] done by their circulation.[16]

Views like this applied with particular relevance to a crime which ought not to be named. In 1833 it was argued that the exclusion of the press from the committal hearing of Tory MP William Bankes had been very unfortunate because it had encouraged the press to rely on the rumours of those in the gallery. This had naturally led to 'many exaggerated reports in the press', in particular the suggestion that the defendant's father had refused to acknowledge him.[17]

The self-proclaimed authority of press reporting nevertheless produced a fundamental contradiction when it was applied to the details of moral offences. The fact that the 'respectable' press was often full of stories of the worst depravity described in the greatest detail, was not lost on their less reputable rivals. One of the scandal-sheets of the 1830s which made capital from this contradiction was the *Age*. This paper was primarily devoted to the sexual indiscretions of the upper classes, so its lectures to *The Times* on morality were not without a certain disingenuous irony. In the wake of the Bankes case, the *Age* declared in pious tones that while it 'usually omit[s] all allusion' to such cases, other journals referred to them over and over again. The papers whom Lord Brougham – one of the chief promoters of the virtues of a public press – described as 'the best possible instructors' turned in this way into 'the worst possible public polluters'. Instead, the *Age* declared, of 'merely noticing the misdemeanour, which would have been the course most consonant not only with public decency, but also with public justice, they gloat on it as a kind of god-send in newsmongery and recur to it with most damnable iteration'. Such people were the same 'gentry' who, when considering journals like the *Age*, 'prate their pompous nothings concerning the licentiousness of the press!'.

The *Age* also suggested that the punishment itself encouraged this sort of disclosure. 'We may just "hint at fault",' it argued, 'against our friends in Parliament, for not considering how far the subjecting certain propensities to penal enactment, and consequently to public investigation is an advisable course for the suppression of that particular class of crime.' Were not the subject 'one we wish to avoid, we rather think that a tolerably cogent list of reasons might be adduced in favour of "re-considering the practice at present pursued"'. At any rate, 'no well-regulated mind' could doubt 'the propriety of imposing some check on that portion of the press, of whom it may be justly said that in such matters they are the veriest sinks and cesspools of pollution, calculated unless placed under proper controul, to engender a moral pest throughout the country'.[18]

In spite of the hypocrisy of the charges laid by the *Age*, some sections of the press were clearly not above using scandalous trials to sell papers. In 1833 a clergyman and tutor named John Bailey brought a libel case against the *Windsor Express* after it had suggested that his nickname among his students was 'Beast Bailey'. This assertion, the plaintiff contended, 'insinuated most clearly, by means of putting the words "beastly" and "beast" in italics, that the plaintiff had propensities of the most odious and unnatural description'.[19] The day after the initial hearing, the *Windsor Express* sought to capitalise on the sensation. It issued a handbill announcing that its next issue would contain a full report 'with some remarkable disclosures as to the character and conduct of Mr Bailey... as well as with regard to his nickname of "Beast Bailey"'.[20]

The unregulated nature of legal reporting also encouraged irresponsible forms of representation, and was another reason to suspect the morality of even the most respectable newspapers. Before the repeal of the Stamp Act in 1855, papers which did not pay the duty, according to Lord Brougham, enjoyed a 'partial monopoly' of indecency. Yet the stamped press was by no means any better and was often full of 'personal slander, not unmixed with obscenity'.[21] A particular problem, according to one editor, was that the sources of police reporting were often highly disreputable. During the first half of the century at least, coverage of legal proceedings was dependant on freelance writers taking notes in the public gallery of the courts and then selling their copy to every newspaper that would take it. John Black, the editor of the *Morning Chronicle*, told the 1843 Lords Select Committee on the laws of libel, that such reporting came 'from a channel not the very best, frequently'. In some courts they had their own reporters stationed, but most reports were provided by these 'Penny-a-Liners'. Sometimes, Black acknowledged, these men extorted money from defendants either by threatening to publish, or promising to suppress, their report. He told the committee that for most of the year these reporters, 'many of whom are men of very bad character', sold their copy to the participants in criminal cases because they could not get it into the papers.[22]

The press also had another unwelcome, if inadvertent function according to some of those accused of sodomy. Publicity, it was claimed, encouraged further persecution. George Lowndes, convicted of an indecent assault in 1841, complained in his petition to the Home Office that the reports of pressmen in the galleries had created an animus against him. 'By a report,' he told the Home Office, 'a public journal may, to all intents and purposes, act as a medium of conspiracy, and an incentive to false accusation.' He particularly lamented that extensive coverage of his case in *The Times*, *Examiner*, *Weekly Dispatch* and *Weekly Chronicle* had prejudiced his case. In particular, he suggested that the police, on reading of his previous offences, had marked him out for special attention.[23]

Lowndes' complaint suggests that the euphemistic language employed in the press was an ineffective method of preventing public knowledge. Instead, it structured a public discourse which made frequent reference to the existence of same-sex desire. Moreover, some of the favourite euphemisms of the press were, in certain contexts, explicitly associated with homosexual acts. An 'infamous crime', for example, was repeatedly defined in law as a homosexual act. This term originally referred to a crime which, if committed, meant that a person was excluded from testifying to a criminal court.[24] By the nineteenth century, however, this usage had slipped into a general adjective of condemnation, applied specifically to homosexual offences. Indeed in all the legislation relating to sodomy, except the 1861 and 1885 Acts, an infamous offence was explicitly defined as sodomy, buggery, or the attempt to commit them. Peel's 1827 Bill for Consolidating and Amending the Laws Relative to Larceny, which sought to change the penalties for threatening to accuse someone of an infamous crime, defined such a crime as

> the abominable crime of Buggery… and every assault with intent to commit the said abominable crime, and every solicitation, persuasion, promise or threat, offered or made to any person, whereby to move or induce such person to commit or permit the said abominable crime, shall be deemed an infamous crime within the meaning of this Act.[25]

This form was reiterated by a renewal of the legislation in 1847.[26]

Although we should bear in mind the danger of 'reading through' Victorian euphemisms to discover our own categories of sexual deviance beneath, it does appear to have been the case that some of these phrases were routinely used to describe same-sex desire. Words like 'unnatural', 'beast' or 'infamous' appear to have been a part of the currency of everyday language, and to have been used to define homosexual acts, if the letters of extortionists are anything to go by. The prevalence of these terms indicates that the terms of press reporting and the law were part of a wider culture which had little doubt as to what they referred. In contrast, colloquial terms like 'molly' or 'margery' were almost never used in such letters and perhaps had a more specific meaning relating to prostitution. When Joseph Drew was in dispute with his employer William Acton in 1841, he sent him a letter threatening to expose his crimes. 'In the next place,' he wrote after a lengthy denunciation of

Acton's character, 'I would ask you *who* and *what* are you? ... There's not the slightest doubt of your being a most *unnatural Beast* [since] your horrible conduct towards the youths of the concern so fully proves your vile and filthy propensities and your natural habits.' Drew found no words to describe such a man except to call him a '*thing* whose very breath would contaminate a City'. He then told him to 'leave off those unnatural *Crimes* that would if they were properly investigated lead to what you richly deserve, *Hanging* or *Transportation*'.[27]

Fears that naming the crime, even in this euphemistic fashion, would cause moral injury were also at the disposal of those who argued against severe punishments for sodomy. Many of those who petitioned for mercy on behalf of the convicted were at pains to point out the contradictory nature of punishment. In Goodyer Long's case, one of the petitioners trying to prevent his execution told the Home Secretary, 'I need not suggest to you that an execution for such a crime is more objectionable than in almost any other case – it must tend to familiarise the minds of the spectators with a species of crime which ought not even to be named'.[28]

Frederick Cox, Chaplain of Buckinghamshire's county gaol, wrote to the Home Office on behalf of George Capel, expressing similar opinions on the propriety of punishment:

> I dare not, my Lord, allude to the crime for which the unhappy man is condemned to suffer; the less that is said of it the better. But, if this be true, how much better would it be, my Lord, to avoid so wide, so universal a promulgation of it, as the public execution of such a criminal would effect. Would not the royal mercy, my Lord, be wisely employed to avert the demoralization, the horror, which would result from such a publication? Would it not be religiously employed, to commute the present sentence into transportation for life.[29]

Others were convinced that press reporting of the criminal process was, in itself, responsible for public knowledge of a crime that would otherwise be completely unknowable. Andrew Elfenbein has pointed out that the anonymous poem *Don Leon* (*c*.1835), which argued for the legitimacy of homosexual desire, made just such a claim. The 'one propensity' of sodomites, it proposed, 'always hides,/Its sport obscene, and into darkness glides/Which none so brazen'd e'er presumed to own/Which left unheeded, would remain unknown'.[30] Prosecution and consequent publication of proceedings was held to be damaging by those who clearly felt that the private sphere should remain private and that discretion should ensure innocence. One correspondent who wrote to the Home

Office in 1830 argued that if sodomy were not a crime, it would not attract the publicity which caused it to spread among those of weak morals. If, for instance, 'no notice were taken of this crime in our civil courts and newspapers', it would probably 'become less frequent, for thousands would never know the present existence of this unnatural offence, nor should we be shocked and disgusted by the frequent public allusion to it'. The criminal process was itself at fault, since trials must produce 'very offensive evidence… the publication of which afterwards for general circulation can produce little but unmixed evil'.[31]

Even though a public discourse about sodomy was fabricated within the constraints outlined here, it was still difficult to legitimise discussion of homosexual acts. When attempts to change the law foundered, they often did so on the difficulty of merely raising the subject in a legitimate form. This was apparent even in the 1830s, when one magistrate, speaking against the retention of the death penalty for sodomy, argued that it only remained on the statute book because of 'the difficulty of finding any one hardy enough to undertake, what might be represented as, the defence of such a crime'.[32] Later attempts encountered similar difficulties. Writing to Edmund Gosse in 1891, John Addington Symonds argued that it was not that anyone denied the existence of sexual inversion, but that 'What everybody dreads is a public raking up of the question'. One judge he had talked to told him that 'he should like the English laws altered but added "there is no one to take the matter up"'.[33]

Changing the law would clearly be seen as legitimising homosexuality, and one of the means of forestalling this was to restrict public speech. However, in spite of the restrictions on naming the crime, or raising the subject of law reform, a persistent popular fascination with the sexual depravity of the upper classes ensured that sodomy trials attracted great popular interest. London's magistrates' courts in particular were treated as a form of popular theatre. When an interesting case came before the bench, especially one involving a gentleman, the court was packed and crowds thronged the streets outside. Far from remaining ignorant of this world and its supposed crimes, people in London and elsewhere took an active interest in it. 'The attraction of the police court,' the Victorian reporter Percy Fitzgerald wrote in his memoirs, 'particularly for the lower classes, has always been extraordinary, and amounts to a positive fascination.' This was also true of 'the superior classes when any case affecting persons of the same degree is in progress'.[34] Crowds of 2,000 or more could congregate around a court deciding the fate of a gentleman.[35]

The same was true of the spectacle of the assizes. In county towns as well as in London, a case involving anyone of any social standing was an object of fascination. The trial of Wiltshire magistrate John Seymour at the Salisbury assizes in March 1827 for sodomy with his servant attracted 'immense interest'. The trial 'brought together, at a very early hour, a large concourse of people of all degrees, by whom the court was filled as soon as it opened'.[36] The explicit detail of sexual acts in such a trial (although it sometimes necessitated the removal of any ladies present) was hardly a deterrent to the spectators. Even the trials of those of low status were the subject of comment in the press and among people generally. When Edward Hill of Stowey in Somerset was accused of an indecent assault in 1830, one witness said he had come to know of the case when he 'heard some children talk about the matter'.[37]

A public discourse on the subject of sodomy was possible, but was necessarily brief and often illegitimate. The trial process and the forms of knowledge which were possible within it structured this discourse and also lent legitimacy to press reports of its operations. Part of the reason why sodomy assumed its status as an open secret was the tension between liberal ideologies of public transparency and a more coercive desire to control obscenity in an age of mass print culture. One way round this dilemma was to separate knowledge of same-sex desire into authorised and unauthorised forms. The former sought and gained legitimacy, which was conferred by the reproduction of legal language, while the latter found few possibilities for legitimate public expression. Yet there were ways of describing the urban sodomite which made use of an existing vocabulary linking the city, deviance and modernity.

THE PRESS, THE CITY AND THE SODOMITE

The nineteenth-century newspaper was a particularly urban form, the leading organs of which, such as *The Times* – the 'paradigmatic Victorian newspaper'[38] – had an avowedly metropolitan focus. This was particularly true of legal columns and of the reporting of sexual offences like sodomy. Metropolitan politics was the focus of the extensive parliamentary reporting characteristic of Victorian newspapers, while London's subcultures and courts were the focus of police and law reports. The interaction between the press and the capital did not go unnoticed. Walter Bagehot's 1853 account of Dickens' urban fiction famously argued that 'London is like a newspaper'. Alexander Welsh has pointed out that Bagehot's dictum describes the press in two ways. Bagehot views the newspaper as both the product of urban life and the cause of a certain way of seeing, which presents the city as a collection of unrelated, even mysterious incidents. As Bagehot put it, 'everything is there, and everything is disconnected'.[39] The press was seen to generate two conflicting forms of understanding. The first sought to provide the fullest possible account of mainly urban political, legal and social events, while the second, as Bagehot and, later, Walter Benjamin realised, produced disorientation in the reader.[40] The bewildering array of *faits divers* generated a sense of disconnection and mystery that, as Bagehot implied, reflected the diversity and ultimate impenetrability of the city itself.

The influence of the press on seeing the city was most obviously at work in the urban literature of the mid century and in the later journalistic exposés of the 1880s. Here, the circularity of the relationship between the diverse events portrayed in the press and a literature of urban 'mystery' is clearly visible. Anne Humphreys and others have pointed out that the most famous, most influential and best-selling of these urban works, G.W.M. Reynolds' series, *The Mysteries of London* (1846–9), took many of its episodes directly from the newspaper and periodical press. As Humphreys and Judith Walkowitz have both noted, the narrative method of the *Mysteries*, which involved revealing the dissimulations, secret conspiracies and shocking facts of modern urban life, had an influence that went well beyond the actual life of the genre.[41] Walkowitz points out that the sexual secrets of the city were commonly presented in the press in the melodramatic terms associated with more popular literary forms.[42] Seeing the city as a mystery was a common feature of social investigation, urban literature and especially the new journalism of the 1880s and was typified by W.T. Stead's 'Maiden Tribute of Modern Babylon' investigation into child prostitution in 1885. Stead's series in the *Pall Mall Gazette*, Walkowitz says, borrowed sensationalist techniques directly from popular Sunday papers, mass literature like Reynolds and from scandalous metropolitan journalism of the 1830s and 1840s.[43]

The urban and metropolitan focus of the press worked with particular power when it considered, like Stead, sexual and moral offences. London's street cultures provided a critical mass of criminal cases and sensational facts, which, as we have seen, appeared regularly in the police columns of the national press. There, reported cases of sodomy and indecent assault were seen to take place repeatedly in the same places and to be committed by particular sorts of people. Gentlemen offenders were regarded by editors and public alike as particularly interesting cases, and their assignations with soldiers, policemen and artisans were the staple of the police report. This picture of the urban sodomite nevertheless contained obvious distortions. Although more criminal cases took place in London alone than in any other county or city in any single year, it was still the case that in some years as many as half the total number of committals happened outside the capital.[44] Yet the vast majority of cases reported in the press occurred in the capital where the concentration of criminal justice generated a mainly metropolitan focus. Although editorial decisions produced a particular vision of urban depravity and those who committed it, this inbuilt metropolitan bias was clearly also a function of the large number of courts, police and sodomites themselves in the metropolis. Through the interaction of subculture, courts and press, urban sensations, such as the depravity of the upper classes or the prevalence of abominable crimes, became the stock-in-trade of metropolitan journalism, urban literature and its several subsequent imitators. In this way, the city, and especially the metropolis, was inextricably associated with sexual depravity in general and in particular with the sodomite.

The way in which the Victorian sodomite took on a modern, urban form happened in specific ways. Although Sander Gilman, J. Edward Chamberlain and Daniel Pick have all presented the association of the city, sexual deviance and degeneration as a particular problem of a post-Darwinian moral and scientific worldview, I suggest here that the association of sodomy and the urban took on a variety of previous forms.[45] There were ways of 'seeing' the sodomite in the city, but it was more common for a studied ignorance to be proclaimed. The sodomite could be effeminate and therefore identifiable, but he was more likely to belong to low life, where financial necessity might be one of his motives. In addition, the sodomite made up the missing component of a mid-Victorian discussion of city 'types'. He hovered on the edge of the urban panorama as one of many deceptive 'impostors' and impersonators. The Victorian sodomite became modern then, as a figure of equivocation, both reported and unseen, flagrantly visible and at the same time invisible and mysterious.

READING THE SODOMITE: EFFEMINACY AND CLASS
One of the principal public means of interpreting the sodomite which developed in mid-Victorian Britain resulted from a complex interaction between images of urban culture, class and effeminacy. Status might be crucial to understanding the sodomite, since financial necessity could be advanced as a motive for selling oneself. On the other hand, there were circumstances in which an effeminate manner could act as a sign of unnatural desire. In spite of the fact that the sodomite was generally seen as a mysterious and secretive figure, it is generally agreed by historians of sexuality that there were popular discourses which associated effeminacy and same-sex desire in identifiable ways before the rise of sexology.[46]

Some of those accused of being sodomites were undoubtedly effeminate, and there were ways of reading them as sodomites which sometimes, but not always, depended on interpreting that effeminacy as a sign of unnatural desire. This form of knowledge, which clearly operated at a popular level to define 'Mary Annes' and 'Margeries' on the street, occasionally found its way into the structured discourse of the courtroom. In 1851, magistrates at Queen Square in the City heard that a 'respectably-dressed old man' named Sharp had been charged with having assaulted a 26-year-old man, Henry Whayman, in Hyde Park. However, the prosecutor's evidence proved extremely unsatisfactory and it was shown that Whayman had brought similar charges before, and also been convicted of an unspecified 'felony'. Sharp's barrister told the court that Whayman was 'one of the most abandoned and disgusting fellows who are prowling about London', since he had clearly made his living from extortion. The judge, Sergeant Adams, told Whayman that he did not doubt from 'looking at his dress, and the way in which he was evidently "got up," together with his general appearance and demeanour... that he was one of those filthy fellows' who walked the parks, 'pouncing on victims'. The jury, he declared, must have reached a similar opinion, since 'his attitude, his dress, his singularly effeminate manner, the peculiarity of his style of headdress and his general bearing [were] quite sufficient to indicate the sort of person he was'.[47] Neither was it only effeminacy which might suggest 'unnatural crimes'. Sometimes it could be assumed that sexual excess could be read on the body in the form of debility or disease. When planning a campaign of extortion against Samuel Wyatt, a man he had never met before, John Sullivan was alleged to have told his accomplice that 'if that is not an old *puff*, my name is not Jack Sullivan, for you can see sodomy printed on his face'.[48]

For much of the nineteenth century, sodomites might be read by their effeminacy, or their faces marked by sexual debility, but as we have seen, these did not necessarily denote a way of being. Neither did the category 'sodomite' necessarily imply gender inversion or even an intrinsic sexual preference. Kaplan suggests, from reading the testimony of a male prostitute, that the word sodomite was explicitly associated by Mary Annes with the specific sexual act which it seemed to describe.[49] There is also often a suggestion in the few remaining documents that at a popular level homosexual desire was in addition to, rather than instead of, other forms of sexual expression. Matthew Sweet's reading of the Victorian pornographic paper the *Pearl*, in which sodomy is presented in just this fashion, would also tend to confirm this suggestion, although that evidence is equivocal.[50] Another fragment, this time written in 1850 by the self-confessed 'dreadfully queer' Alfred Allen, consists of sexual propositions to a potential lover. Allen claimed to have nearly 'taken liberties with a servant maid of ours (twice I was in danger of affiliation)', before coming to his senses and realising that his love would be better spent on a young man.[51]

Kaplan's account of the Cleveland Street scandal indicates that the category 'sodomite' might be seen not only as specific to the act of sodomy, but also as intimately related to age and social position. The sodomite who emerged from Cleveland Street was either a corrupted working-class youth who had been perverted by 'gold laid down' or an aristocratic seducer.[52] Anti-aristocratic abuse of this kind borrowed extensively from a language of social purity that not only attacked the alleged aristocratic involvement in seduction and White Slavery, but also defined sexual depravity of all kinds as a form of dissipation, excess and cruelty. Yet before social purity and its melodramatic vocabulary of seduction and innocence, sodomites could be associated with the other end of the social scale, in particular with an urban 'residuum'. In the latter case, financial necessity might be regarded as a prominent motive for selling oneself. Being a sodomite might then be thought of as situational. Even those who participated in sexual acts could consider themselves diverted from the path of morality by their poverty or their youth. The letters of extortionists are frequently couched in terms of financial 'reparation' or 'compensation' for the wrong done to the writer. Henry Wood's 1857 letter to James Ware, for instance, demanding money for the various 'sods tricks' committed upon him, told his victim that 'if I had been Better off in the world you would not have done such a thing a second time I can tell you'.[53]

A calculation of this sort was made in the estimation of the character of George Osborn. He was an associate of the extortionist and former policeman Edward Glynn, and a man who also made his living by 'thieving and practising unnatural offences' in the 1870s and 1880s. Osborn was sentenced to a life term of penal servitude for extortion in 1886 and, according to the police, 'although quite a lad, was regarded as a notorious sodomite, and an associate of blackmailers'. However, his sojourn in prison had had 'a wonderful effect on him', for on his application for his release from parole conditions in 1901, he was described as married with a child and 'leading a thoroughly respectable life' in Paddington. Under these circumstances, the police concluded, 'it is not at all likely that he has any intention of reverting to his former life'.[54]

Osborn's appeals for remission provided the Home Office with an opportunity to consider his life as a 'notorious sodomite' as a case study, thereby giving us a narrative of same-sex desire very different from the sexological histories of 'inversion' being provided around this time for medical and homophile texts. Osborn's sodomite status was determined by the fact of his background, but only in the sense that poverty, idleness and immorality had been the driving forces in his life. His father, who was an unemployed stablehand and who at the time of his son's arrest had not worked for five years, told the police that his sons were 'a source of trouble to him for years past', as 'they would not work'. Their mother, a laundrywoman at St Martin's Baths, was also said to have known of her son's lifestyle and to have assisted him by procuring clients.[55]

Idleness, financial necessity and an association with the urban 'residuum' impelled George Osborn to obtain a living in his own way. There are clear parallels with the account of sexual agency provided by social purity. Just as W.T. Stead and other social purity activists defined prostitution as the corruption of girls by their environment, family life and necessity, the police saw Osborn as a temporary, although notorious, sodomite. Two overlapping ways of understanding the connection of sodomy and the city can be observed. The sodomite could be effeminate and defined by his look, dress or manner, or he could be part of urban low life, a man whose crimes were clearly a function of environment. However, the sodomite became urban not only through his place at the bottom of a metropolitan social structure, but through other ways of reading the urban landscape.

READING THE CITY, READING THE SODOMITE

Part of the equivocal and undecidable nature of the sodomite was his supposed penchant for concealment. This image did not only draw on a commonsense understanding of how a man might get away with an unnatural crime by covering his actions in secrecy. Sexual subcultures were visible and problematic in nineteenth-century London. Not only were cases of a 'shocking description' a 'frequent occurrence', but also the presence of sodomites and blackmailers was 'notorious'.[56] Instead of taking accounts of the invisible sodomite at face value, we should see his 'secrecy' and equivocal status as part of a literary and cultural tradition, which defined the city as a place of imposture and impersonation. This vocabulary of imposture was a particularly common method of interpreting those men who dressed in women's clothes and walked the city streets. I suggest here that we take this Victorian language of 'impersonation' seriously, rather than dismissing it as a misconception or as a self-serving obfuscation of the sodomite's 'real' identity and nature. The language of impersonation had a particular mid-Victorian resonance that bridged a gap between older views of the 'passing' man or woman and more modern versions of urban sexual degeneration. The male cross-dresser was therefore read as an 'impersonator', as someone who had assumed a disguise for the purpose of concealment, not because it was part of his nature. In this way, the idea of impersonation collapsed sexuality, passing, modernity, new urban practices and imposture into one amorphous category. Part of this interpretation of the sodomite was undoubtedly a distancing device, keeping the sexual aspect of his effeminacy dissociated from his desire by stressing the instrumental nature of his dress and manner. But it was also paradoxically about recognising the cross-dresser's connection with unnatural desire and placing the sodomite as a quintessentially urban figure.

Passing and impersonation, then, had particular connotations, which have been lost in most histories of male homosexuality. One reason for this is that it has become common in the history of sexuality to see older versions of sexual meaning as giving way completely to more modern, contemporary and scientific descriptions and identities. Thus, sodomy, a category of sexual acts, gave way to the idea of the homosexual as a type of person, just as the mannish lesbian replaced the female romantic friend. This search for what Sedgwick has called 'great paradigm shifts' in the history of homosexuality has, as she has noted, tended to imply that older models of meaning and identity simply die away and cease to coexist with newer, more coherent descriptions.[57] The result of such reasoning is to presume that the sexual categories of the present are stable, knowable and fixed. The ambiguity of passing, impersonation and masquerade means that these terms are placed into just such a category of the obsolete, to be superseded by scientific discourses of the self such as transvestism and gender dysphoria.

Yet Marjorie Garber, James Vernon and Terry Castle have all shown that masquerade and impersonation, when applied to figures of equivocal sexuality, had a history that began in the eighteenth century and was by no means exhausted in the twentieth. Conceptions of impersonation, when linked to sexual deviance, have a more complex history than is implied in the simple assumption that these ideas represent archaic misconceptions which have been replaced by more 'accurate' terms. In *Masquerade and Civilisation* (1986), Castle saw the masquerade as a particularly Augustan craze, a phenomenon closely associated with the eighteenth-century city. She presents the masked ball as a Bakhtinian carnival, a paradigm of an emerging modernity in which the world is inverted and the very naturalness of selfhood and identity is called into question.[58] The fashion for masquerade, she suggests, reflected the increasing possibility of social mobility and urban anonymity. However, Castle argues that this form of what was mainly entertainment for social elites had faded away by the 1790s, to be replaced by an obsession not with the shifting nature of identity, but with strict social and personal boundaries.[59]

Cross-dressing has not only a specific history, but also an ambiguous relationship to same-sex desire. In different ways, both Garber and Vernon see the cross-dresser as a protean figure, who cannot be completely subsumed by available discourses of gender reversal, sex change, transvestism, homosexuality or passing.[60] Both suggest that the cross-dresser does not simply hide a 'true' identity or sexual orientation, but disrupts the easy opposition between male and female, gay and straight by overlapping all available categories. For Garber the cross-dresser is a 'third term' who 'offers a challenge to easy notions of binarity'.[61] Cross-dressing, Garber says, is simultaneously over-determined in its association with a 'hidden' sexual deviance and underestimated as a harmless 'lark'. He/she is neither one gender nor the other, but an 'or and', who 'puts in question the idea of one: of identity, self-sufficiency, self-knowledge'.[62] In a similar way, Vernon rightly cautions against finding a stable and knowable gay or lesbian identity in the various forms of cross-dressing. His account of the interwar woman Valerie Arkell-Smith who passed for years in various male guises, but most famously as the war hero 'Colonel Barker', suggests that in spite of the available vocabulary of sexual science, he/she retained a sense of mystery. Her sexuality in particular remained ambiguous, in spite of attempts to place her as a sexological case history.[63] In these circumstances, language other than that of sexual science was used to describe her, in particular that of passing or masquerade.

Even though impersonation and masquerade had a complex association with sexuality that pre and post-dated the Victorian age, it nevertheless took on a particular nineteenth-century form in response to the problem of urbanisation. While Castle suggests that an Augustan obsession with surfaces celebrated the shape-changing nature of the carnivalesque, the Victorians were more disturbed than excited by dissimulation. Profound Victorian anxieties about imposture represented the obverse of a desire to order and 'read' the urban landscape. These worries also responded to a perceived need to divide the amorphous urban crowd into identifiable 'types' which was one of the first cultural reactions to the industrial city. The 'reader' of the urban crowd in literature, from Dickens to Poe and Baudelaire, was the *flâneur* or the 'street philosopher', the man able to look upon the 'panorama' of the city and draw general conclusions about human nature.[64] His appearance signalled a cultural response to the city which sought to reassure the middle-class reader that the urban world might be pacified and ordered. Urban literature, from the *flâneur* to Dickens and Reynolds' *Mysteries of London*, along with the sensational 'descents' into 'Darkest London' of the 1880s, presented the city as a series of signs which might be read by the initiated. Reynolds in particular presents the city as a network of secrets, which he then proceeds to unmask in an attempt to reveal the trickery that maintains an aristocratic and unequal network of power. He compared his own method to the effect of viewing an object through a microscope. To the superficial observer, it appears 'fair and attractive', but Reynolds' magnification will show that 'it swarms with disgusting, loathsome and venomous objects, wearing human shapes'.[65] Guides to urban physiognomies, which provided practical advice on how to interpret and place urban faces and bodies, were also a common mid-Victorian form.[66]

Richard Sennett, Elizabeth Wilson and, more recently, Simon Gunn have all dwelled on the Victorian obsession with public appearance.[67] Gunn suggests three reasons for this preoccupation. Firstly, it reflected the mass production of fashionable dress, which meant that clothing could no longer be a reliable guide to status. Secondly, the rebuilding of industrial cities after 1850 and the consequent development of gothic and classically-influenced prestige architectural projects turned the centre of these towns into what Gunn calls a kind of 'monumental stage-set'.[68] Thirdly, towns became the backdrop for a form of ritualistic public presence involving a form of promenading *flânerie*, which was a crucial demonstration of middle-class social power. For the urban middle classes, being seen in the city represented their commitment to urban order, civility and publicity itself.

The literature of *flânerie* and urban investigation, then, mirrored and helped to constitute social practices of display and demonstrations of status. The urban wandering of the street philosopher held the same attraction as the rituals of the middle classes: the possibility of imposing order on apparent chaos. Yet, as Gunn points out, the desire for order and legibility generated anxiety about who exactly was who. 'Fake swells', idle 'mashers' and cads of all description might be got up like gents, but they were still disreputable under their clothes. Prostitutes who endeavoured 'to imitate the style of ladies at Evening Parties and Theatres' might be impossible to distinguish from respectable women.[69] In Birmingham in the early 1880s, there was even a vogue for impersonating Oscar Wilde. Gunn also points out that the provincial metropolis was not without its own population of cross-dressing deviants.[70] Even outside London the city was full of potentially malevolent impostors, impersonators and equivocal figures whose real purpose might never be understood.

For street philosophers, nothing might be as it seemed. Richard Maxwell has explained that more than half of the characters in urban literature like Reynolds' *Mysteries* are impostors, whose true, often malevolent nature is ultimately revealed.[71] In Reynolds' 1846 story 'The Rats' Castle', his worthy and moral protagonist, Richard Markham, is at one point being shown round a criminal 'rookery' by his detective guide. Markham, whose own manly, open sincerity and frankness is the counterpoint to the array of impostors, ticket-of-leave men and false beggars, asks the constable why he did not arrest them all, to which the policeman replies, 'Lord Sir! ... If we took up all persons that we know to be impostors, we should have half London in custody'. The police only interfere, he points out, 'when we see cases so very flagrant that we can't help taking notice of them'. 'What a city of deceit and imposture this is!' Markham exclaims, 'painfully excited' by such strange details.[72]

In spite of their interpretive ambition, the literature of *flânerie*, the *Mysteries* genre, sensationalist social investigations and the press reports of urban depravity on which they drew all ultimately present the city as an intractable puzzle. There were always more secrets to uncover, more mysteries to detect, elements of the crowd which resisted the gaze. For Reynolds, there was always more to reveal, and the serial form of his stories meant that the reader had still to be initiated more deeply into the secrets and mysteries of London. The word London constituted 'a theme whose details, whether of good or evil, are inexhaustible: nor knew we, when we took up our pen to enter upon the subject, how vast – how mighty – how comprehensive it might be!'.[73]

The conventions of urban literature shared a great deal with its newspaper source material. The disorientating diversity of isolated criminality which emerged in police reports of the press was mirrored by the bewildering array of impostors and types who inhabited the pages of urban literature and street philosophy. Yet it was not only status that might be deceptive in the city. To those attuned to a certain kind of observation, the city was also a place where even gender might be deceptive, and where the usual signs of masculinity and femininity were inverted. The sodomite also appeared in the Victorian city in this contradictory guise, as an impostor, an impersonator and a figure of gender reversal, whose true purpose was concealed by his dress, his class or his location. As we shall see, this urban imagination was applied specifically in the interpretation of those arrested for wearing women's clothes. Sexual subcultures, in spite of their all too public manifestations, remained a typically shadowy presence. Only occasionally is reference made in the literature of urban investigation to the worst nocturnal abominations lurking in the city streets. George Augustus Sala's story 'The Key of the Street', in which he finds himself locked out and condemned to wander the streets, notes that at around one o'clock in the morning, few people remain outdoors. Instead it is 'The great-coated policeman, the shivering Irish prowlers, and some fleeting shadows that *seem* to be of women' who have 'taken undisputed possession of Bow Street and Long Acre'.[74] These shadowy pseudo-female figures of Covent Garden were clearly not the only equivocal figures inhabiting the nocturnal world. From the 'Swell Mob', a term for young pickpockets who dressed in the highest fashion and affected great respectability, to prostitutes and the fake 'gents', false Wildes of Birmingham and Champagne Charlies 'doing the la-di-da', the city was a place where imposture was seen to thrive as a daily practice.

Gender Inversion in the City

For those attuned to a particular kind of gaze, the city was also a place of gender inversion. An interesting source in this respect is the diary of the Victorian *flâneur* Arthur Munby. In addition to his more famous historical role as the husband of the maid-cum-diarist Hannah Cullwick, Munby enjoyed taking long walks through the city, often coming across what he felt to be typical examples of gender ambiguity. Munby's obsession with the physique of working women speaks partly of a typically Victorian association of sensuality and the lower classes, but also indicates a displaced erotic fascination with the masculine. On many of these travels Munby encountered and was fascinated by the equivocal figures of vigorous, manly women, some of whom had even assumed men's clothes. In addition to women who had assumed masculine dress, 'because it's a greater spree', more ordinary working women also caught Munby's gaze.[75] These 'phenomena', whom he met throughout the 1860s were, he acknowledged, 'totally uninteresting to the well regulated mind', but 'very satisfactory to mine'. They were women who clearly contradicted the ideological status of the middle-class woman and who had, of necessity, adopted a masculine role. For Munby, the city was alive with such gender reversals, including women like May Sullivan, 'queen of the dustwomen'. She, Munby noted with approval, was 'full chested, square shouldered', and walked down the street in an attractive 'erect, manly' fashion.[76] Another object of his fascination was the masculine street singer Madeleine Sinclair, whose true sex was a matter of guesswork for city crowds. Seeing her dancing a highland fling in 1862, Munby recorded that 'no one could make out whether she was a man or woman'. Her hair and hips were feminine, but, he recorded, 'her large bony hands, and her tall strong figure, became her male dress so well that opinions were about equally divided as to her sex'.[77] In spite of the evident femininity of some of those he encountered, Munby found a 'sort of manly beauty' in many of them.[78]

He was less pleased by men who assumed feminine airs. In April 1864, for instance, he noticed an advertisement for a dance at a low pleasure garden in Camberwell, 'admission *one shilling*', and was intrigued by the question of 'who would be attracted by such a ball?'. On arriving, he found a wooden shed in which 50 or 60 people were present, 'most of them in fancy dresses of a tawdry kind'. Several of the girls were 'drest in men's clothing, as sailors and so on: one, as a volunteer in uniform, I took for a man until somebody called her Jenny'. In addition to this familiar spectacle, 'not a few of the youths were elaborately disguised *as women* of various kinds; some so well, that only their voices showed they were not girls – and pretty girls. This is a new thing to me, and is simply disgusting'. However, even though dressing as a woman was in itself an outrage, 'it was clearly "only a lark", and the youths affected a quiet and feminine behaviour'.[79]

Yet gender reversal was not the only way in which urban types attracted and diverted the gaze of the flâneur or avoided the supervision of authority. In spite of the superficial gender inversion adopted by those men who wore women's clothes in public, they were interepreted not as congenitally effeminate, but, in ways which might have been dictated by urban literature, as 'disguised'. In these cases, the question of effeminacy was raised, but not as a means of describing the supposedly natural inclinations of the sodomite towards gender inversion. There were other, forgotten vocabularies of desire operating in which wearing women's clothes was regarded simply as an instrumental act of trickery intended to entrap unknowing men into unnatural lust.

'Impersonations' of this kind did not only have resonance in urban literature. By the 1850s, they had also taken on a new meaning in a more general sense. Laurence Senelick has noted a transition in the meaning of impersonation during the mid-Victorian period. Before the mid century, it had tended to refer to the personification of certain qualities or characteristics, but by the 1850s impersonation had come to denote the assumption of a character in its modern sense of imitation or mimicry. This latter connotation meant that impersonation increasingly referred to the assumption of an authentic persona, which could then be read as a copy of the dress, habits and ways of the person or gender being impersonated. Private theatricals in which respectable men assumed women's dress were also a mid-Victorian invention, and amounted to a positive craze. Peter Farrer's careful trawl through the Victorian and Edwardian periodical press has uncovered a suppressed fascination with stays, tight-lacing, petticoats and female attire.[80] In public performance, impersonation also took on a specific set of meanings. Peter Bailey has observed that the conventions of the music hall, in which many female and male impersonators appeared, encouraged a kind of knowing complicity in its audience. The audience inserted their own words and meanings into 'indecent' music hall songs, appropriated characters and plays and as such became used to 'reading' the spaces and gaps where sex – which was otherwise unmentionable in a public theatre – might be placed. The theatricality of impersonation in this context, Bailey implies, represented a knowing 'conspiracy of meaning' between performer and audience about the incipient indecency of music hall.[81]

Alongside this new, theatrical version of impersonation, older, less overtly sexual meanings continued to exist. The sexual suggestiveness and authenticity of impersonation merged with an older discourse which described gender reversal as an instrumental form of passing. The collapsing of theatricality into sexual and gender deviance is particularly evident in the examples of various 'woman husbands', passing women, female sailors and *flâneuses*, who occasionally turned up in the police column. The assumed chastity of women, especially in the absence of men, tended to obscure any sexual intent on the part of cross-dressing women, leaving only an assumption that they had assumed men's clothes for more prosaic reasons.[82] Escape, freedom of movement or earning a living were assumed to be the principal motivations of female cross-dressers. The process by which overlapping discourses of passing, sexuality and gender deviance were used to describe the figure of the female cross-dresser applied equally to the cross-dressing sodomite.

The numbers of cross-dressers in London has been a matter of recent debate. Charles Upchurch's work on the trial of Boulton and Park suggests that they belonged to self-identified networks of 'margeries', most of whom were middle class, and whose existence threatened the self-image of the Victorian bourgeoisie.[83] It is certainly the case that those arrested in London and other cities appeared in the press with a degree of frequency throughout the nineteenth century. Their crime was usually to have contravened the Vagrancy Act, either by loitering, or more usually by 'wearing female attire with a supposed unlawful purpose'. Most of them were young and tried to explain their actions with the almost standard admission that it was a foolish 'lark', a bet or a joke.

The apparent prevalence of such cross-dressing and prostitution was remarked upon by magistrates. They heard from the police that men who appeared before them were by no means alone in their assumption of women's clothes. When John Travers was arrested for accosting men in Pall Mall, it was noted that his 'was the second or third case of this kind which has been brought under the notice of this court within the past few weeks' and that Travers had 'associates' in his enterprise.[84] Neither were the activities of men like Travers confined to the metropolis. One Manchester policeman told magistrates in that city that 'in society, there existed a class of men, almost unknown to many gentlemen, who prowl about the streets almost to the same extent as unfortunate women'.[85]

Women's clothing worn in public by men operated as a sign of sodomy, but not in an obvious sense. It was read as a form of passing or impersonation, but such readings did not represent an unwillingness to name the crime with which it might be associated. On the contrary, the suspicion that female attire might in these circumstances be a sign of sodomy was naturally raised. The magistrate deciding Travers' case, Mr Hall, told his court that everyone 'who had any experience in life, and knew to what extent vices and crimes of the most abominable nature

Name	Offence	Date	Location of offence	Age	Occupation
Bird, James	Meeting together	1847	Shad Thames	Young man	
Campbell, George	Incitement	1854	Turnagain Lane, City	35	Lawyer
Challis, John	Incitement	1854	Turnagain Lane, City	60	
Crane, Richard	Female attire	1863	Holloway Hill	33	Grainer
Hollingsworth, Lewis	Female attire	1841	Tredegar Square	Young man	Schoolboy
Jones, Horace	Female attire	1859	Coventry St	Young man	Medical student
Lawson, William	Female attire	1877	Glasgow	Young man	
Newman, Henry	Lewd acts	1879	Wardour St	23	Boot closer
Paddon, George	Female attire	1863	Hackney Road	Young man	
Pearce, William Henry	Female attire	1876	Bishopsgate	16	Actor
Robertson, John	Female attire	1877	Glasgow	Young man	
Scott, Elijah	Idle and disorderly	1850	Minories	Young man	Runaway slave
Smith, Arthur	Lewd acts	1879	Wardour St	Young man	
Smith, Henry James	Female attire	1869	Lambeth		
Tetbenham, James	Female attire	1840	Tavistock Square	28	Footman
Thurston, Walter	Female attire	1870	Holborn		
Travers, John	Loitering	1846	Pall Mall	Young man	
22 men	Drag ball	1880	Manchester		

Table 1: Cases of Cross-Dressing reported in the press, 1800–1890.

prevailed in this large town, must deduce from the circumstances the most unfavourable conclusions'.[86] However, the association of women's clothes with sodomy was made through the idea that such 'disguise' facilitated the commission of crime, and not via an assumption that outward appearance reflected inner disposition. It was natural to conclude, Hall said, that Travers had a 'most atrocious' purpose, and that his clothing was probably assumed 'to conceal crime of the foulest character'.[87] Similarly, Elijah/Eliza Scott's dress was, in the view of Guildhall magistrates, 'a disgraceful disguise' assumed 'for the worst purposes'.[88] A declaration of similar intent might even be made by cross-dressers themselves. One such man claimed that his clothing was no more than a camouflage which might allow him to 'see a little of London life, without mixing with its abominations'. Even though the magistrate appears to have accepted this explanation, he informed the prisoner that to indulge in such 'extraordinary freaks' was, to say the least, a 'very imprudent course'.[89]

Men such as these were often thought to have assumed women's clothes in order to deceive the unsuspecting into unnatural intimacies. This interpretation appeared to have two functions. An assumption that a 'disguised' man was merely an ordinary female prostitute might excuse a police officer from taking action. Police witnesses therefore often claimed not to have seen a man in women's clothes, but a real woman. The authenticity of the performance was crucial to establishing that this impersonation might work, thereby reducing the blind-eyed complicity of police and society in tolerating and even generating the abominable crime. The officer who arrested John Travers made the standard claim that he had known of the man's existence for a while, and had seen him several times loitering about courts and alleys in the West End. However, 'supposing that he was a woman of the town', the officer simply and repeatedly 'ordered him to move on'.[90] When Constable Carney of 'K' division arrested George Paddon in the Hackney Road in July 1863, he claimed to have been entirely taken in by his appearance. It was only the 'astonishingly large crinoline' which he had been wearing which had attracted the officer's attention. Paddon's clothes were described at length in order to establish the authenticity of his imposture. These included the latest fashions for female prostitutes: the crinoline, 'of very extensive dimensions', a silk dress with an over dress and a lady's French coat trimmed with black lace 'of the newest mode' all of which were produced in court. According to Carney, whose remarks provoked knowing hilarity, Paddon looked, 'very nice indeed – quite the lady (considerable laughter)', and he affirmed that he 'should never have taken her for a man but for the crinoline (uncontrollable laughter)'.[91]

It was not only the flagrant cross-dresser who was defined by his invisibility. As we have seen, the haunts of sodomites included those parts of the city, such as the parks by night, which represented grey areas of police jurisdiction. We have also seen that gentleman made up one of the largest single groups of reported offenders. The slumming gent, then, was an urban character whose intentions might be just as mysterious as John Travers or George Paddon. Gentlemen who trawled the streets looking for sex could also assume the character of an impostor. The sodomite's *flânerie* alone might make him a figure of suspicion. In one case, a man walking around a notorious area of the West End between Orange Street and Trafalgar Square was deemed to have been 'roaming about for some unexplained motive', suggesting that 'his conduct in that respect is suspicious'.[92]

Practices of disguise might also be employed in a deliberate fashion. In February 1843, for example, two men who gave the names George Stacey and Richard Simpson were arrested in Hyde Park and charged with 'vile conduct towards each other'. Stacey was a butler, and although Simpson had a relatively humble appearance he was supposed to be 'a man of greater consequence than he appears' and had a 'military air'. He had 'assumed the appearance of a footman to disguise his rank', but was reported to be a baronet. Even after being arrested, some men were able to use the legal devices available in order to conceal their identity. These involved assuming the identity of their social inferiors and using every means available to conceal their identity, including simply refusing to reveal who they were. For instance, in June 1835 a man charged with an indecent assault on a soldier gave the name Edward Barton, which nevertheless was 'believed to be a fictitious one'. He finally confessed that he was 'in a public office, but refused to give any further explanation'.[93]

The magistrates' court might also be a place of concealment and imposture. As we have seen, lodging the responsibility of press reporting in the hands of 'penny-a-liners' could facilitate the perpetuation of anonymity through secret deals with defendants. The Clerkenwell magistrate John Greenwood was of the opinion that the practice of selling copy or extorting money on the promise of removing the names involved in a case was common. He had, he said in 1843, 'known of the suppression of names, and other names substituted', a practice which was likely to be the outcome of collusion between reporters and defendants.[94] Other ways were also found to protect the names of those arrested. Stating one's occupation as 'labourer' rather than gentleman might offer some protection from publicity. One 'James Thomas' took this route to anonymity. He was charged with indecency in company with a soldier named George Green (who did give his real name) in

February 1846. The case had, however, 'excited a great deal of interest, on account of it being understood that the elder prisoner, although described as a labourer, is, in point of fact, a man of large fortune and of station in the church'.[95] Throughout the committal hearings and the trial, Thomas was able to keep his identity secret and was finally acquitted when the witnesses for the prosecution failed to appear amid suggestions that they had been bribed.[96]

Although exposure was considered part of a condign punishment, magistrates were often powerless in the absence of other evidence to discover the real name and social status of defendants. The magistrates and police made strenuous efforts to discover Richard Simpson's real identity. One gentleman 'connected with St. James's Palace' claimed that he recognised the prisoner as a person of wealth and believed he was a deputy-Lieutenant of a county who was in the habit of attending court-levees and drawing rooms. According to this witness, Simpson was one of a number of 'gray-haired rich old debauchees [who] were in the habit of attending on court-days, and he had told the police in attendance to watch them as he knew their filthy propensities'.[97] At his second examination, Simpson's solicitor told the court in response to their protests that his client was concealing his identity, that 'You have a name given, and there is not a particle of evidence to show that this name is not the real name of the prisoner. In the absence of evidence to the contrary, you are bound to suppose that the prisoner had given his real name'. The *Morning Chronicle* was appalled that Simpson was able to escape exposure with such ease. 'It appears,' it wrote, 'that the magistrates are invested with no sufficient authority to compel a party, who chooses to assume a fictitious character to disclose his real name and condition.' One of the consequences of this was that 'persons of wealth and station charged with infamous offences are enabled to elude the punishment of public exposure, and to escape the consequence of their guilt at the cost of a little temporary inconvenience and an inconsiderable sum of money'.[98] This had also happened in a recent case where 'a disguised gentleman taken in the Park on a revolting charge' preserved his incognito but was generally assumed to be a dignitary of the church.[99]

In these readings of sodomy, those accused of unnatural offences or strongly suspected of being sodomites were men who deliberately and naturally chose to conceal themselves. Therefore when sodomites appeared in full view in the crowded spaces of the city, the contradiction which ensued tended to encourage the assumption that the sodomite could only exist in this public way by passing as a more acceptable figure, a woman or a gentleman. Just as the police, courts and press drew a line between public and private and enforced that distinction, so the sodomite, in his many guises, was supposed to exist on an identical margin, sometimes revealed, but much more often concealed. These were themes which were to resonate throughout the 1871 trial of Boulton and Park.

SODOMITES, SWELLS AND IMPERSONATORS: THE TRIAL OF BOULTON AND PARK

Historians have tended to assume that no one knew of or saw sodomy in the mid nineteenth-century city and that, as a result, no one knew what to make of cross-dressers like Ernest Boulton and Frederick Park. The trial of these 'female personators',[100] and their subsequent acquittal on the charge of conspiring to commit sodomy, is now one of the central parts of any history of male homosexuality and is justly one of the most famous criminal cases of the nineteenth century.

In April 1870, Ernest Boulton and Frederick Park, dressed in women's clothes and in character as 'Stella' and 'Fanny', were arrested as they left the Strand theatre. It emerged at the committal hearings that they had been in the habit of attending fancy dress balls in fashionable hotels and walking the West End in female attire, under the gaze of the police, since at least 1867. They had even attended the 1869 Varsity boat race in women's clothes. It was soon revealed that Boulton had been living with a penurious aristocrat named Lord Arthur Clinton, who was the son of the fourth Duke of Newcastle, a former government minister.

Further enquiries brought the police to a number of other young men who had accompanied Fanny and Stella on their urban wanderings, some of whom fled abroad rather than face justice. Lord Arthur meanwhile had the convenient misfortune to die of scarlet fever just before the scandal broke. Two other men were arrested, the American consul in Edinburgh, John Safford Fisk, and a Post Office official named Louis Hurt, both of whom had in their possession a number of love letters, along with photographs of Boulton and Park in female attire. When the police raided the latter's rooms in Wakefield Street, St Pancras, they discovered a large quantity of dresses, jewellery and make-up. The letters which passed between all four men – which spoke of the 'matrimonial squabbles' of Boulton and Lord Arthur and expressed Fisk's love for his 'angel', his 'darling Ernie', in the most extravagant terms – seemed to suggest that a network of sodomites had been exposed.

It appeared to the police that Boulton and Park were prostitutes. They seemed to have been using their Wakefield Street address to change into female clothes and wander Fitzrovia and the West End. They had, it emerged, been thrown out of the Alhambra theatre more than 20 times and had been ejected from the Burlington arcade on more than one occasion. The police had seen them in the street in the early hours, accosting gentlemen, 'As strangers, and as young women would who are out in the street at that hour of the night'.[101] The accumulation of evidence against them and the fact that the police were 'literally inundated with communication respecting this case from all parts of the country'[102] eventually led to their arrest. At Bow Street they were given a medical examination, which seemed to show that they had been habitually engaged in acts of sodomy. However, although the trial was backed by the government and conducted personally by the Attorney General, Sir John Duke Coleridge, its progress faltered and all four men were acquitted.

The interpretation of Boulton and Park has gone through distinct phases. William Roughhead, writing about the case in the 1930s, assumed that their antics had been 'mostly innocent', and were the result of a typically Victorian love of sickly, sentimental romanticism.[103] Later, H. Montgomery Hyde argued more convincingly that Boulton and Park were simply homosexuals against whom there was no adequate evidence.[104] More recently, Jeffrey Weeks and Alan Sinfield have suggested that the courts went so far as to celebrate their ignorance of homosexuality. This ignorance prevented conviction, since it could be persuasively argued by the defence that Boulton and Park were nothing more than foolish young men. Neil Bartlett and Charles Upchurch both suggest in different ways that the acquittal of Boulton and Park represented a kind of wilful ignorance, a knowing refusal to recognise that London contained a street culture of sodomites. Their acquittal meant that British society and its middle-class men could be exonerated of any suspicion that either might be implicated in the production of such horrors.

The trial has also provided historians with a number of questions, not least of which is how Fanny and Stella managed to escape the full force of Victorian justice.[105] They were, by our own standards, camp, extravagant, effeminate, all incontestable signs of an inherent homosexuality. Why, Alan Sinfield has asked, 'were Fanny and Stella and their friends not demonized, victimized, punished? That is what we have been used to'.[106] For Sinfield and Jeffrey Weeks, the acquittal of Boulton and Park resulted from the fact that homosexuality in its modern form was not yet understood. Nobody knew of London's secret world of sodomites, and therefore could not recognise the signs of sodomy like effeminacy, cross-dressing and camp when they saw them. There was simply no frame of reference in which to place Fanny and Stella's behaviour.

It was this supposed lack of interpretive apparatus which, according to this argument, gave weight and credibility to the often laughable arguments put forward by the defence. The defence argued that their clients' assumption of women's clothes in the streets was simply a result of their excessive love for theatricals, which had been demonstrated in numerous private gatherings as well as on the provincial stage. Boulton had played a female role opposite Lord Arthur in a charity performance of *The Morning Call* in Scarborough in 1869, while he and Park had undertaken a number of female roles during a theatrical tour of Essex towns the year before. These facts provided the defence with the barest justifications for the camp quality of the letters and their lives. Attempting to account for the love letters, in particular for phrases like 'my darling Ernie', Fisk's barrister told the jury, 'I have never been in America Gentlemen, but I had derived the impression that far-fetched metaphors and a certain extravagance of language was the common characteristic of Americans'.[107] As for the cross-dressing, that was the result of their passion for theatricals. Intimacy was a function of this performance, since 'great familiarity' was 'bred upon the stage'.[108]

The apparent success of these risible arguments shows, Bartlett argues, that only very few people 'saw' same sex passion when they looked at Fanny and Stella. Bartlett also argues that the trial revolves around one question: who saw that they were sodomites, and how? He suggests that the fact that they were sodomites and that London contained a street culture to which they partly belonged was unknown to most people. However, those in power saw what they were, and were determined to declare them and other sodomites non-existent. This was the purpose of the trial, which ended with the perverse but socially necessary verdict of acquittal.

Precious little space is left to interpret Boulton and Park, but I want to argue here that there was an interpretive framework in which to place their behaviour that derived from the intersection of class, idleness, effeminacy and imposture. In addition, the most frequently used description of the defendants as 'the female personators', or 'the men in women's clothes', had a specific connotation which did link impersonation with same-sex desire.

In spite of the outcome of the case, it was obvious even to the judge that cross-dressing was associated with unnatural crimes. Alexander Cockburn, the Lord Chief Justice, argued that one of the central questions of the case was the significance of Boulton and Park's dress. In particular, he said, the jury should consider whether the defendants' cross-dressing and the fact that they had exhibited themselves in public 'in the disguise which they had assumed' meant that 'the defendants had the intention of inducing persons with whom they might be brought into contact to have the unnatural and detestable connection with them that the indictment suggests'. It may be fairly said on behalf of the prosecution, he continued, that:

> what other inference can you legitimately draw if you find men painting and powdering themselves and tricking themselves out in tawdry tinsel

finery, assuming not only the appearance of women to whose sex they do not belong but of fallen women of the lowest description[?]

It may, he continued, 'be fairly asked what inference can you draw except that they have some sinister purpose like that which is suggested'.[109] As for their assumption of female roles in private life, the way the two men addressed each other as sisters, along with the apparent marital relationship between Lord Arthur and Boulton was clearly unhealthy. Did that not, he asked the jury, 'lead your mind irresistibly to the conclusion that there existed a relation analogous to and unnaturally analogous to that of husband and wife'? It certainly had that aspect, he continued, 'and a very ugly aspect it is'.[110] The public were similarly undeceived by Boulton and Park. After the committal hearings, in June 1870 a London schoolteacher received a threatening letter, which promised to 'expose you and punish you in the same way as Boulton and Park will be'.[111]

In spite of the clarity with which the Lord Chief Justice saw their unnatural intentions, many people and social groups were clearly complicit in Boulton and Park's antics. The language of impersonation and authenticity was therefore generated in this context not only to excuse the inaction of the police. On the night of their arrest, they had met and befriended a 24-year-old gentleman named Hugh Mundell, who eventually became one of the principal witnesses in the case. He was convinced Boulton and Park were women, despite the fact that when he had first met them some time before they had been dressed as men. The authenticity of their impersonation was stressed by Mundell as a means to explain his own actions, rather than those of Fanny and Stella. According to Mundell's testimony, while they were in the box at the Strand theatre another man told him that Boulton and Park were men. Mundell's acquaintance told him that 'it was the best get-up in London… and would deceive anyone'. Despite this, the young man claimed to have persisted in his belief to the contrary and, although he was beginning to entertain doubts about the more mannish Park, he was 'certain Boulton was a woman'. Eventually, Mundell said, they had given him a note on which was written the words, 'we are men', but he still refused to believe them. Echoing assumptions about the functional purpose of such 'disguises', Mundell is reported to have said that Boulton and Park 'looked so much like women that I was led away'.[112]

The arresting detective, William Chamberlain, was also party to this imagined authenticity and imposture. Chamberlain and other witnesses who had been familiar with Boulton were keen to stress the fact that they had been taken in. The detective told the court that he had seen the men for some time past in the haunts of prostitutes such as the Haymarket and the Holborn Dancing Casino. When asked if he knew they were men, Chamberlain replied, 'Well, I had seen them and I believed them to be women' and despite the fact that 'I was told differently... I did not think differently'.[113] Another witness, who had been keen to demonstrate his innocence at the committal hearing, said that he had flirted with Boulton at the Globe restaurant in Coventry Street. However, he had believed him to be a 'fascinating woman', despite the fact that Boulton wore men's clothes. Boulton, he said, 'went on in a flirting way and I kissed her or him [laughter]. I then had not the slightest doubt he was a woman'.[114]

Complicity in the crimes of Boulton and Park went beyond the police and immediate witnesses. Although Boulton and Park were seen as part of an urban world of prostitution, deception and depravity, their effeminacy could be portrayed in a far more innocent light. They could be presented as an integral part of the middle-class public world. The fact that Boulton played his female roles in private life, it was argued, rendered such conduct practically conventional. In particular, the defence sought to show that Boulton, even with his apparently 'unnatural' feminine ways, had been part of a wider society, which had welcomed him as a 'character'.

In 1869 Boulton and Park performed their impersonations on a charity tour of villages and towns in Essex. During June and July they played six towns to the same adoration and favourable reviews which the Scarborough show had received. At Romford, the show had even been sponsored by a local clergyman and a Baronet. For the defence, this demonstrated that their impersonations were entirely innocent, or that – more disturbingly – a great number of respectable people had connived at, and participated in what later came to be seen as an immoral spectacle. After their tour of Essex, Boulton in particular was the recipient of bouquets, 'mash notes' and the adoration of the local press. As 'a Correspondent' to the *Illustrated Police News* argued soon after their arrest, 'the public should... learn that there are very many others besides the unfortunate prisoners who must take to themselves some share in the disgrace of the exposure'.[115]

Others must have been thinking about the part they had played in Boulton's small fame. A Scarborough photographer, who had taken the photographs of Boulton in women's clothes which were later presented in evidence, declared that Boulton's performances in the town were 'very favourably criticised' and had been attended by 'the very best that we have in town at that time of year', including ladies. As for the photographs, there had been a 'great demand' and they had sold 'as fast as we could print them' to the tourists and gentlemen of the town.[116] While in Essex, Boulton had appeared in character at house parties held by local worthies, and had even been invited to go hunting in drag.

Boulton and Park's effeminacy was not criminal in the village halls of

Essex or in the studios of Scarborough, or even in the hunting field, but was only suggestive of 'unnatural intimacy' when they descended from the drawing room and went into the street. As Upchurch suggests, by crossing the line which separated these places and practices from respectability, Boulton, and especially Park (the son of a judge), were committing crimes against their class as much as against morals when they went abroad dressed as fallen women.

The case against the four men also depended on placing them as marginal to their class. The constant harping of the prosecution on Boulton's lack of means clearly sought to position him as a man dependent for his income on the funds of his aristocratic lover. But the recurrence of this theme in the Attorney-General's case positioned Boulton more forcefully as an idler who had explicitly rejected the mores of his lower-middle-class upbringing. Moreover, if Boulton and Park represented a betrayal of their social duty, then Fisk, Hurt and Lord Arthur Clinton were no less guilty, and no less amenable to the seductions of urban life. Although Boulton and Park have not surprisingly hogged the historical limelight, partly as a consequence of the fact that the trial revolved around proving their guilt, little attention has been paid to their gentlemanly suitors. Louis Hurt and John Fisk were hardly the idle swells of music hall legend or the socially marginal 'mashers' of the police report. Although Hurt's position as a senior clerk in the Post Office did not match his pretensions to gentility, Fisk was in a prestigious position at the American Consulate in Scotland. They were nevertheless both assumed to be part of an urban culture of 'sprees' on the town in which idleness, dissipation and financial necessity propelled its participants to ever greater heights of immorality.

'Fast' gentlemen like Fisk and Hurt could also be seen as unmanly and even effeminate. Sinfield has pointed out that leisured inactivity, which was normally associated with the aristocracy, was at odds with Victorian notions of duty, moral purpose and manliness and as such contributed to the association of sexual deviance with Wildean decadence after 1895.[117] Stefan Collini has also noted that Victorian ideals of manliness were equated with public duty and the development of a self-commanding 'character'.[118] Moral purpose, in the form of a dutiful career, was the cornerstone of masculinity. Giving in to one's selfish passions and base desires of any sort, was therefore unmanly in the truest sense. Before Wilde, then, effeminacy might describe the frivolity of the 'swell' or the 'masher', the fast young man who imitated the dress and spendthrift habits of his social superiors, just as easily as it described the cross-dresser. There is a clear lineage here between the Regency fop and the *fin de siècle* decadent, which is bridged by the swell, the Champagne Charlie and the masher, all of whom were first cousins to the *flâneur*.

Effeminacy could therefore be employed to describe the forms of dissident masculinity exhibited by Mundell, Clinton, Hurt and Fisk in a way that did not immediately suggest an unnatural passion. Their seeming lack of dutiful purpose and apparent success in presenting a respectable façade was in some ways just as worrying as their intimate connection with unnatural lust. In particular, their apparent public morality and actual private depravity generated the same doubts as to authenticity which were associated with more overt forms of 'personation' like that of Boulton and Park. The dandy, the swell and the masher were united by their duplicity, their lack of the masculine qualities of frankness, openness and candour. The dandy, as James Eli Adams observes, could be seen as effeminate without necessarily being associated with same-sex desire because of the studied theatricality of his bearing.[119] The letters of Fisk and Hurt, with their expressions of intimacy and effusive spontaneity placed them as effeminate in different ways to the unmanliness of Boulton and Park. The trial of Boulton and Park nevertheless opened up a space by which the dandy could begin to be associated with same-sex desire. The dandy and the swell, in the form of the recklessly 'extravagant' Fisk and Hurt, embodied the dangers of spontaneity and also indicated the perils of subtlety and dishonesty in masculine self-presentation.

Fisk and Hurt, like Boulton and Park, appeared to set themselves not only against sexual morals, but also against ideals of manliness. In contrast, the gentleman, who represented the highest ideal of Victorian manliness, was defined by his 'moral transparency' and his inability to dissimulate. The gentleman was 'essentially a man of truth, speaking and doing rightly, not merely in the sight of men, but in his secret and private behaviour'.[120] For him, 'discourtesy is a sin and falsehood a crime'.[121] In contrast, Fisk, Hurt and Clinton put candour, authenticity and masculinity in question by stressing the performative quality of gender. To borrow from Judith Butler, fake gents of all kinds highlighted the fact that masculinity relied on a form of enaction or even performance, and in doing so pointed to the inauthenticity or theatricality of all such identities. Fisk, Hurt and Lord Arthur Clinton were just such dandified fakes, who, although outwardly respectable, had privately derided the most hallowed of Victorian conventions. Not only had they lavished affection and gifts on other men, they had mocked marriage itself. Specifically, Fisk, for all his high character, had wondered aloud in his letters to Boulton whether he should maintain his respectable front by marrying a young 'fool' with £3,000 a year.[122]

Although, prior to the trial, Fisk and Hurt maintained their public face of gentility with some ease, Boulton and Park's other associates were more easily placed in a culture of unmanly swells and dissolute aristocrats. Hugh Mundell and Lord Arthur Clinton were more representative of the leisured immorality which Sinfield describes and were portrayed by one anonymous pamphlet as part of a large urban population of loafers. While this was hardly the language of social purity, which identified aristocratic 'minotaurs' as the characteristic sexual predators of the urban 'Babylon', such men were nevertheless the embryonic murderers and sociopaths of the future. However, they were not necessarily identified as members of a sodomite subculture. The principal defendants were, according to the anonymous pamphlet *The Lives of Boulton and Park*, part of a particularly dangerous group of young men who simply would not work, and whose idle hands had been put to a number of nefarious uses including prostitution, murder and gambling. 'That at the present day,' it said, 'we should have in England a large percentage of our population who will not work, but prefer to prey upon those who do, is a fact as alarming as it is true.' The writer urged parliament to pass legislation forcing 'idle and disreputable' men to work. Men not only like Ernest Boulton and Hugh Mundell, but also perhaps the extortionists George Osborn and Edward Glynn, should be forced by law 'to seek some means of employment and not to haunt low taverns, live upon the prostitution of the unfortunate class, or glean a livelihood by billiard marking or card sharping'.[123] Writing in 1888, Percy Fitzgerald recalled that the case was symptomatic of the moral failings of the upper classes of the period. It was, he wrote, 'but the outer eruption of a deeper social disease within', the symptoms of which were the freaks of dissolute young men. At that time, he added, 'there were a number of young aristocrats 'on the town', whose low and vulgar extravagances excited much attention and scandal', one of whom was Lord Arthur Clinton.[124]

Boulton and Park should be placed in a tradition which collapsed images of the city, sexual deviance, modernity, deception, effeminacy and social status into the all-purpose categories of 'impersonation' and disguise. Imposture also spoke to a particularly Victorian obsession with appearance and dissimulation. Yet in using this language the courts did not fail to see sodomy, but instead made the 'natural' assumption that the defendants had been indulging in an unnatural vice. Their suitors, Fisk, Hurt and Lord Arthur, ignored in most accounts, were also effeminate in their own way, distanced from manly virtue, frankness and restraint. The sodomite, then, became urban and modern in a complex and indirect way, via his association with the city, its low life and its deceptive surfaces.

The presentation of shocking crimes in the press, which was necessitated by the liberal mission of the newspaper, informed a genre of urban literature and investigation reliant on the same techniques and forms as the newspaper police column. This incestuous meeting of genres ultimately helped to produce the terms which defined the sodomite as quintessentially urban, metropolitan and modern. The sodomite was imagined in urban form. He could be effeminate in a variety of complex ways, either as an identifiable 'puff', whose face and dress gave him away, or as a deceptive, idle, fake gent. Wearing women's clothes might be read as a similar form of dissimulation, an authentic performance which paradoxically recognised and distanced his crimes. In this way 'personation' could be read as one of the techniques of the supposedly secretive and deceptive sodomite, who assumed such a 'disguise' in order to go unnoticed. For all his flagrant exhibitionism, Boulton's 'authenticity', like that of other cross-dressers such as George Paddon or John Travers, made him invisible, but only to those fearful of complicity. Boulton, Park, Fisk and Hurt finally escaped justice, not because of the determined ignorance of those who claimed to be 'taken in' by their female characters, but because of a skilful defence and an unusually sympathetic judge.

For the Lord Chief Justice, the trial confirmed the virtues of circumspection. As we have seen, Lord Cockburn had a well-developed suspicion of police authority, and one of his favourite themes in his summing up was the misplaced zeal of the arresting officers. He implied that because the prosecution's case had been so badly prepared, the Attorney General and the police should take a large share of blame for the sensation that had resulted from the case. He reprimanded both the police and the prosecution for the conduct of their case. The Metropolitan Police had not only exceeded their authority in arresting Fisk in Scotland, but had acted 'without the authority of anybody'.[125] As for the medical examination conducted by the police surgeon, Dr Paul, without the authorisation of a magistrate, he had no more authority to examine the defendants 'than if he had caught a man in the street and asked him to unbutton his breeches and let him see what was behind'.[126]

In addition to the unfavourable attitude of the judge, the prosecution's case had a central, fatal, weakness. It proposed to establish that a conspiracy had existed between the defendants and others by proving that the crime of sodomy had been committed. Thus, the entire case rested on the ability of the prosecution to prove that either Boulton or Park had committed sodomy. However, the medical evidence did not stand up to the attack of the expert witnesses for the defence and as a result acquittal was the only possible result. Boulton's body was as difficult to interpret as his effeminacy. The evidence which the police surgeon, Dr Paul, had obtained from his unauthorised examination at the magistrate's court, later turned out to have lasted no longer than three minutes behind a screen in a poorly-lit charge room. That might have been sufficient in other, less well-defended cases, but the evidence it provided in this case was flatly contradicted by Alfred Swaine Taylor, the leading medical jurist in the country, and by a host of other doctors.

The trial of Boulton and Park struck several chords with its audience: the problem of police authority; the complex association of effeminacy, class and same-sex desire; the deceptions of appearance which went on in cities; and the dissolution and idleness of *déclassé* young 'swells' on the town. The trial was a disaster for the police. They had gone to court, caused a sensation, then failed to secure a conviction. As the *Illustrated Police News* put it, the public were, 'unfortunately but too familiar with the evidence in this objectionable trial', and 'it would have been well if the prosecution had been abandoned at the very outset of proceedings'.[127] The historical paradox of Boulton and Park lies in the fact that they were undoubtedly seen as figures of unnatural desire, and yet it could not be legally proved that their behaviour added up to a specific form of guilt. Yet they were characteristic sodomites, in that they 'impersonated' women in a manner that was seen as 'authentic'. Seeing this authenticity was not only about distancing homosexual desire. It was also about recognising it. The idea of impersonation therefore collapsed several different categories of representation. Boulton and Park belonged to an urban discourse of sensation which defined the city as a place of imposture and passing, while at the same time recognising its association with sexual depravity. Boulton and Park were paradoxical in another sense as well. For their contemporaries, to make an open declaration of unnatural desire in the way they did was unthinkable. Sodomites belonged in secret corners, in nocturnal *flânerie*, not in broad daylight at social events where they could be fêted and welcomed. The cross-dresser was both eminently thinkable and, at the same time, unthinkable.

4

Respectability, Blackmail and the Transformation of Scandal

The world of the street intruded in many ways into the realm of respectability. Not only did the sodomite bridge the worlds of the effeminate swell and the streetwalker; he occasionally threatened the world of the respectable in a far more direct manner. Blackmail, which was an integral part of the sodomite's urban world, was a common feature of the Victorian city. Threatening to accuse a man of being a sodomite in the hope of extorting money from him even had a name: 'the Common Bounce'. Throughout the century, extortion was regarded as a possibly more serious crime even than sodomy itself. A striking feature of such cases is the willingness of workmates, acquaintances and strangers to make casual accusations of capital crimes on the flimsiest of pretexts. False accusation was, then, perhaps a more pressing urban danger than has hitherto been realised. In addition, blackmail represented the meeting of two worlds: the sexual underworld of the streets and the ordered realm of the respectable man of character. The blackmailer also produced an alternative public discourse to the authorised language produced by the courts and the press. He or she clashed with the formalised, orthodox and legitimate knowledge of the legal system and the press who reported it. In this way, extortion and its near relatives, scandal and slander, all threatened the social boundaries which helped to keep order in masculine public life, and especially in political life, and called for new legal sanctions to be applied against it. Yet they could not be stamped out. Even worse than the realisation that some parts of the city were dangerous places where the blackmailer held sway, was the fear that aspects of the legal system actually facilitated this clash of social worlds and enabled such disorderly speech to take place. The nature of homosexual blackmail therefore presents us with a set of individual moments when naming the crime threatened to escape the discursive boundaries that were the agreed limits of public discussion. The insinuations and allegations of the blackmailer threatened to make sodomy public in unpredictable ways. Blackmail could make public life intolerable for men, and therefore had to be controlled.

Scandal also had a role in maintaining social and moral divides. The scandal raised by the blackmailer and the press could, like secrecy, be turned to particular political and social uses. William Cohen has argued that late-Victorian scandal had wider consequences than simply revealing the indiscretions of individuals. Instead, the principal function of scandal was not necessarily to disrupt, but to re-establish the boundaries of public and private, secret and open, even while ostensibly revealing 'hidden' facts. By bringing sexual matters to public attention, and by treating homosexuality as a 'secret vice', Cohen argues, scandal announces these things 'in such a way as to establish their status as private'.[1] Scandal therefore warns sexual dissidents against the dangers of publicity, and as such was vital to the establishment of homosexuality as secret.

However, scandal and slander were not only techniques used by the powerful to condemn social and sexual deviants. Instead they were often unpredictable and threatening to the order and peace of public men and therefore required constant policing, distancing and control. Scandal had a dual character for the Victorians. As Cohen suggests, it played a part in establishing social and sexual boundaries, but at the same time it threatened those boundaries, and hence demanded that it be marginalised in law and society. Yet the tactics of the blackmailer were not always regarded as illegitimate. This chapter details the transformation of scandal, slander, blackmail and insinuations of guilt by association, as they moved from tacitly accepted aspects of public and political life, through criminalisation, to their re-emergence as central tactics of the 'new journalism' which developed in the 1880s. Critics of the new journalism who wished to maintain the decorum of public life argued that the ways in which newspapers generated and reported scandal were the same as the techniques and tactics of the blackmailer. This process of reappropriating homosexual scandal as a political tool was seen to begin with a group of Irish nationalists in the early 1880s. Men in the circle of Charles Stuart Parnell and his party, such as the editor William O'Brien, were at that time dedicated to disrupting English politics by any means. As such they had placed themselves on the margins of legitimate political debate. They put themselves beyond the pale by their very willingness to make use of the underhand methods of the extortionist and to reinvent these tactics as part of the public interest. Yet they were by no means alone in adopting such methods. Even the respectable press and the government itself were not beyond employing the services of notorious blackmailers to slander their opponents. In this way, the techniques of scandal and blackmail were seen to re-enter mainstream political life as a quasi-legitimate part of public discourse.

SODOMY, WEALTH AND RESPECTABILITY

The majority of reported cases of extortion, as 'homosexual' blackmail was known in the nineteenth century, occurred across class. The blackmailer who confronted a social superior faced the problem that a combination of wealth and respectability usually guaranteed that the weight of the law was behind gentility. Not only did material wealth enable gentlemen to obtain expert legal advice, but also the benefit of any doubt was usually extended to men of good character and high social status. These facts were, it seems, widely appreciated. A valet who tried to make allegations of sodomy against an MP in 1846, for example, was advised that 'he was acting an unwise part', and that 'at all times a servant was placed in a weak situation against a gentleman, let it be what it might'.[2] A suitable distance between urban subcultures and masculine civility and order could therefore be maintained.

There were, however, some ways to connect wealth with sodomy in public discourse long before the emergence of either the aristocratic seducer of social purity legend, or the equation of Wildean decadence with unnatural lust which marked discussions of homosexuality in the 1890s. Yet for the most part, apparently respectable gentlemen who succumbed, like the army officer William Arden who was executed in 1823, were regarded as anomalous. However, Arden and 'his crew' were therefore worthier of comment than sodomites of low status. A broadside published to celebrate the occasion of Arden's execution entitled *A Doleful Dirge on the Wicked Men* expressed particular horror that he had been 'born of good degree', and that he had run a respectable London establishment: 'a fair and proper house he kept/in Pulteney Street as well.' That he was a captain in the army made it even more horrid that he should 'condescend to do/such crimes we dare not name'.[3] In spite of this confusion, explanations of sodomy, published in broadside form and drawing on Biblical inspiration, did have a frame of reference for men like Arden. One in particular argued in religious terms that men could be lured into immorality by wealth, and specifically by abundance and lassitude. Charles Clutton, it was said, gave way 'to… excess and intemperance', because he made more money than his fellow soldiers. His crime therefore verified 'the truth of the Scripture in the prophet Ezekiel, "Behold, this was the iniquity of thy sister Sodom, pride, fulness of bread and abundance of idleness."'[4]

The rich might also be explicitly associated with the privileges of privacy. In the opinion of the London magistrate Hesney Wedgwood, sodomy was not a crime confined to the poor and degraded. Indeed, it had a particular status among the upper classes because it was impossible to detect when committed in the privacy which these social groups could afford. Wedgwood, who was the magistrate at Union Hall in Southwark, argued that not only was the punishment for consenting sodomy out of proportion to the crime, but also that there was 'a shocking inequality in this law in its operation upon the rich and poor'. It was the only crime, he suggested, 'where there is no injury done to any individual and in consequence requires a very small expence to commit it in so private a manner and to take such precautions as shall render conviction impossible'.[5]

Perhaps these accounts of the association between wealth and sodomy found a distant echo in the interpretation of the decadent figures of the 1890s. Nonetheless, most Victorian accounts of sodomy stress that it was the outcome of a pre-existing career of moral degradation, or, as we have seen, something done out of financial necessity. Yet perhaps something of Ezekiel can be found in William Acton's description of sodomy as one form of over-indulgence. For Acton, unnatural desire was the final stage in a process of decay which had begun in youth. Excessive sex at that stage polluted the body and the mind, producing a series of insatiable sexual impulses. Youthful indiscretion deadened the moral sense and weakened the body, thereby opening the way to ever-greater debauchery as a means to raise a jaded desire. Adulthood, which usually provided the means and the will to indulge a greater array of perversions, only made the condition worse. Variety and 'local stimulants' might satisfy these failing powers for a while, but they were bound to fail. 'Unnatural excitement' was finally attempted 'as a last resort', and the only check 'to the lust of the opulent satyr, is his finding himself the hero of some filthy police case – then, maybe, a convict or a voluntary exile'.[6]

Common assumptions about sodomites, then, tended to protect the respectable from overt suspicion and to insulate upper-class privilege. A wealthy man might become a sodomite, but would have had to pass through a career of depravity which would have left other traces on his character that might give him away. A respectable man of good character, on the other hand, was defined by the regularity of his habits and the status of his connections. The Victorian idea of good character, as Stefan Collini has argued, described that which was deemed to be ethically good.[7] A man of good character was also likely to be in full possession of himself, in the sense that he was able to postpone personal gratification for the sake of morality and responsibility. In terms of reputation, character stood for the fact of being known to possess this capability. Therefore, good character had two principal components: the habit of self-command which defined the rule of the will over one's own desires, and being known for such a faculty amongst one's friends and associates. Masculine respectability and good character, then, were mainly about moral self-possession, the dominion of the will over the passions and the ability to postpone personal gratification, all of which were essential measures of middle-class rectitude.

Assumptions made about the low morals and degraded character of sodomites therefore tended to insulate any man of character from suspicion. Contesting the accusations of the blackmailer, then, was partly about using one's social status and good character to face down any allegations. There were other ways in which the respectable or wealthy could defend themselves against legal inquiries. The advantages conferred by wealth could translate into procedural tactics which could lengthen or abbreviate the trial process. These methods, as well as the assumed connection between morals and respectability, helped to maintain social and moral boundaries.

The Use and Abuse of Procedure

The advantages available to the defendant of apparent good character and respectability were not only rhetorical, but were also practical. When gentlemen were arrested, they were able to use the very real procedural advantages available to those in a position to afford them. Even without the exaggerated assumption of innocence afforded to men of good character and connections, the criminal process tended to be weighted in favour of those with enough money to make use of its opportunities for gaining advantage. Through the use of bail, special juries, and the transfer of cases to superior courts, the trial process was lengthened, making it more expensive, while the delay created could be used to buy off witnesses and prosecutors.

If the offence was an indecent assault, the defendant was entitled to bail. If he could afford it this provided an ideal opportunity for either escape or tampering with witnesses. In November 1842, the realisation that inadequate levels of bail surety meant that it was open to just these abuses drew a thundering editorial from *The Times*. A defendant of 'gentlemanly appearance', who was 'discovered to be a man of considerable property, and most respectably connected', had been befriending and assaulting some of the pupils of Harrow School, for which he was arrested and charged. Bail was set at £500. This was pitifully inadequate, according to *The Times*, which argued that in the case of men of property:

> we are justified in finding the gravest fault with magistrates who satisfy themselves with the imposition of a sum which, large as it may sound to the ears of a poor man... is plainly and disgracefully insufficient to enforce the appearance of a man of fortune threatened with certain disgrace and punishment.

The man would undoubtedly forfeit his £500 and 'disappear from England'. This way of proceeding not only enabled the purchase of impunity but was nothing other than 'a most obnoxious form of class legislation – a mode of exempting the rich from the *real* force of the laws by which the poor are unsparingly (and rightly) coerced'.[8]

Even when the case went to trial there were ways in which a wealthy defendant could secure an advantage. Before the advent of police prosecutions, the expense of a trial could be compounded in a number of ways which made the case into a contest of resources. One of these was the removal of cases to the court of Queen's Bench by a writ of *certiorari*. Trials for indecent assault were often tried before sessions rather than assizes, particularly in London, but a writ of *certiorari* could be applied for in order to move the case to a higher court like the Queen's Bench, thus vastly increasing the expense of the process. When this happened, court documents would have to be reproduced, the expenses of which were often paid by the parties. However, a writ of *certiorari* could be a double-edged sword, as Hay has pointed out. Moving a case in this manner also invalidated any recognisance posted in the lower courts, thereby removing any obligation on witnesses and prosecutors to appear. In that case, they could simply bring an accusation without having any intention of proceeding to trial.[9]

Another way of using the power of privilege was to empanel a special jury. Several high-profile cases throughout the century were tried in this way, including that of MP William Bankes in 1833, Boulton and Park, the trial of Wiltshire magistrate John Seymour and others.[10] The ostensible object of a special jury was to enable the defendant to benefit from being tried by men of his own social status. In London at least, special juries were made up of 'every person who comes up to a certain qualification as banker, or esquire, or of a higher degree'.[11]

Special juries were most frequently used in the court of Chancery and the divorce court to make sure that the jury was educated enough to follow the evidence, but in sodomy trials their principal advantage was to increase the expense of proceeding and gain the sympathy of one's social equals.[12]

A group of 48 jurors was originally chosen, from which both lawyers were allowed to strike 12 men each, allowing at least some attempt to create a sympathetic group. The failure to appoint a special jury could even be grounds for casting doubt on the validity of conviction. Patrick Strachan complained in 1844 that his conviction was unsound because he had been tried by a common jury made up of 'mechanics of the lower grade', who were 'ignorant and illiterate' and 'loaded with the prejudices they had imbibed from the fabrications in the newspapers'.[13] The use of a special jury also required that the parties pay the fee of the jurymen, which was one guinea each. A special jury, according to one City official, was 'a privilege to the parties' and 'they pay very dearly for it'.[14]

Special juries and delaying tactics were two methods by which the legal process could be used to protect the privileges of wealth. Men of apparent wealth and good character might therefore be preserved from the threat of credible accusation and ultimate punishment. Servants and other men of low status 'in a weak position' against a gentleman were disadvantaged by legal procedure and by assumptions made about the equivalence of morality and respectability. However, on the city streets, no such advantages were available to resist the threats of the blackmailer. In the court the gentleman held all the cards, but in the streets and parks, the blackmailer ruled.

BLACKMAIL, EXTORTION AND CHARACTER

According to the Irish nationalist Michael Davitt, who became familiar with all kinds of criminals during his stay in Dartmoor in the 1870s, no major city in Britain was free of street blackmailers. The bounce was 'of the commonest occurrence in most large cities, especially in London' and was frequently 'the means of extracting large sums of money from many gentlemen in society who would be proof against any other species of robbery or fraud'.[15] Of all the scoundrels who 'stalk abroad in the world unhung for undetected enormities', Davitt declared, the bouncer was the most infamous. They preyed on aged victims by training 'young lads, generally thieves whom they are bringing out', to follow respectable men 'and endeavour to entice them to some out of the way place where the scoundrel who is watching pounces upon the victim'.[16] Areas of London notorious for sodomites, especially the West End and the Strand, were also well-known places of blackmail. However, scandal and accusation had not always been uniquely associated with street robbery. On the contrary, slander, scandal and the other tactics of the extortionist had begun the century as a tacitly accepted part of public life. During the next 80 years, scandal moved from being a feature of the political landscape to the margins of public life and back again. By the 1880s,

what was seen by some as slander again became a key political tactic and
was presented as a moral and social necessity. Scandal was legitimised as
a necessary aspect of the public interest.

In *Radical Underworld*, Iain McCalman established that blackmail of
all kinds was a constant accompaniment to public life at the beginning
of the century and was even regarded as an accepted political tactic.[17] In
Regency London it was possible, he implies, for threats of prosecution
and exposure of all kinds to be used without completely marginalising
the accuser. As the century progressed, however, it became harder to
make such accusations and retain respect for one's character. Threats
and blackmail became increasingly divorced from respectable public life,
partly as a result of the cultural investment in moral character and partly
through the action of the courts and parliament against blackmail and
libel. These crimes gradually became indelibly associated with a criminal
underworld and the lack of moral character, and hence lost their pseudo-
legitimate place in civil society.

A particularly popular form of blackmail at the beginning of the century
was the threat to publish defamatory material as a short book or pamphlet
in order to gain office or preferment. Spencer Perceval was even alleged to
have become Prime Minister in this way, by threatening the Prince Regent
with publication of details of his life with Princess Caroline. Informers
and government spies were also discovered to operate large-scale schemes
for preferment. In the case of one man, his blackmails resulted in 'obtaining
money… appointments or promotion for his family and friends'.[18] This
form of extortion, McCalman suggests, was, 'if not a respectable, then at
least a tacitly accepted and widely practised political mode'.[19]

The robust rituals of Regency politics also encouraged the kind of
slanderous assaults that became increasingly subject to legal sanction
as the century progressed. The radical orator Henry Hunt recalled in
his memoirs that his opponents were not above sexual allegations, and
that he was determined to respond in kind. He claimed that a 'little
gang of desperadoes' were always placed in front of him at public
meetings during the Westminster election of 1819. Their heckling
started with 'Hunt, where's your wife?' and was followed by 'a volley
of such beastly and disgusting ribaldry as would have disgraced the
most abandoned inmates of the lowest brothel in the metropolis'. Hunt's
response was to recall the arrest of the Vere Street coterie, a group of
men who had been arrested in a molly house raid and subsequently
pilloried to great public sensation nine years previously, but who clearly
remained lodged in the popular mind. He claimed that 'no one would
resort to such cowardly, base, and horrid language, but some monster
who was connected with a gang like that of Vere-street notoriety'. It

was later shown, to Hunt's satisfaction, that one of his tormentors was actually prosecuted for sodomy.[20]

As Hunt's memoirs suggest, accusations of sodomy were a constant theme of attacks on public figures in the early part of the century. McCalman points out that a particular object of suspicion was the Tory Duke of Cumberland who was repeatedly singled out by radical printers for abuse. In 1810, Sellis, the Duke's valet, had died in suspicious circumstances, allegedly after he had discovered his master in a sexual act with another man. The Duke was then supposed to have murdered him with a razor and to have tampered with the jury at the coroner's inquest, an accusation that was still being routinely repeated in 1830 when Cumberland's supposed sodomitic lust provided an easy radical shorthand for the moral corruption of anti-reform forces.[21] Personal and political disputes also threatened to degenerate into accusations of sexual indecency. Some of the most famous figures of this period, including William Cobbett, were subject to the accusation of 'unnatural propensities'.[22] The attacks on the Duke prompted one of his pamphleteering defenders to label the era encompassing the previous 20 years 'the age of Cant'. There was, Theodore Norton exclaimed in 1832, a 'ferocious appetite for slander', particularly among those who claimed devotion to morality. Men with this propensity abounded in the present generation 'to such an extent... that future historians will be justified in asserting that 'the land stank, so numerous was the fry'.[23]

Scandalous papers like the *Satirist*, *Crim. Con. Gazette* and *Paul Pry*, flourished during this 'age of cant', and argued, in the manner that Norton had identified, that their activities were a moral necessity. The *Crim. Con. Gazette* even borrowed radical gestures to elevate its declared purpose, which was to 'arrest as much as possible the progress of aristocratic vice and debauchery'.[24] In spite of the fact that they financed themselves through a combination of sensationalism and extortion, these papers took what moral high ground was available to them. 'Was there ever a period,' one editor asked, when considering the moral hypocrisy of the upper classes, 'at which the vigorous hand of the satirist was more necessary?' The justification of the public interest, so dear to later Victorian editors, was not far from articulation in these journals. Was there a time, they asked, 'when society from high to low needed castigation so unsparing?'[25] The taste for this kind of journalism was also, according to one witness, a middle-class preserve. Looking back from the comparative order of 1843 on the supposedly riotous Regency, Stanley Giffard, the editor of the *Standard*, told a Lords Select Committee that there was a smaller audience among the 'middle orders' for such 'scandalous or libellous publications' than there had been 20 years previously.[26]

The continuing vibrancy of gutter journalism also appeared to marginalise scandal and place it beyond the pale occupied by the respectable press. Lord Brougham suggested in 1834 that the emergence of obscene journals over the period since 1820 had 'formed a sort of drain for the other newspapers to carry off their worst trash'.[27] As a result, the daily papers were less preoccupied with slander than they had been. Another consequence of the increasing orderliness of print culture was that certain sexual matters were similarly marginalised. Contrary to Brougham's assertion, even scandalous papers like the *Age* were prepared to trumpet their own virtuous disinclination to name the crime of sodomy. Similarly, unstamped papers like the *Poor Man's Guardian* were unwilling to match the respectable press in the extent of their legal coverage.[28] In addition to this reticence on the subject, it also became far harder to make accusations of sodomy without at least being implicated in the crime or suspected of being a sodomite oneself. The judge presiding over one extortion trial in 1835 told the prisoner that he believed it was:

> the melancholy experience of those tribunals before whom guilty individuals of this description have been convicted, to discover that such charges are rarely if ever made except by those debased beings who are conscious of the horrid offence in their own bosom.[29]

There was also an explicit association between sodomites and extortionists, since the latter were assumed to be men who had grown 'old and unfit for their beastly traffic' and had, as a result, taken up careers as 'panders' and blackmailers.[30]

In addition to the association of blackmail with sodomites, legal sanctions were increasingly directed against the extortionist. From the late eighteenth century onwards, an array of legislation and case law was directed against 'homosexual' blackmail. Legal developments partly reflected a growing disquiet in English culture about attacks on character and reputation. Richard King's accounts of London street life, *The Complete Modern Spy... for 1781* (1781) and *New Cheats of London Exposed* (1795), mention gangs of extortionists as a particularly dangerous urban hazard. In addition, a new awareness of these dangers, along with a series of legal rulings, led to a reinterpretation of the nature of reputation. During the late eighteenth and early nineteenth centuries, the crime of extortion under threats to accuse a man of unnatural crimes gradually became a special type of robbery with its own legal status. As Anthony Simpson has pointed out, in the period between 1776 and 1841 this kind of extortion became easier to prosecute and was susceptible to harsher punishments than other forms of robbery or threats to reputation. Threats of 'heterosexual' immorality were customarily prosecuted using charges like perjury or conspiracy, both of which were difficult to prove. However, Simpson shows that 'homosexual' blackmail was not only prosecuted using charges of extortion, which had a relatively low requirement of proof, but was also established as a capital crime.[31]

'Abominable extortion' gradually became a special type of robbery, singled out from other forms of robbery with violence. Until two legal decisions in the 1770s, a successful conviction for robbery under threats or menaces could only be obtained by proving that a threat of force or personal violence to the victim had been made. However, in three cases in which extortion had taken place under accusation of unnatural crimes, it was established that threats to the character and reputation of the victim were equivalent to the threat of personal violence. These cases, according to Simpson, were 'the only exception in a legal tradition which was otherwise quite strict in regarding force as an essential ingredient of the crime of robbery'.[32] In *R v Jones* (1776), it was recognised that such a threat did constitute robbery, since 'a sufficient degree of force had been made use of', but, as W.H.D. Winder pointed out, physical force had in fact been used in this instance. In *R v Donally* (1779), however, it was asserted by Justice Willes that the threat of accusation was 'equivalent to actual violence; for no violence that can be offered could excite a greater terror in the mind, or make a man sooner part with his money'.[33] By 1796, in *R v Hickman*, Mr Justice Ashurst could argue that terror inspired by a threat could be of two kinds, 'an injury to his person, or a terror which leads him to apprehend an injury to his character'.[34] In that case, a threat to accuse a man of committing unnatural acts was 'a sufficient force to constitute the crime of robbery by putting in fear', since 'to most men the idea of losing their fame and reputation is equally, if not more terrific than the dread of personal injury'.[35]

Although legislation again followed case law in this area, parliament was no less stringent in the identification of this type of extortion as a separate offence with its own status. An Act of 1823 made accusations of certain capital and other serious crimes into a species of robbery, while the 1827 Larceny Act singled out threats to accuse someone of an infamous crime and defined it as statutory attempted robbery.[36] In addition, the 1827 Act removed the need for the victim to be put in fear. This legislation specified that it was necessary only for the accusation to be made and for property to change hands for the offence to be complete.[37] The Larceny Act was extended in 1847 in a manner that appears to have further simplified the law in relation to accusations of sodomy. It became unnecessary for property to change hands, and, as one lawyer successfully contended, 'the offence was committed immediately the accusation was made with the evil intent stated in the indictment'.[38] As a result of all this legislation, the truth or falsity of the allegations made by an extortionist and the success or otherwise of the threats could not be at issue in court.[39] The effect of these laws was to define character and reputation as needful of the protection of the state. The principal result of these legal changes, Mike Hepworth has argued, was that character and reputation came to be seen as both socially valuable and inherently unstable, as well as a vital component of the public interest.[40]

Alexander Welsh has explained the Victorian obsession with blackmail and secrets, which he finds in the Victorian novel, in two main ways.[41] First, he argues that social change created an increasingly anonymous society in which privacy took on a new meaning and force. Migration and mobility created strangers, so that general opinion rather than personal ties came to be the principal basis of reputation and self-worth. More fluid social structures also enabled escape from past places and difficulties and opened up new spaces not only for privacy, but also, more importantly, for secrecy and revelation. Secondly, Welsh identifies a 'pathology of information' developing in the first half of the nineteenth century. The expansion of print culture, the press and the state created new forms of mobile information and generated corresponding questions about the use and misuse of knowledge. The vast expansion of mail following the establishment of the penny post in 1839 and the development of the telegraph system after 1845 were central to this process of making and using new types of knowledge. In addition, the development of the law of blackmail and threats highlighted the new status of such information. Welsh notes a movement away from the idea that threats should only be illegal when they might 'overcome the ordinary free will of a firm man' and towards the suggestion that criminality should depend on the nature of the evil being threatened.[42] These legal interpretations represented a shift away from the 'archaic' idea that an individual should take it upon himself to resist such threats through the firmness of his will and towards a recognition that free-floating information which one could do nothing about might be an insuperable problem. The 1849 decision in R v Smith, which put forward the latter view, Welsh argues, represented a recognition of the fact that the individual was powerless before a revolution in knowledge. It also indicated that men and women could not have control of all the information that affected their reputation.[43]

The blackmail plots which abound in Victorian literature, and especially in the sensation novel of the mid-century, responded to these complex trends. The literary result, Welsh argues, is that the nineteenthcentury English novel 'repeatedly dwells on the hero's fear of publicity'.[44] As we have seen, the liberal rhetoric of public transparency, which was one of the articles of faith of any newspaper editor and reforming politician for most of the century, produced a corresponding dilemma about what it was proper to know and who should know it. Welsh points out that such liberal language, when combined with the Victorian information revolution, resulted in a fascination with secrecy, secret plots and societies. 'It is possible,' he writes, 'that more people believed in the secret power of a few in the nineteenth century than at any other time in history.'[45] In law as in society, publicity, secrecy and revelation were prominent obsessions.

Another contributing cause to the rise of blackmail which Welsh does not mention is the expansion of criminal justice and the increasing likelihood that accusations might lead to a court case. Blackmail clearly grew in power at a popular level because of the increasing numbers of sodomy trials and the resulting public awareness of the crime. On the streets of the Victorian city, the blackmailer was assumed to pose a secretive, strange and baleful threat to all men. In addition, allegations of sodomy appear to have been made casually and to have been taken seriously even before a legal investigation was made. It was all too possible for popular suspicions to lead to violence and even death without a proper inquiry. When labourer George Capel was thought to have committed sodomy in 1834, 'the culprit received cruel usage from his neighbours'. His house was broken into, 'he was dragged from his bed, knocked about in a terrible way' and, despite his protestations of innocence, 'hurried to the canal into which he was thrown, nor was he taken from thence till it was thought he was killed'.[46] In 1825, a man named John Axx was forced from his home by three men impersonating constables, who demanded and received 18 shillings from him. The men arrived at Axx's house, 'told the prosecutor that he must leave Leicester; they said they would not leave the house until they saw him out', after which he stayed away for more than three months.[47]

Given the seriousness of the crime of extortion and the potential result for both victim and blackmailer, it is striking that some of the accusations that reached the courts had an indiscriminate and everyday character. John Yoread told the police that he had accused Dr Kahn, proprietor of the risqué Anatomical Museum in Regent Street, because he knew a boy in Birmingham who had got two or three hundred pounds from a gentleman in this way.[48] In another case, R v Redman, it was shown that the prisoner had tried to use accusations of sodomy to sell his horse. The accused had gone to one of his associates and told him that his son had committed sodomy on a mare belonging to him. He then informed the boy's father that if he refused to buy the horse he would accuse the child of having committed the offence, which on the father's refusal he duly did. 'Failing in his attempt to dispose of the mare, he preferred the charge against the boy,' which at that time carried a maximum sentence of life imprisonment. The charge was dismissed and proceedings were undertaken against the owner of the horse for extortion, for which he was convicted.[49] A similar case had arisen in 1821 over a dispute about payment for the repairs to some shoes. This had led one of Thomas Skinner's workmates to accuse him of having committed sodomy with a mare. Skinner was convicted and sentenced to death, but escaped the gallows thanks to the efforts of a City of London official.[50] In spite of their apparently casual character, systems of extortion could result in the transfer of enormous sums of money. In 1862, one of the directors of a City bank was induced to pay nearly £3,000 over an 18-month period, roughly equivalent to £90,000 in today's values.[51]

The anonymous letter was one of the typical crimes of the powerless.[52] Threatening letters had a distinguished history in nineteenth-century England, being associated with popular protests like Luddism and the Swing Riots. For the blackmailer, letters had the obvious advantage of breaking down social boundaries and of reaching into the heart of respectability. One of the most fearful aspects of extortion was that it was directed at men of fortune who were most in need of protection. The fear inspired by blackmailers James Dovey and Roger Adams merited the death penalty, *The Times* argued, because:

> If there be any possible offence in the calendar, besides murder, for which capital punishment can properly be inflicted, it seems to be a crime like that of these persons – a crime which lies within the compass of the meanest individual, and against which the strongest or most prudent has no protection.[53]

The advantages of status and procedure which attached to the wealthy were clearly rendered irrelevant by the crime of anonymity. Victims might not even be known to the sender. Threatening letters were not always related to any sexual encounter, and in some cases the victim was chosen opportunistically on the grounds of his respectability and fortune. When William Whatoff was transported for life in 1842 for threatening to accuse two Leicester solicitors, his father argued in his petition to the Home Office that the offence was only committed from youthful indiscretion. He had been led astray by an accomplice who had told young Whatoff that the accusation was true. Apart from that, his father stated, he had 'never had communication with, or knowledge of, the parties injured until the very period that injury was inflicted upon them'.[54]

Doctors, bankers and members of the aristocracy were frequent targets. As Table 2 shows, most of the reported and prosecuted cases of extortion took place across class. Wealth of any description clearly attracted the attention of potential extortionists. The victims of Rebecca Hamilton, for instance, were a group of city merchants. In the spring of 1857, these men received a series of letters threatening them with denunciation. Most of them were unknown to their assailant and had clearly been chosen by virtue of their fortune and respectability. Two of Hamilton's victims, City merchants named Welsh and Margetson, had employed her in their warehouse, but the others, Dr William Allingham and George Hitchcock – also a merchant – and other gentlemen 'of the highest respectability and influence in the City' were apparently unknown to her. Hamilton had worked for Welsh between January 1855 and March 1856, during which time he had received letters instructing him that ' on receipt of this you are to enclose a sovereign in a letter'. If he neglected to comply he was warned that he would 'at once be denounced as a sodomite yourself and Partner' and that there were 'witnesses to prove the fact against you'. William Allingham had received similar instructions, and Hamilton had threatened not only to 'accuse you of an unnatural crime with your assistant' but also to 'Ruin your practice', whispering 'throughout all the City you are a sodomite vagabond'.[55] While Hamilton's blackmails were unsuccessful, and she was traced through the postal address she had given, the anonymity of the postal service put a wide variety of people at risk. Even William Gladstone received threatening letters. Gladstone's assailant, Charles Boydell, wrote from Vienna in 1885 threatening to accuse him of 'infamous crimes' unless he received £300. In addition to menacing public figures, it was Boydell's custom to peruse the announcement columns of English newspapers and to write to newly married men and women threatening them with the exposure of their past indiscretions.[56]

As Michael Davitt suggested in his memoirs, the streets were the favoured territory of the bouncer. Some areas were doubly perilous not only because blackmail could circumvent social and physical boundaries, but because of its seemingly pervasive nature. Like some malevolent secret society, extortionists were said to have laid down 'systems' of accusation and to have perfected techniques by which gentlemen were 'laid under contribution'. In addition, the Victorian picture of the criminal, which frequently located him or her in a 'mob' or group, often presented urban extortionists as members of large and powerful criminal gangs. Small groups of men clearly worked together, but trial proceedings often implied an established network of blackmail. In 1850, for instance, a group of men conspired to accuse a shopkeeper named Samuel Wyatt of having committed an indecent assault on one of them. The prosecution maintained that the prisoners were:

Name of offender	Date	Occupation of accuser/prosecutor
Norton, James	1838	Tailor/Minister
Dunkley, Thomas	1825	Labourer/Labourer
Whatoff, William	1842	Not stated/solicitor
Macdonald, John	1850	Not stated
Cornwall, Peter	1843	'young ruffian'/Gentleman
Coney, John	1828	'squalid young man'/Butler
Amor, Thomas	1829	Part of criminal gang/banker
Denman, Frederick	1825	Secretary/chemist
Porter, Susan	1847	Not stated/army officer
Tarbuck, William	1849	Tallow chandler/gentleman
Cooper, Samuel	1849	Soldier/clergyman
Tiddiman, Henry	1850	Bus conductor/tobacconist
Bennett, John	1850	Sugar refiner/tobacconist
Laidler, William	1850	Waiter/tobacconist
Sullivan, John	1850	Fancy willower/tobacconist
Jones, John	1850	Labourer/tobacconist
Cracknell, Horatio	1866	Carpenter/Doctor
Taylor, Charles	1876	Not stated/Doctor
Wilmot, Thomas	1854	Not stated/Warehouseman
Nash, William	1884	Land agent/JP
Pickering, John	1884	Soldier/not stated
Mills, James	1863	Clerk/Earl
Skinner, Thomas	1821	Cobbler/labourer
Hamilton, Rebecca	1855	None/Merchants
Newbery, James	1846	Groom/MP

Table 2: Occupation of Blackmailer and Prosecutor in selected reported Nineteenth-Century Extortion Trials. Source: Press Reports, Trial Proceedings.[57]

part of a gang of persons infesting the metropolis, and who under different disguises, made it their business to seek out persons of a nervous or weakly temperament and by making the most odious charges against them, succeeded in extorting from their fears in many instances large sums of money.[58]

One of the locations associated with such gangs was the print shop. As Lynda Nead has argued, the print or picture shop was frequently regarded as a moral contagion because of the often obscene nature of its display.[59] This was particularly true of the picture shops of the Strand and the neighbouring Holywell Street, which was the centre of Britain's pornography trade. Print shops, Nead suggests, were dangerous because they represented a form of promiscuous exhibition, which could attract a varied and indiscriminate crowd. The young, women and the working class could therefore be exposed to the polluting effects of obscenity in spite of the efforts of parliament and the law to protect them. In addition, the picture shop could not only be a place of licence for sodomites but might also be a location for heterosexual indecency and casual contact between men and women.

For the blackmailer the attraction of crowds was clear. They provided an ideal cover in which a casual brush of bodies could be used as either a sign of sexual interest or as a pretext for an accusation of indecent assault. In the spring of 1843, *The Times* reported that 'for some time past the attention of the police has been attracted to the numerous cases of persons committing the most flagrant assaults upon persons looking at the pictures in the windows of the respectable printsellers at the west end'. Most of these delinquents 'escaped in the crowds attracted'.[60] One accusation of assault, however, turned out on further inquiry to have been made by a man named Long, who was, according to the magistrate 'not only unworthy of belief, but who was, in fact, a member of a gang of an infamous character'. Sergeant Gray of 'C' division testified that Long was 'one of the gang who infected print shop windows and accused persons for the sake of extorting money'. He had 'for about 15 years earned his living in the most disgraceful manner'.[61] By July, complaints about indecent assaults at print shops had reached such a pitch that 'as a preventive the Commissioners of Police have sent out at various times numbers of constables in plain clothes; [but] still the nuisance persists'.[62]

It was not only the streets, but also the other haunts of sodomites which were associated with the practice of extortion. The parks, which were known for their disreputable soldiery, and West End urinals were places where it was sometimes unwise to go alone. Three men, William Campbell, George Burnett and Herbert James, were charged in November

1867 with 'loitering about different West End urinals for an improper purpose'. Two policemen, giving evidence, told the magistrate that the men were well known for 'following persons who entered those places, and attempting to extort money by certain threats'.[63] At the hearing of Henry Spencer in March 1871, charged with being in a urinal for an improper purpose, his barrister 'thought the magistrate would agree with him that it was becoming altogether dangerous to go into one of those places at all'. Mr Tyrwhitt did agree. 'It was well known,' he said, 'that urinals were visited by such scoundrels as Parker either for the purpose of robbery or something worse.'[64]

The crime statistics compiled by the government give little indication of the disquiet raised by the crime of extortion. The figures clearly reflect the difficulty of facing such an accusation, and perhaps indicate that extortion more often than not went unpunished. Moreover, the contrast between the low level of prosecution revealed by the official figures and the inflated attention which blackmail received in the press is revealing. In 1838 the prevalence of 'homosexual' extortion was officially recognised. In that year the crime of 'obtaining property by threats to accuse of unnatural crimes' was included in parliamentary statistics of the different types of robbery. Between 1838 and 1890, only two such cases per year on average reached court, although 14 cases did so in 1850.[65] However, other categories of threats could contain similar crimes, such as that of 'sending threatening letters to extort money', of which there were 4.3 per year between 1835 and 1890. It was also calculated that a proportion of those charged with robbery were extortionists. From the official statistics, Humphrey Woolrych argued in 1833 that as many as 20 per cent of those who had been charged with robbery in some years (over 1,000 offenders) were in fact 'abominable extortionists'.[66]

It was not only the sheer volume of extortion which caused concern. Blackmail threatened men in two ways: firstly by attacking their socially necessary reputation and character; secondly by its apparent ubiquity. As we have seen, character, which had a particular meaning and value within Victorian discourses of masculinity, was increasingly regarded as the basis of the social order. Sentencing two men to seven years penal servitude for extortion in 1866, the judge told them that theirs was a most serious crime since, 'True or false, there was no offence which so easily robbed a man of his character – dearer to him than his life – sowing discord between him and his friends if they believed it and proving itself in every way to be the most hateful species of slander that could be imagined.'[67] In 1838, the judge at the trial of James Norton, a tailor convicted of extortion by threats to accuse the Rev Gilbert Chestnutt of an abominable crime, told him that:

The robber on the highway who was bold and wicked enough to hold a pistol at the head of his fellow man, and demand his money or his life, was an innocent offender compared with the cowardly assassin of honour and reputation, who sheltered by darkness and secrecy, would seek in cold blood to gratify his sordid views by wounding the peace and blasting the happiness of his terrified victim. Such has been your crime... You have endeavoured by means the most wicked and odious to destroy the character of a gentleman of unblemished reputation.[68]

The scandalous *Crim. Con. Gazette* also took up the subject of blackmail following the Chestnutt case. This paper was itself known for its slanderous and indecent content, but nevertheless counselled fortitude in the face of such threats to character. The proper way to deal with a blackmailer was to confront him and face down his threats. Such advice was particularly necessary, the paper argued, because similar threats might be levelled against anyone. The *Crim. Con. Gazette* implied that all men were potential victims, and that:

to be mixed up with an offence so abominable as the one under review, is horrible in the extreme [and] there is no denying; as however, it heretofore has been, so may it again be, the misfortune of any man, although free from the taint of suspicion, to be ensnared in a similar way.[69]

The ease with which such accusations were made and the fact they placed the social order in danger necessitated harsh penalties. Mr Justice Willes said in 1866 that in extortion cases, 'a sentence must be passed, which, if possible, would protect society'. Accusations like this also produced promiscuous knowledge, which harmed more than just the man in question. If the charge were false, Willes went on, 'nothing could exceed the injury to unoffending men, for, false as it might be, foolish persons would always be found who would believe that such a charge could not be made unless there was some foundation for it'.[70] Those who did bring such prosecutions were praised for undertaking a dangerous but necessary social duty. In 1863, Mr Justice Crompton told Earl Spencer, who was prosecuting a sender of threatening letters, that 'in general, when men were attacked by such miscreants, they were too apt to yield to intimidation, [and] it was a matter of congratulation to find one so true to himself and to the community at large as to bring the matter under the cognizance of the law'.[71]

Although prosecuting an extortionist was a public duty, the law by no means provided a complete solution to the problem of blackmail.

The danger of extortion was enhanced, according to some critics, by certain features of the criminal process itself. Douglas Hay has argued that the theoretical and practical dependence of the criminal law on the action of the private prosecutor made it especially vulnerable to the contaminating influence of private interest.[72] He also suggests that malicious prosecution for all types of crime was a much greater proportion of all criminal trials than has usually been assumed. As a result, extortion was particularly dreaded by jurists and writers on the law, because it represented the abuse of both prosecutorial duties and of the justice system in general. In London, malicious prosecution was a particular problem because of the great number of courts which were constantly in session. In addition, the public presence of the police made recourse to law a natural way to solve personal disputes.

As Hay points out, the Grand Jury system, which decided whether a true bill of indictment should be returned, aroused particular concern. Until 1859, it was possible under a 'voluntary bill' for an accusation to be made directly to the Grand Jury, in secret and without the knowledge of the other party and also without the necessity of an examination before a magistrate. Accusations of this kind were likely to lead to an arrest and a trial of which the accused person had no warning, no chance of preparation and no way of knowing the charge or the name of his accuser.[73] 'How long,' the *Satirist* asked, 'is the infamous system which endows men with the power to inflict irreparable injury upon innocent people to exist?'[74] The temptation to reach some sort of financial arrangement in such circumstances must have been great. Another critic of this system, W.C. Humphreys, wrote in 1842 that the secret investigation before a Grand Jury 'is not only useless, but worse than useless, by assisting rather than suppressing crime'.[75] At every session of the Central Criminal Court, and at the sessions of Middlesex and Westminster, voluntary bills were presented. The effect of this, according to Humphreys, was that 'the accused man's fears are worked upon, and exposure by a criminal trial, perhaps for an infamous offence, is considered a blight to every hope, both of himself and his connexions'.[76] However, money could be offered to prevent a trial. 'Thus,' Humphreys lamented, 'extortion, conspiracy and false accusation are encouraged by the Grand Jury system.'[77]

Another source of dangerous publicity of all kinds was the practice of magistrates giving 'information' or 'advice'. This usually involved an *ex parte* declaration in a magistrate's court by someone complaining about an offence which was supposed to have taken place. Its ostensible purpose was to inquire about whether a criminal prosecution might be brought. The tireless efforts of Lord Brougham to purify the public sphere were also directed against the magisterial practice of information, which, he argued, encouraged the 'detestable traffic' of extortion. It was common, he said, for a sitting magistrate to be approached by a party who assumed that he had a potential case against someone else. Brougham argued that the magistrate should never hear requests for advice since they might mean that unsubstantiated allegations would appear in the press as a result. Instead, what was plainly required was for the magistrate to 'shut the mouth at once of the applicant, and to say that he, the magistrate, has nothing to do with the case, and no right to hear a word about it'.[78] In spite of the existence of these flaws in the justice system, there was, Hay argues, considerable reluctance within the legal profession to interfere with the integrity of the prosecutor by increasing the penalties for malicious prosecution.[79]

Extortion and accusation were therefore simultaneously encouraged and discouraged by certain aspects of the legal process. A promiscuous public discourse was produced in this way, which circumvented the prohibition on naming sodomy or making slanderous accusations. Blackmail also gained in power in the nineteenth century, partly because of the greater likelihood that any accusation might result in a criminal trial, a press report and public exposure. Even though it was increasingly subject to legal sanctions, slander never went away, it was simply marginalised to the fringes of the public world, where the park, the street and the scandalous journal became its natural habitat. However, tactics explicitly associated with criminals, and specifically with extortionists, were to make a comeback. During the 1880s, unsubstantiated accusations, slander and scandal became an almost legitimate part of political and public life once again.

THE TRANSFORMATION OF SCANDAL

1. The Dublin Castle Affair

Criticisms of the partiality which seemed to be inherent in the legal process partly reflected particular anxieties about knowledge and speech. In particular, such criticisms emphasised a persistent disquiet about who could lay claim to the authority of accusation and produce legitimate speech about a nameless crime. As we have seen, part of this debate about authority and legitimacy revolved around the press. Clearly, there was a public discourse which represented sodomy trials before the arrival of the 'new journalism' in the 1880s, and we have seen that such representations were regarded as bordering on the scandalous. However, authority to print these details was gained by presenting these columns as part of the inherently public legal process. Authoritative accounts were also deemed to be in the public interest and acted to prevent ill-informed and illegitimate knowledge. Before the 1880s, press reports of sodomy and sodomites reproduced a sanitised version of legal reporting, leaving out 'disgusting' evidence, but also asserting authority via the imitation of the legal transcript. In this way, only legal evidence could be presented. Suspicion or scandal was confined to those immediately involved in the case, with public discourse forced into a rigid form. The blackmailer, on the other hand, generated not only particular accusations, but brought popular suspicions and promiscuous speech to the public world. His or her accusations were defined by their lack of authority and the absence of anything that the courts or the respectable press might recognise as substance.

I want to show here that those who criticised new journalists for bringing homosexuality into the public realm during the 1880s saw the new evening press as having a deep affinity with the blackmailer. The papers which broke both the Dublin Castle affair in 1883–4 and the Cleveland Street scandal in 1889–90 were seen as illegitimate sources of knowledge and accusation. For their critics, these papers were spreading around unfounded accusations, and publishing them in a public form, in the same way that an extortionist would. The defenders of the evening press, on the other hand, presented such tactics as a necessary means to further the public interest. To complicate matters, proponents of the new journalism argued that such methods were at the heart of journalistic practice and had been for a long time. It was sheer hypocrisy to pretend otherwise.

Scandal resulted from the clash of these two worldviews. On one side were the government and *The Times*, which steadfastly refused to widen inquiries into either scandal or to make unsubstantiated allegations. Politicians and editors who stuck by tried and trusted methods of representation and reporting worried that public life might be made intolerable for men if this kind of guilt by association were allowed to be aired. Legal evidence ratified by the authority of the courts and by police investigation was their criterion of legitimacy. Keeping allegations under control, then, was one way of safeguarding the public realm as a place of ordered civility and masculine privilege. On the other side of this divide were those who were in some senses marginal to public and political life: Irish nationalists and the new popular press. For them, allegation and insinuation were in the public interest and private rather than police investigation was the best way round corrupt public officials and a politically dominant aristocracy. Accusations of indecency were needed to shake up the social order.

The Dublin Castle affair of 1883–4 represented a major shift in the attitude of the press. Very few, if any, scandals which linked sodomite subcultures with mainstream political and public life had been the subject of extensive press investigation since the Duke of Cumberland affair, which, although based on events that happened in 1810, had been a persistent radical theme until well into the 1820s. Although same-sex desire had occasionally touched the lives of the powerful in the meantime, newspapers of all kinds had seemingly been unwilling to make capital out of the potential connections between the life of the streets and the corridors of power. It was judged sufficient to print the bare details of each case, without speculating on additional facts or enlarging the investigation. Men of influence, such as the Halifax MP Edward Protheroe, had been connected with the world of the sodomite, but had been able to use the law and its reports in the press as a means to forestall scandal by exonerating themselves. In 1846, Protheroe had prosecuted his valet for sending threatening letters, the offence earning a sentence of 20 years transportation.[80] The following year, the MP was again in court charged with assaulting a man who had appeared at his house and accused him of 'decoying lads' to his residence. Again, being enmeshed in a court case only worked in his favour, by producing a public declaration of innocence. The magistrate in the latter case dismissed the charges, saying that Protheroe's apparently aggressive reaction to his accuser was only natural, and that he would leave the court 'quite free of any imputation, no charge having been exhibited against him'.[81] Protheroe's last entanglement with low life did not even reach the papers. In 1850, his name was mentioned in a separate extortion case, but he received almost no publicity. One of the gang involved, a young man named Henry Tiddiman, became a principal witness for the prosecution, whereupon his former comrades tried to make his long-term connection with Edward Protheroe into a form of guilt. Had he not, they asked in court, 'taken persons to Mr Protheroe; lads, youths which Mr Protheroe likes (you know the sort of persons to suit Mr Protheroe) and shared the money between them and yourself?'. Tiddiman denied it, stating categorically that he had never 'been in custody for *smashing*', and neither had he been in the former MP's bedroom.[82] This time, Protheroe's name was not even mentioned in the press.

Individual instances of scandal did punctuate the mid century, but the relationship between same-sex desire, politics and scandal remained a relatively unproductive one. Although the 'unnatural propensities' of cadets at the Royal Military Academy in Woolwich and the prevalence of nameless crimes among convicts in Van Diemen's Land (now Tasmania) reached the press, debate was confined to the correspondence columns, and centred on the justice of the charges, rather than the implications of guilt. In spite of the fact that *Reynolds' Newspaper* dwelled on the 'aristocratic' nature of the Academy, wider political points were left unmade.[83] The relationship between same-sex convict colonies and unnatural propensities was more troubling, however. In 1845, rumours about the convict colony at Van Diemen's Land and the private character of its Lieutenant Governor, Sir John Eardley-Wilmot, reached the metropolitan press. Gladstone, who was Colonial Secretary at the time, panicked and dismissed Wilmot on the basis of what the Governor called 'the most extraordinary conspiracy that ever succeeded in defaming the character of a public servant'. A commission of enquiry set up in Australia had concluded that there was no case to answer, but Wilmot was not reinstated.[84] A brief debate in the English press ensued, and broadsides were even written and published but, as Robert Hughes has shown, the impact of the scandal was primarily private and confined to those involved in the making of colonial policy. Hughes discovered that the report on sodomy in the penal colonies which was finally produced by Parliament in 1847 excised all the original references to homosexual behaviour.[85] Its publication in pamphlet form, which its author was hoping to effect, was also, naturally, discouraged. As a later attempt to use the issue for political ends showed, making connections between privilege, power and same-sex desire was a highly problematic matter.

An attempt to revive the question of Van Diemen's Land was made in the 1850s by the former Chartist leader John Frost, but in this case his marginality and lack of authority caused the miserable failure of his campaign. Frost, who had led the Newport rising in 1839 and been transported to Australia as a result, tried to appropriate the issue of convict settlements for radical politics. On his return to England in 1856, Frost tried to put some life into a moribund radical movement in a series of public meetings. One of his major themes was that the Palmerston government and the established political order was morally corrupt. This fact could be demonstrated most obviously by considering its brutal regime of transportation, which was producing a number of 'horrors', including the widespread commission of sodomy among convicts in Van Diemen's Land. Such a situation, Frost argued, not only risked divine retribution, but also showed the wickedness inherent in the British political system. The cruelty which it produced would, he suggested to a meeting of 20,000 people at Primrose Hill in 1856, 'bring down on the nation the vengeance of God, who, for crimes of a similar kind, destroyed the fairest spot in the world'.[86] Although he completed a successful lecture tour, and succeeded in gaining large audiences, Frost was laughed to scorn by the mainstream press, who presented him as a failed rabble-rouser with 'ridiculous pretensions' and disorganised followers.[87]

Why did the Irish succeed in generating a *political* scandal where others like Frost had failed? Part of the answer lies in the changed nature of the press and its relationship to investigative reporting. Although it has been argued that investigative journalism was a 'weak part of the late Victorian press', newspapers were nevertheless developing these techniques in the 1870s and 1880s.[88] Gary Weber has pointed out that the new journalists of the 1880s were also more interested in personal details about public men, and were prepared to argue that such interest was 'healthy and rational'.[89] By the early 1880s, political campaigns generated and orchestrated by the press were beginning to be customary features of public life. W.T. Stead's serialisation of Andrew Mearns' expose of urban poverty, *The Bitter Cry of Outcast London*, appeared in 1883, while the *Pall Mall Gazette* series 'The Truth About the Navy', exposing the apparent inadequacy of British naval defence, appeared at the same time as William O'Brien's allegations surfaced in Ireland.

So-called 'society' journalism, which usually printed upper-class social news and gossip had also changed with the emergence of Henry Labouchere's paper, *Truth*. Labouchere, as Richard Dellamorra notes, was helped in his mission against the 'classes', a social group to which he himself belonged, by his assiduously cultivated status as an outsider.[90] His Radical Liberalism and association with Joseph Chamberlain and Home Rule for Ireland also made him politically marginal to his aristocratic peers. Under Labouchere's ownership, *Truth* became a weekly assault on the rich, powerful and corrupt. Its methods were also innovative. According to Weber, *Truth* placed a great deal of emphasis on investigative journalism, and was the first English newspaper to employ a permanent staff for such purposes. The result of this new ethos of reporting was that people bought *Truth* to see 'who was going to get it next'.[91]

Another factor in the transformation of the press and its techniques was the increasingly close relationship between editors and politicians. According to J.O. Baylen, the government and senior political figures were much more willing to use the press to bring pressure for change in the 1880s than ever before.[92] Stead himself recognised his overtly political function by styling his new methods 'Government by Journalism' and celebrating the editor as the 'uncrowned king of an educated democracy'.[93] Stead's *Pall Mall Gazette* was the particular instrument of choice for the Liberal imperialist *éminence grise* Viscount Esher, who used it not only to pressure the government over its imperial policies, but also to influence the passage of the Criminal Law Amendment Act of 1885.

Labouchere and William O'Brien must also take their place as two of the key progenitors of new journalism. Like Labouchere after him, O'Brien and his paper, *United Ireland*, also had a specific set of targets, dogged persistence and a large amount of information to back up their allegations. In addition, O'Brien had far more influential political backing than someone like Frost, at least from his supporters in Ireland and in the House of Commons.

The Dublin scandal began with a series of insinuations against Crown officials who ran Ireland from Dublin Castle. For O'Brien and the Nationalist cause, the scandal presented a heaven-sent opportunity at a time when the movement was labouring under the British policy of coercion. The Nationalist Movement, according to O'Brien, was 'in a state of utter prostration', its leaders had only just been released from prison and it was discredited in English eyes by association with political violence. In particular, it had suffered from association with the Phoenix Park murders of 1882, when the Chief Secretary and his deputy had been stabbed to death by a nationalist group in a Dublin park. The Castle scandal, which began to emerge in the summer of 1883, made O'Brien's *United Ireland* newspaper one of the few centres of active agitation against the British. It was, O'Brien later recalled, 'a weekly insurrection in print'.[94]

O'Brien's first target was the head of Dublin's detective division, James Ellis French, about whom rumours had begun to circulate in both London and Dublin. Irish MPs had been criticised for drawing attention to these rumours in the House of Commons, but O'Brien promised that he would reveal all. He would continue, he said, until

the life and adventures and what is called the 'private character' of various crown employees in Ireland, from Corry Connelan [Inspector-General of Prisons] to Detective Director and County Inspector James Ellis French are fully laid bare to the universe![95]

French responded in the usual way by issuing a libel writ against *United Ireland*. However, O'Brien was far from deterred. Ignoring potential complaints about his methods, he instructed his own agents and informers to investigate the 'sweetsmelling' French's private life. French tried to place obstacles in his way. Not only was the detective destroying all incriminating evidence, O'Brien alleged, but he was doing so with the full cooperation of his colleagues in the Dublin police force. O'Brien nevertheless promised further revelations based on his own, rather than on legal, investigations. 'We promise the public such an exposure,' he told his readers, 'as will surprise persons who do not know as much as we do about this ex-official and his class.'[96]

At the end of November 1883, French finally served his libel writ against the paper. However, the case could not be heard until the following spring. Between the serving of the writ and the trial, which finally took place in June 1884, French was said to have fallen ill, suffering from a 'nervous debility', 'softening of the brain' and paralysis.[97] This delayed the trial still further, pending inquiries into French's mental fitness. In spite of the absence of legal judgement, *United Ireland* was prepared to imply that French was a known sodomite. The government, he said, 'knew all along what French's character was, it had become notorious in the Force' that he was 'a ruffian guilty of the most frightful and abominable crimes that man could commit'.[98]

O'Brien's disappointment at not being able to engage in a show trial with French was brief. He immediately moved on to his next target. In May 1884, he began to make similar allegations against Gustavus Cornwall, the Chief Secretary of the Post Office in Ireland. Using a private detective as his agent, O'Brien later claimed to have amassed details of a 'criminal confederacy which for its extent and atrocity almost staggered belief '.[99] O'Brien now extended his allegations to include the Crown Solicitor, George Bolton. Within two months, both Cornwall and Bolton had issued libel writs against *United Ireland*. At the same time, Home Rule MPs raised the matter in the House of Commons, demanding the appointment of a select committee to investigate the whole affair.[100]

By June 1884, the tide appeared to be turning O'Brien's way. French's libel action against him was dismissed with costs for the defendant on the grounds that no action had been taken on the writ. O'Brien also got his show trial in the form of an action on Cornwall's libel writ. At the beginning of July, with O'Brien's conduct rapidly becoming a national *cause célèbre* in Ireland, the National League established a fighting fund for his benefit. By the end of the month, his tactics of provoking the Castle were vindicated. On 11 July, the jury returned a verdict for O'Brien in the Cornwall libel trial. Within the week, Cornwall had been arrested, along with French, and a Dublin merchant named James Pillar, whose house in the Rathmines Road was an alleged meeting-place for all those involved. In addition three young 'Mary Annes' of no noticeable occupation, Patrick Molloy, Michael M'Grane and Clark Cooper, were also arrested. All were charged with conspiracy to commit sodomy, while some, including Cornwall, were charged with sodomy and a series of indecent assaults. The arrests did not stop there. On the 25 July, Captain Martin Kirwan of the Dublin Fusiliers was apprehended and inquiries spread to military circles in London. At the end of the month, a private in the Grenadier Guards and an army doctor, Albert de Fernandez, were brought to Dublin to face charges of procuring men for sodomy. Two other Dubliners, Robert Fowler and Daniel Considine, were also arrested at the end of July, and charged with keeping an 'improper house'.[101]

O'Brien's tactic of suggesting guilt by association was making public life intolerable for the British officials running Ireland. As the Chief Secretary noted, mud flung by the Nationalists could have repercussions for the private lives of government officials. During the Commons debate over the case, he noted that 'We are not conducting a debate; we are conducting something like a legal inquiry into private character.'[102] The character of all those involved was put at risk in this way, extending even to those at the top of Ireland's administration. O'Brien's ally Tim Biggar declared at a mass meeting in August that 'the head of the gang who was morally responsible for this misconduct was Earl Spencer'.[103] O'Brien himself added that 'With the poor wretch himself [Cornwall] we have no quarrel beyond the disgust of ordinary humanity against his crimes'. His real quarry, declared *United Ireland*, were Cornwall's superiors: 'with them we shall grapple and fearlessly we shall unite the verdict of every decent and honest citizen as to what manner of men they be.'[104]

As Sally Warwick-Haller has suggested, this was too much for the Lord Lieutenant, Earl Spencer, and his deputy, Charles Trevelyan. Spencer wrote to Gladstone that 'this touches my honour... I feel very deeply about it', while Trevelyan asked the Premier in July 1884, at the height of the scandal, to relieve him of his duties. Spencer argued that administering Ireland involved 'the sacrifice of one man's nerves, health, happiness, and self-respect; ... as recent events prove, by a terrible and ever-present risk to his character and reputation'.[105] The scandal also began to have consequences for other Irish officials, some of whom received threatening letters at this time, accusing them of unnatural offences, and demanding money to prevent their exposure.[106]

The similarity of O'Brien's work to the disreputable scandals raised in the lowest newspapers and to the tactics of the extortionist was not lost on the British press. O'Brien's description of the evidence at the trials was more explicit than usual. It directly named the crime of sodomy, and even went so far as to describe the alleged nature of Cornwall's kisses. In addition, O'Brien's use of initially unsubstantiated personal attacks divided the English and Irish press along national lines. *The Times* portrayed the attacks on the Castle as the simple result of partisan politics. The scandals offered little more than 'perennial exercise to the exuberant and inexhaustible Celtic rhetoric' and were treated 'with entire disregard of the results of legal investigation'.[107] Nationalist attacks were motivated, *The Times* argued, by the need to invent 'respectable' reasons to attack the successful administration of the Crimes Act, the central plank of Gladstone's policy of coercion. Whatever his moral shortcomings, Bolton was attacked because 'as Crown solicitor he was engaged in the conduct of the some of the most critical prosecutions conducted by the Government'.[108]

The principal criticism made by the English press, however, was of the indecency and intemperance of Nationalist coverage. Even Stead's *Pall Mall Gazette* recoiled from a full presentation of the facts.[109] The *Saturday Review*, according to *United Ireland*, 'piously intimates that it cannot enter into the class of particulars which are relished by the readers of the Irish Nationalist Press'. The latter's parliamentary reporter wrote from London that it was 'amazing how thoroughly the situation is appreciated' given the attempts by the English press to hush things up.[110] O'Brien also denounced 'The scoundrel press of London, which held its peace when this unspeakable Castle-cloaked conspiracy was proved up to the hilt'.[111] He and his followers represented themselves as champions of the press, while the National League proposed a resolution of gratitude to him for 'vindication of the cause of morality and freedom of the press'.[112] Yet O'Brien's success was dependent on his embracing the underhand tactics of insinuation, guilt by association and private investigation. Indeed, he could only raise the scandal in detail and employ the methods he did because he and his paper were outside the umbrella of legitimacy enjoyed by most of the British daily press. For most of his British critics, O'Brien's nationalism automatically rendered him disreputable, thereby licensing the tactics he employed.

Some of O'Brien's methods generated a series of delicate questions as to his status in raising the case. His assistant during the scandal had been a disgraced Scotland Yard detective named John Mieklejohn, who had served a prison term for his part in the 'Turf Scandal' of 1877, a system of extortion against illegal bookmakers. Like the blackmailer, Mieklejohn had 'explored the lowest depths of vice and crime and was familiar with all their scabrous secrets'. While his detective collected evidence, O'Brien committed his second cardinal sin in the eyes of the London press: raising the question of guilt by association. George Bolton and a series of other minor officials who had nothing to do with French or Cornwall were put in the same category of moral corruption. After O'Brien had secured the verdict in the Cornwall libel case, the Dublin *Evening Telegraph* argued that had he not 'shown cause for the shocking charges advanced it is not too much to say that society would have closed its doors against him, and that he would have been looked upon as a social plague'. At that stage, O'Brien's status in public life had been deeply ambivalent. He was 'either a foul libeller and inexcusable disseminator of immoral filth, or he was a gallant knight-errant'.[113]

Yet success for O'Brien was widely interpreted as having justified his methods. The *Freeman's Journal* wrote that the popular rejoicing at the verdict in the libel trial showed that the public had grasped the 'real significance of the struggle to the death that has just been fought out'.

The political and moral corruption of British rule had been fully demonstrated. 'Despotic forms of government', it went on, 'and odious vice have had in the history of the world an association so common as to be justifiably held as cause and effect'. The reigns of autocrats, it noted, from the last days of the Roman Empire to those of Napoleon III have 'been remarkable for the growth in rank luxuriance of all forms of unnatural vice'. No one in Ireland would believe that 'the Government which detected the Phoenix Park murderers, could not have detected French and Cornwall'.[114]

For O'Brien, success in the Cornwall libel case represented vindication. It did not matter that both Cornwall and the hapless French were acquitted after disagreement of the jury in both cases. The damage had been done, not only to the Dublin administration, but also, in the eyes of the British press, to public morality. Although O'Brien's status as an Irish Nationalist made it easier to dismiss his campaign as 'Celtic rhetoric', his methods were replicated by the London press in another scandal centred on homosexual desire.

2. Cleveland Street

The Cleveland Street scandal of 1889–90 demonstrated a similar clash of worldviews. During the course of the affair, the government sought to control knowledge of the case and to restrict what could be said publicly about those involved. On the other hand, the evening press, egged on by Home Rulers and Radical Liberal MPs like Henry Labouchere, found new reasons to generate allegations that did not have the sanction of legal investigation or judgement.

The affair began on 4 July 1884, when a Post Office messenger named Charles Swinscow was found to be in the possession of more money than he could have earned legitimately. He was questioned and admitted that he had received the money as payment for having sex with men at Number 19 Cleveland Street, off Tottenham Court Road. Another messenger named Alfred Newlove had induced Swinscow and at least two others to go the house with him for the same reason. The house was run by a man named Charles Hammond, assisted by the self-styled 'Reverend' George Veck, and its clients, according to the Telegraph boys, were army officers, businessmen and aristocrats. On 7 July, Newlove was arrested. Attempts were also made to arrest Hammond but he had already escaped to France and eventually ended up in Seattle. The house at Number 19 was found by the police to be closed.

On 25 July, the police passed the matter to the Director of Public Pros- ecutions, Sir Augustus Stephenson. At the end of July, the Commissioner of the Metropolitan Police, James Munro, reported to Stephenson that one of the aristocrats identified by the Telegraph boys was Lord Arthur Somerset, equerry to the Prince of Wales and son of the Duke of Beaufort. On 29 July, some of the messengers implicated in the scandal were taken to Piccadilly to see if they could identify any of the gentlemen who frequented the clubs in the area. Constable Sladden reported that they had seen and identified a man whom they claimed was one of the patrons of Number 19. Sladden followed him, later identifying the man as Lord Arthur. At the end of August, in an attempt to collect corroborating evidence against Somerset, the police went to interview another boy named in the enquiry, Algernon Allies, who was living with his family at Sudbury in Middlesex. Unfortunately for them, Allies had been tipped off about their visit and had destroyed a number of incriminating letters.

At the beginning of September, Somerset took four months leave from his regiment and went to France. The first newspaper article on the case appeared on 14 September in the society and sporting journal *Man of the World*. It reported that Lord Arthur had left for the continent on leave and in the next paragraph reported the rumour that an enormous scandal was about to break. Readers were left to draw their own connection between the two stories. Newlove and Veck were tried, on 18 September, for procuring the Telegraph boys and attempting to commit sodomy and respectively sentenced to four and nine months imprisonment. The witnesses in that trial, almost all from the ranks of the GPO, were again taken by the police to stand outside Pall Mall clubs to see if they could identify any men as the clients of Number 19.

At the beginning of October, Lord Arthur returned from the continent to attend his grandmother's funeral at Badminton, but the police took no action, despite having seen him there. At this point, the Prince of Wales intervened, sending two emissaries, Sir Francis Knollys and Sir Digton Probyn, to meet the government's law officers and find out whether Lord Arthur was to be charged. Probyn had a brief meeting with the Prime Minister, Lord Salisbury, and immediately returned to Pall Mall to try to find Lord Arthur, but according to Montgomery Hyde, found he had already absconded.[115] Henry Labouchere later alleged that Salisbury had told Probyn that a warrant was about to be issued for Somerset's arrest. Labouchere also suggested that Probyn had warned Somerset in turn, thereby enabling him to escape justice. What did happen was that a warrant was issued against Somerset for gross indecency on 12 November, but by that time he had already left the country.

By the middle of November, the newspaper coverage was beginning to escalate. Labouchere's *Truth* harried the government at every turn. In particular, Labouchere alleged that a cover up had been perpetrated in order to protect the aristocracy, and that the Tories were implicated. A campaign against 'the classes' on behalf of the 'masses' began. A series of allegations against the morality of the aristocracy in the evening papers culminated with the publication of a story in the *North London Press* which named both Lord Arthur and the Earl of Euston as frequenters of Number 19. Lord Euston immediately launched a libel action against its editor, Ernest Parke. Even though Euston admitted going to the house in Cleveland Street the previous summer, he claimed he had been duped into going by the promise of '*poses plastiques*', the coy phrase used to describe what was essentially a strip show. He had, he said, gone to see the poses of women, not to consort with men, and when he had realised what sort of place it was he had hurried away.[116] Parke lost the case and went to prison for libel. In spite of this setback, Labouchere continued to harass the Tories, demanding a select committee to investigate, but made no headway. By February 1890, the scandal had begun to die down.

The factor which allowed Labouchere to make his allegations was the seeming inaction of the government and police. Yet this inaction was, I suggest, a reflection of a desire on the part of law officers to control scandal and hence to govern public knowledge. As we have seen, both government and police opted for a generally cautious approach when dealing with sodomy cases. The avoidance of scandal was uppermost in the minds of officials. This was a mindset which informed many of the decisions which were taken in the Cleveland Street case. At the outset of the scandal, Home Office officials went to some lengths to prevent Lord Arthur's name from being known, even within their own department. He was initially referred to in correspondence as 'Mr Brown', 'LAS' or with a series of dashes. In some of the case papers, his name was covered up with small strips of paper to prevent knowledge from spreading among junior clerks and civil servants. When details of the case, thought to be known only to the law officers, were repeated by Labouchere in the House of Commons, one official concluded that it was 'not wise' to 'rely on the loyalty of public servants in these matters'.[117]

Decisions of this kind reflected the dominant legal opinion, frequently expressed by judges, that public discussion of cases resulting from the multiplication of allegations and inquiries was their most pernicious aspect. This was a view shared by most barristers and jurists, and it was imported into Home Office practice by the transplantation of many members of the legal profession into the senior ranks of government service. Not only was Stephenson a former barrister, but many of the senior civil servants involved in the Cleveland Street scandal had also served an apprenticeship in the legal profession. Godfrey Lushington, the Permanent Under-Secretary at the Home Office, had first come into the civil service as a legal adviser in 1869. The Home Secretary, Henry

Matthews, the man most likely to have stalled the prosecution of Lord Arthur Somerset, had been a distinguished barrister since being called to the Bar in 1850. He had also been part of the defence team at the trial of Boulton and Park. Matthews had defended Fisk at that trial, and can hardly have been uninfluenced by its outcome in the face of what appeared to be the strongest evidence.

Stephenson's initial objection to proceedings was his dread of giving publicity to the case by making it a government matter. He and Matthews agreed at this stage that the best policy was to keep the scandal at arm's length. He wrote to Munro in July pointing out that prosecutions for sodomy and indecent assault were traditionally the responsibility of the police. Stephenson referred the Commissioner to the fact that policy in 'cases of this character' had been decided in a series of conferences in 1880 and in August 1884 (at the height of the Dublin Scandals) between the Home Secretary, Howard Vincent (Commissioner of the Met), Sir John Maule (DPP) and Stephenson himself as solicitor to the Treasury. At these conferences, Stephenson had:

> urged on grounds of public policy the expediency of not giving unnecessary publicity to cases of this character – and that therefore the prosecution should not be at the instance of the DPP and conducted by the solicitor to the Treasury, but should be conducted by Messrs Wontner as solicitors to the police... Under these circumstances I submit to the Chief Commissioner of police that he should direct Messrs Wontner to undertake the conduct of the prosecution as a police prosecution.[118]

A police prosecution not only exempted law officers from involvement, but seems to have had the effect of restricting the charges to those directly involved. Publicity was thereby contained. At any rate, such a direction from the DPP and the Attorney General hardly represented a signal of encouragement to the police to proceed with further inquiries. Stephenson was only too happy to send the papers to other departments and to abdicate responsibility for the case, at one stage pointing out to the Home Secretary that Section 10 of the DPP regulations required that he cede the unwelcome duty of decision to the Attorney General.[119]

The letters which were sent between the Home Office, Treasury, DPP and the police at this time show a complete lack of unanimity over how to proceed. While Munro agreed with Stephenson that giving the case to Wontners would restrict publicity, he disagreed with the larger implications for policy and hesitated to assume the full responsibility for the case himself. Munro told Matthews that he did not 'consider that this prosecution [against Lord Arthur] is in any sense a Police

Prosecution' and reminded him that 'there are no funds at the disposal of the Metropolitan Police to meet the legal expenses which must necessarily be incurred'. He therefore referred the matter back to Matthews, who, he suggested, should direct the DPP as he thought fit.[120]

When the government did act, it had made a delicate calculation of the necessity of scandal. By August 1889, Stephenson had estimated that the scandal resulting from inaction seemed likely to be greater than that resulting from proceeding against Lord Arthur. He wrote to Matthews on 31 August, arguing that whatever the necessity for corroboration, the 'moral evidence against LAS is overwhelming'. He told Matthews that he was 'fully sensitive of the public scandal – and the desirability of avoiding it – which a charge against LAS would create – and deeply sympathise with his family'. As to the need for corroboration, further inquiries would be certain to produce it, but 'whether or not such enquiry should be made – depends upon consideration of public policy – on expediency – [and] in my judgement much can be said both for and against such enquiries'. Despite these reservations, he warned that the 'public scandal involved in a criminal charge against a man in his position in society is undoubted – but in my opinion the public scandal in declining to prefer such a charge – and in permitting such a man to hold Her Majesty's commission and remain in English society is much greater'.[121]

In addition to the procrastination of the leading law officers, the government maintained a cautious attitude to some of the witness testimony. This feeling reflected the dubious status of the evidence which could be provided by someone who had willingly participated in the crime. The male prostitutes and Telegraph boys in the case were not only immoral, but their allegations were also seen by the law officers as inherently untrustworthy and little better than slander. One of these men, who became Ernest Parke's star witness in the Euston libel trial, was Jack Saul, who had lived by prostitution since at least 1879. He claimed at that trial to have known Hammond, who managed Number 19, and Lord Euston. Although Saul was interviewed by the police in August 1889, and implicated a number of men as well as Lord Euston, his status as a professional prostitute enabled the Home Office to dismiss his evidence as tainted. Despite the network of immorality which Saul described, the Attorney General, Sir Richard Webster, expressed the view that the statement was 'in my judgement utterly unworthy of credit'. Further proceedings on the grounds of allegations made by him were unsafe, and, Webster concluded, his evidence 'could not be used without inflicting irreparable injury upon other persons against whom there is at present no trustworthy evidence whatever'.[122]

The fate of Saul's testimony in the Euston libel trial tended to confirm these suspicions. The judge in that case, Justice Hawkins, said that it would be difficult to imagine a 'a more melancholy spectacle or a more loathsome object' than Saul. Inspector Abbeline had, Hawkins noted, obtained Saul's evidence in the summer of 1889, but had not acted on it because to have done so would have been to give credibility to evidence which would not have stood up in court. It would have placed the criminal trial on the same level as the informal tribunal of the blackmailer. It was, Hawkins said, 'the height of cruelty to make a charge of an abominable crime against a gentleman, unless there was in the command of those instituting the prosecution evidence that it was right and reasonable to submit to a jury'. Given the status of the witnesses, this could not be said to be the case.[123]

Allegations by self-confessed prostitutes could not, in the view of the law officers, be used as the basis of a wider investigation. The majority of the press, however, disagreed. Labouchere was the chief tormentor of the Tory government, assisted by the new evening press. His methods were by no means universally acclaimed, but the disdain of some editors did not prevent Labouchere taking up the scandal in order to try and further a radical agenda by discrediting the Tory government.

Most of the popular press joined in with Labouchere's campaign. *Reynold's Newspaper* pointed out that Lord Salisbury's brother-in-law, the Earl of Galloway, had been arrested in Scotland for exposing himself to a little girl.[124] The fact that the police and Procurator Fiscal had apparently done nothing about the case, showed that there was one law for the rich and another for the poor. In an echo of Irish commentaries on the Dublin scandals, the *Referee* commented that the affair was 'positive proof that while the masses are made virtuous by force, the classes can with impunity be as wicked as ever were Greeks or Romans in the days of their greatest degradation and debasement'.[125]

O'Brien, Parke and Labouchere presented facts which otherwise might have been seen as slander as necessary to the public interest. The radical press presented their stance, just as O'Brien had done, as a necessary break with previous conventions of decency which had enabled all sorts of high-born criminals to escape. Silence, according to the *Star*, had broken down under the weight of revelation. Although the paper asked 'of the man whose mind is not diseased' by vice or fanaticism 'whether this sacred and holy ignorance is not better than the hideous enlightenment from which we can now no longer escape' it was clear that 'The Convention of Silence – to which we ourselves confess to have been partners – has been broken, the secret is no longer to be kept, and the whole situation is revolutionised.'[126]

For the *Star*, the exposure of such horrors was a new social duty:

> Now that the exposure has come it must go on to the end – without
> pause, without veil, without mercy. We must probe this hideous evil
> down to its lowest roots; for there is not extinction of disease without
> the most searching and merciless dissection of its causes and origin.
> We must have no more concealment, no more shielding, no more
> intervention... on the part of anybody, however exalted, however
> powerful, from whatever motives. Justice, having entered on the path
> of enquiry and pursuit, must be allowed to advance, quick and sure-
> footed, to its allotted goal; until she has laid her heavy and inevitable
> hand on the shoulders of every offender – ay, though he bore a name
> illustrious by centuries of descent and by pages of brilliant exploits.[127]

In addition, Parke's defence at the libel trial was not that he sought to
justify the charges by showing them to be true, but that he had published
the accusations against Lord Euston for the public benefit.[128] Parke's
barrister, future Liberal leader Herbert Asquith, 'doubted whether there
would be any argument on that point'.[129] Parke also appealed beyond
the court to the sense of English fairness which was an explicit part of
radical campaigns. The *North London Press* spoke of the 'solemn duty to
the public' it was carrying out, and promised to 'submit our cause to the
British people' and to 'ask them to stand by and see fair play'.[130]

In spite of the widespread radical support for Labouchere and Parke,
they were by no means universally acclaimed, especially when the Euston
libel trial went against them. Some of these criticisms came from the
usual quarters. *The Times* in particular decried Labouchere's efforts and
sought to associate him with the partisan tactics of the Irish. In calling
attention to 'the unsavoury subject' of the Cleveland Street cases,
Labouchere had repeated the allegations from which 'the [Irish]
Separatists of the baser sort have been trying to manufacture political
capital for many months past'. These rumours, *The Times* accurately
surmised, had been 'put about for political purpose' and 'repeated during
at least half a year in the most unscrupulous and despicable of the
Separatist organs'.[131]

Yet *The Times* and the government were far from guiltless in their methods and had played a central role in the legitimisation of slander and scandal. In the two years leading up to the Cleveland Street scandal, they had
collaborated in an attempt to bring down the leader of the Home Rule
party in Parliament, Charles Stuart Parnell, that had itself employed blackmailers to collect and disseminate incriminating information. In 1887
and 1888, *The Times* published a series of letters appearing to implicate
Parnell in the Phoenix Park murders. A parliamentary investigation (the

'Special Commission') into the letters followed, and in February 1889 it was established that they were not the work of Parnell or his party but had been forged by a disenchanted nationalist and notorious political blackmailer named Richard Pigott in collaboration with *Times* journalist Edward Caulfield Houston. To say the least, the irony of the situation was not lost on Labouchere and his supporters in the evening press. If anything it had been *The Times* and the government that had started the process which brought scandal, slander and even blackmail back into the heart of political life. *The Times* was clearly not above using the same methods of underhand investigation, incriminating letters and unsubstantiated allegations which it now accused Labouchere and the Irish of employing. Cleveland Street represented a satisfying revenge, made all the more delicious by the fact that seemingly underhand methods might now have the inadvertent sanction of government. The *Star*, edited by Irish Home Ruler T.P. O'Connor, relished the parallels with the treatment of Ireland. 'Nemesis was the presiding deity in the House of Commons last night,' it wrote after the debate on the affair, 'nemesis for Pigott in Cleveland Street.'[132] Political blackmail in the form of the Pigott forgeries had brought back not just the techniques of the extortionist, but actual blackmailers themselves into semi-sanctioned public roles. It was no wonder that Labouchere regarded his hitherto illegitimate methods as fair. Cleveland Street represented an open season, a no-holds-barred retaliation for the Pigott affair.

However, not all editors were convinced by Labouchere, Parke and the rest of the evening press. As Morris Kaplan has observed, Parke's failure to substantiate his allegations against Lord Euston in court led to him being dropped by some of his former radical allies.[133] Other criticisms of the evening press came from predictable sources. Sir Charles Russell, who had so conclusively demolished Pigott's testimony before the Parnell Commission, now stood on the other side. As Lord Euston's barrister, he declared that Parke was little better than a street criminal, since he had scattered allegations about 'vaguely and without particularity'.[134] Others were also critical of Parke and his methods. Augustus Moore, the editor of the society journal the *Hawk*, saw talk of a 'sacred duty' of investigation as little more than 'flap-doodle'. For Moore, Parke was on the same moral level as Pigott. In comparison to Parke's offence, the *Hawk* declared, 'Pigottism sinks into insignificance'. Parke had, 'without one particle of evidence or excuse, except to advertise his paper', accused a man of 'the most odious offence against common humanity which the mind of man can conceive'.[135] In addition, Labouchere's indiscriminate accusations were seen as making public life impossible in the same way that O'Brien's earlier allegations had ruined the peace of Ireland's English rulers. After the noisy Commons debate on the affair at the end of

February 1890, *The Times* declared that Labouchere had been suspended not only 'for a gross breach of the rules of the House of Commons', but also 'for a deliberate disregard of all those decencies of debate which make parliamentary life possible for civilized men'.[136]

Labouchere was clearly aware of the implications of his own actions. His earlier self-justifications had shown that he, and the new journalism which he practised, had come a long way. Ten years before Cleveland Street, Labouchere had shown that he was sensitive to the difficulties which investigative methods presented to the orderly conduct of public life. Gary Weber describes Labouchere as trying, like other embryonic new journalists, to walk a tightrope between salacious gossip about individuals and the public interest. 'If [a journal] pokes and pries into the privacy of domestic life,' he had written in 1879, 'if it is vulgar and offensive in its tone... and if it trades in baseless slanders, calumnies and aspersions; its career will be a short one.'[137] At that time, he surmised that sensation would make circulation fall. The new journalism had proved quite the opposite, and moved *Truth* and its imitators towards the investigation of privacy and domestic life.

Personal gossip and accusations that might in some contexts be regarded as 'baseless slanders' tended to convince some of the virtues of silence. Labouchere and his critics both implicitly realised that freedom from slanderous accusations and even the overt protection of upper-class sexual privilege had worked in favour of public men. Silence was equated with a particular kind of masculine civility. This realisation was the consequence of cumulative efforts to bring sexual matters to public attention and have them debated in legitimate public ways. By 1889, it was commonplace for those critics of male sexual licence in the social purity movement to argue that silence on sexual matters was the same as protecting the supposed male right to the bodies of female prostitutes. Josephine Butler and her supporters had argued that men had prevented serious discussion of prostitution and its effect on women by claiming that sexual matters should not be approached in public and especially not by women.[138] Stead's Maiden Tribute affair, the Dublin Castle and Cleveland Street scandals all suggested to many that the same 'silence' protected all kinds of sexual and moral privileges. The freedom that most public men enjoyed from sexual slander and guilt by association might even be regarded as an indispensable condition of public life. The Tory *Globe* pointed out that the rigid policing of slander afforded privileges to men on both sides of the political world. Under the headline 'Three Questions for Mr Labouchere to Answer', it demanded to know whether the 'champion of Truth and the Rights of the People' would answer some questions. '*Who was Prime Minister*', it asked, and:

who was Attorney-General, and what party was in power when the brother of a well-known Gladstonite nobleman was accused of the same crime as Lord Arthur Somerset? Who on that occasion gave the accused person three days' warning to quit the country, and told him that upon the expiry of that time a warrant would be issued for his arrest? And what use did that titled criminal make of the 'law' which he was thus given in place of the law by which he might justly have been condemned to penal servitude? If Mr Labouchere does not know the answers to these questions, Mr Gladstone or Sir Charles Russell may be able to tell him.[139]

Freedom from the suspicion of sexual depravity, then, could work both ways. The policing and definition of slander and the prevention of promiscuous knowledge was seen to have a protective effect on the civility of masculine interaction and on public life as a whole. The illegitimate status of unsubstantiated allegations of sodomy tended to prevent such suspicions being aired. They remained the province of the blackmailer and the scandal sheet and their proper location was the street. However, during the 1880s it became almost acceptable to rely on blackmailers themselves for evidence of secret crime. It also became legitimate to raise alleged private 'infamy' in a public forum like Parliament, or to debate it at length in the press. A justification was required for these often private investigations of sexual morality and was found in the language of Radical Liberalism and new conceptions of the public interest.

The new journalism challenged the legal, social and political marginality of scandal. By recognising that scandal had an important function in cleansing the public world, new journalists altered its status in fundamental ways. Even though, as Cohen argues, scandal might still perform the function of re-establishing sexual and discursive boundaries, it was nevertheless reinvented as a political tool. The boundaries that had confined scandal to small-circulation papers like the *Age* and had rendered many different forms of slander and accusation illegal and marginal were beginning to break down in the 1880s. Editors still maintained the convention that sodomy should not be named or approached, but as the subsequent career of scandal indicates, it was becoming possible to raise homosexuality as a public issue and retain one's status. The career of slander in the nineteenth century represented the separation and meeting of worlds. The popular and promiscuous discourse of the blackmailer had separated and then united again with the legitimate public world of press and politics. From the Wilde scandal, through the public attacks on Edward Carpenter's 'infamy' in 1912, and on to the Pemberton Billing affair of 1918, the public interest could justify the investigation of homosexuality, its nature, causes and consequences for society.

After 1889, it was apparent that the disorderly urban world of the blackmailer and that of the legitimate politician or editor were not that far apart. Disreputable characters like O'Brien's detective Mieklejohn and *The Times*'s hired blackmailer Richard Pigott, directly connected public life with the urban world of the extortionist, the threatening letter and with insinuations of guilt by association. Accusations of homosexual desire, then, had a chequered career in nineteenth-century England. They moved from an occupational hazard of public life in the early part of the century through criminalisation and were finally transformed into a tactic of political life. During the scandals of the 1880s, it became apparent to some that a controlled public discourse had not only acted as a means of marginalising deviance, but had also protected public men from slander and had insulated the privileges of their class.

Part III

5

'A Strange and Indescribable Feeling'

Unspeakable Desires in Late-Victorian England

Just as new ways of describing scandalous desires were emerging, new forms of homosexual subjectivity were being defined. In a broad sense, the particular forms of experience associated with the late-Victorian homosexual are threefold. Firstly, there is the relationship or transaction across class which was almost wholly defined by its economic character and its structure of power and subordination. These relationships, explored in the work and lives of John Addington Symonds, Wilde and later J.R. Ackerley, were characteristic of their typical location in the Victorian city, and took some of their form from the public, economic nature of an urban sodomite subculture. Secondly, there is the very Victorian tradition of camp. The word appears first in its modern association with homosexuality in the letters of Boulton and Park. For them, camp was an activity and an adjective that described their curious mixture of women's clothes, public display, theatricality, impersonation and effeminacy. A number of studies have suggested that camp emerged in response to the constraints of the 'closeted' pre-Stonewall era. From Susan Sontag onwards, there has been much debate about the meaning of camp, but it seems obvious that the actual *practice* of camp performs the same dynamic of simultaneous concealment and display which is explored in this book.[1] Camp too was defined by its relationship to questions of disclosure that belong particularly to nineteenth-century England and to Anglo-American culture more generally. Finally, the structure of silence, negation and simultaneous incitement to discourse that I have described in the previous four chapters fostered among homosexual men a strong fascination with transcendence. Comradeship and spiritual love belong to many different traditions, but they were also part of the same moral world as the notorious but perhaps temporary urban sodomite and the concealed/revealed camp young man. In this chapter, I will explore one way in which a fascination with transcendence of body, desire, self and even speech came to define a homosexual sensibility.

The 1890s represent a key moment in the history of homosexuality, when, it is generally argued, what had been a nameless crime became visible, identifiable as modern, and subject to new scrutiny and investigation. I have suggested up to now that this process of recognition was predominantly one in which political imperatives united hitherto separate, but nevertheless interpenetrated and visible, worlds of knowledge and experience. Although it was the case that the volume of scientific and literary works about homosexuality began to expand in the 1890s, and that such investigations increasingly challenged social, cultural and literary boundaries, I want to show here that not only did new theories of homosexuality influence individual men, but also that secrets, silence, transcendence and negation were paradoxical methods of adapting sexological discourses and resisting condemnatory accounts of homosexual desire. I want to alter the metropolitan focus of the historiography (and of this book) and to explore self-making and subjectivity as a means of both resisting and making use of secrets. The 'closet', then, the secret repository of a nameless desire, might be seen in a perverse manner as an enabling form. In particular, I want to show that secrets and evasions were important resources of subjectivity in an age before it was thought wise or healthy to act on one's every desire.

Until now, we have considered how homosexual desire was talked about and described in the public locations of courtroom, newspaper and city street. In this chapter, I want to explore the lives of men in ordinary life, who did not or could not stand outside the society or the morals of their time, and who were not attached to a sodomite subculture. I want to explore the ways in which they developed an interest in new theories of homosexuality and used those theories to understand their own desires and attachments. In contrast, most histories of homosexuality (including this one) have tended, mainly for practical reasons, to concentrate on metropolitan or literary figures, an approach epitomised by the amount of attention devoted to Oscar Wilde and to other canonical figures of the *fin de siècle*. Such attention has tended to obscure other sources of knowledge and identity and has concentrated on the combination of sexual science and an effeminate Wildean archetype as the epitome of the 'modern homosexual'.

Wilde, then, is seen as the originator of the homosexual identity which was to emerge in his shadow in the twentieth century. His encounter with Victorian justice has also provided historians with the paradigm of the persecuted homosexual. However, I argue in this chapter that there were other, more or less forgotten histories of homosexuality and its emergence, which can be tracked using sources which are not metropolitan and did not emerge from an urban subculture of 'renters', sodomites and their clients. These people represent an alternative history of homosexuality to that of Wilde, the urban, criminal sodomite and the 'modern homosexual'. This part of the book therefore shifts away from the metropolitan and public focus of the previous ones and away from legal sources towards literary ones. Instead of indictments I engage here with private diaries, personal intimacies and provincial politics. These sources may seem a long way from Cleveland Street, or from Bow Street magistrates' court, physically as well as figuratively, but that is their value. We have seen how the metropolis, the city, the law and the press structured a public discourse about homosexuality. Missing from those accounts are discussions of private desire and intimacy which try to resist the condemnatory discourses associated with public discussion of unnatural crimes. Also absent are the views of those who stood apart from the subculture of the street and park.

The letters and diaries left by a group of men in Victorian Lancashire give us the distance from London that lends perspective to the view of late nineteenth-century homosexuality. They also show how new theories of homosexuality produced by sexologists and homophile writers like Edward Carpenter were actually taken up and applied by individuals to their own lives and desires. These sources, for all their peculiarities, are therefore an invaluable means of understanding the way in which even private desires might be simultaneously recognised as homoerotic and yet remain unnameable or ineffable.

The men that I will be discussing here used literature to understand themselves. They lived in Bolton and the surrounding area and formed themselves into a small, sect-like group in order to read and appreciate the works of the American poet Walt Whitman and other apostles of comradeship. They formed a particular attachment to Whitman because they saw in his writings the basis of a new social order which could be founded on harmony between the classes and based on the idea of a transcendent and ineffable 'comrade love'. Whitman's poetry provided the ideal context for them to explore the meaning of romantic friendship and comradely attachment. They, unlike Wilde, did not have the resources or perhaps the wit to invert the moral order with which they lived, and they therefore had to live substantially within its confines. Their writings therefore tell us a great deal about the significance of comrade love in otherwise 'ordinary' masculine relationships. They also show that comradeship was a sign under which many different types of masculine intimacy could be articulated.

The Bolton Whitmanites also illuminate the principal theme of this book and of much recent historiography: the way in which knowledge of homosexuality was structured by its unnameable quality. Even when it was directly encountered, same-sex desire remained somehow ineffable. In their determination to avoid the condemnation of their peers, and to resist prevailing accounts of 'degenerate' intimacy, the Bolton group followed in the tradition of 'unspeakability' which has been outlined in the previous chapters of this book. We have seen that the legal process produced ways of distancing homosexual desire even when it was directly encountered. The relationship between the law and the ineffable quality of private desires explored here is one of affinity rather than causation. They both occupied a similar discursive space, in which homosexuality could be simultaneously approached and distanced. Yet the Whitmanites represent a departure from this theme in one important respect. They show that one effect of publicly discussing homosexuality during the 1890s was to throw new suspicion over direct expressions of masculine intimacy. The Bolton group lived on the cusp of change, and the records they left document the arrival of a certain kind of mistrust of manly association.

However, they also show that there were ways round this kind of suspicion. They demonstrate how intimate but masculine attachments could be justified and explained in this climate without rendering them subject to condemnation as 'morbid' or 'unnatural'. To avoid these imputations, the Bolton Whitmanites adopted and developed a concept of an alternate spiritual personality which would experience inconvenient desires. The literally 'unspeakable' and ineffable feelings some of the group felt for each other could be displaced onto this spiritual plane, and remain, to a large degree, 'unnamed'. Indeed, the unnameable quality of homosexual desire was one of their principal resources. It enabled them to develop intimacies which at a later date would have seemed suspicious, not to say pathological.

In reading the Bolton group, I want to move away from the idea that the unsayable quality of homosexual desire in Victorian England was only a sign of repression. Neither do I argue that closeted lives of misery and desperation were the unique result of these discursive prohibitions. Instead this cultural moment provided, paradoxically, a series of opportunities for those who felt attracted by same-sex desire. However, in spite of the fact that some of the Whitman fellowship expressed an intense interest in sexual inversion, they cannot be claimed wholeheartedly for a gay history. Many of the men involved were not avowedly homosexual. Among those that did express an interest, loving marriages and intense friendships with women were not unusual. Instead of glibly asserting the 'hidden' homosexuality of this group, then, and reading their elaborate denials of homoerotic intent in their passionate friendships as symptoms of mere repression, their unmistakably homoerotic feelings for each other should be seen in their own terms and words. They were not necessarily homosexual in the modern sense, since they lacked the post-Freudian imperative to act on one's desires, but an intense love existed between some of them which became a means to experience homosexual desire. Their separation from any sexually dissident subculture meant that when they did recognise an intense intimacy among themselves and perhaps in others, it required a new vocabulary of evasion to be spoken of, and new understandings of consciousness in order to be acknowledged.

THE EAGLE STREET COLLEGE

The context for these movements of sympathy and intimacy was a small group of friends, known later as the Bolton Whitman Fellowship, and to themselves as the Eagle Street College. Their association grew up in the 1880s out of a common friendship which had begun in the previous decade. The regular meeting of these friends, which often centred on discussion of a particular author, issue or text, was soon dubbed the Eagle Street College by its members after the address of its gatherings and in ironic imitation of more formal educational institutions. The core of the group was never more than eight or nine men, with occasional additions of friends and visitors. These were J.W. Wallace (affectionately known as 'the Master' of the College) and the 'Fellows', Dr John Johnston, Wentworth Dixon, Fred Wild, William Ferguson, Samuel Hodgkinson, Thomas Shorrock, Richard Greenhalgh, Charles Sixsmith, Frederick Hutton, Will Atkinson, Walt Hawkins and a group of around five or six other occasional members. Wallace was an architect's assistant who had risen from a humble background, Johnston a GP, while the others worked in the textile industry as managers and businessmen, apart from Hutton, a clergyman, and Wentworth Dixon, a solicitor. They were initially united by little more than friendship. As Wallace later recalled, the men had begun to call on him regularly every Monday shortly after the death of his mother in January 1885. They soon agreed to devote some of this time to discussion of subjects of 'more permanent interest and value' than mere current events. According to Wallace, the group 'never formulated any programme... nor thought of organising a society for any specific purpose'. Only a few of them had received an education beyond school and professional training in their respective fields, and they were not connected with literary events even in Bolton. At the beginning, Wallace wrote later, the group was no more than 'a little company of men of widely different characteristics, ideas and training, who were united only in a common friendship'.[2]

They had, by Wallace's own admission 'no remarkable gifts or attainments' which lifted them above the run of Bolton's middle classes, but the group nevertheless had a 'certain emotional atmosphere' which grew out of long acquaintance and mutual acceptance. As a result, they felt able to speak their minds on matters of importance to them, such as religion and philosophy. 'Each one of us,' Wallace recalled, 'felt that this friendly and perfectly free interchange of ideas on such subjects did us all an invaluable service,' as well as leading 'by imperceptible stages, to a deepened intimacy, in which the inmost quests and experiences of the soul were freely expressed, and each grew conscious of our essential unity, as of a larger self which included us all.'[3]

Far from being a tiny provincial reading group, the College had links to some of the most significant figures of the 1890s. They corresponded with and visited Walt Whitman himself, and were friendly with the leaders of the early Labour party. They also formed strong links to the Labour Church and to other socialist groups of the period. Some of them also attempted to influence the Independent Labour Party (ILP) by convincing its leaders that an ethos of comradeship would be productive, and that Whitman's 'teachings' would provide the spiritual energy which the movement required. By 1891 the College had expanded their horizons to the extent that two of the group actually went to meet Walt Whitman at his home in New Jersey. They were introduced to a corresponding circle of Whitmanites in America, some of whom had also begun to formulate new ideas of spiritual comradeship. Through the American Whitman circle they became acquainted with Whitman's personal physician, Richard Maurice Bucke, and his attempts to explore the unconscious through his idea that the personality could develop a higher form of 'cosmic consciousness'. The interchange with the American Whitmanites, and with Whitman's followers in England, especially John Addington Symonds and Edward Carpenter, produced a flowering of ideas which sought to approach and understand homosexuality as a form of 'alternate' selfhood.

Although they were friendly with unconventional men of letters and dissident ideas, the College was similar in many ways to other forms of masculine association. Its members generated a manly camaraderie common to other clubs and groups. Johnston in particular was an active member of similar and more conventional groupings such as local professional bodies, as well the Boys' Brigade, local Scottish associations and cycling clubs, all of which had a clubbable, masculine ethos. The College shared with these groups a masculine heartiness, summed up by Johnston's 'Song of the Eagle Street College'. This recalled some of what Johnston called the 'hearty good feeling and the ceaseless flow of merriment' which permeated their meetings. Hailing the group in dialect form as 'the Pheelosiphers' and the 'Wans for Knowlidge', the song went on to declare that 'The Talks ov the bhoys are varied an' frae;/From Brownin' an' Whitman to a Parish Church shprae,/For be jabers, there's mortial few things won't agrae/Wid the bhoys ov the Aigle Shtrate Collidge'.[4]

This cheerful self-deprecation was one of the consistent strands of College life throughout its long existence. Given this and other continuities, it would be somewhat artificial to divide the activities of the College into periods or phases. However, the changes in the group do clearly fall into three stages between about 1885 and 1900, which mirrored the fortunes of both progressive thought and the possibility of imagining new forms of masculine comradeship. The first, from 1885 to 1891, was a relatively quiet period during which the foundations of group solidarity and interest were laid. Much time was spent pondering the meaning of Whitman's *Leaves of Grass* and considering the nature of the message it contained. In particular, there was a simultaneous fascination with homoerotic desire in the poems and a consistent effort to exonerate Whitman from its taint, an effort which the College continued to pursue throughout its existence.

After 1891 and Wallace's visit to Whitman, the College, inspired by its 'Master', took on a more millennial feel, with Wallace attempting to forge links with the emerging ILP. Also at this time the College cemented its connections with new intellectual currents through their friendships with Edward Carpenter and with Richard Maurice Bucke. These years, between 1891 and 1894, were the headiest days of the College, and perhaps of their own brand of comradely socialism, and culminated in the arrival in Bolton of a young American singer and composer named Philip Dalmas in the summer of 1894. This remarkable man seems to have been the focus of many of the hopes and aspirations of the College, especially those of Wallace, Johnston and Sixsmith. In particular, he aroused intense feelings of love and admiration, and seemed, like Whitman, to personify the 'new spiritual personality' which was to herald the new world.

In the years following 1894, however, the diaries and letters seem to exhibit a palpable sense of a lost possibility, a quietening of the tone and the implicit abandonment of any 'mission' to the people. It would be tempting to place this apparent sea change in the context of the trial of Oscar Wilde and its cramping effect on male intimacy. It is certainly true that Johnston's diaries from 1895 have either not survived or were not kept, a void that might encourage all manner of speculation. Yet there were other events and trends which dented the millenialism of the College and the possible association of social reform, comradeship and homosexuality. Chief among these was the overall transformation of the socialism of the 1880s and 1890s from a holistic attempt at universal transformation into a narrower party political grouping. It was not only the Whitmanites who felt this lost opportunity. As one trade unionist put it, looking back on this ferment from the 1920s, this 'fanatical time' had really been a period of evanescent excitement, and was 'in fact too exciting to last'.[5]

Therefore, through the Bolton Whitmanites we can see that it was not only the post-Wilde moral atmosphere which transformed ideas about homosexuality, comradeship and manly intimacy. There were other factors involved too, in particular the marginalisation of ideas like 'cosmic consciousness' and spiritualism from scientifically authorised discourses like psychology and psychoanalysis. These developments tended to defeat the talk of 'alternate selves' which had sustained the College and given power to the idea of comrade love. Yet although the climate was less conducive after about 1895, the ideal of spiritual love and of homosexuality as a form of acute sensibility, which the College fostered in its links with Edward Carpenter, nevertheless remained.

The fortunes of the College, then, reflected the possibility of imagining comradeship and homosexuality as powerful social entities that might solve the question of class cooperation. It might appear that Bolton was an unlikely location for these developments, but in many ways it was a typical place for such imaginings. Although the College was intimately connected with local institutions and life in Bolton, their focus was on universal ideals rather than locality. Indeed, there was little that was unique to Bolton which could have inspired the meditations of the College on politics, culture and the spirit. The town was an almost archetypal location for the millennial hopes and fears brought on by the anticipation of a mass culture and mass electorate. It had a large labouring population based in the textile and engineering industries, the more skilled sections of which had formed powerful amalgamated trade unions. By the 1890s, settled patterns of employment, unionisation and wages had produced a stable, and even aspirational, working-class culture. Part of this culture was a characteristically Victorian interest in self improvement, fostered by a liberal upper strata of cotton spinners, the 'barefoot arisocrats' of Bolton's working class who have been described by one historian as a 'status-conscious artisan elite'.[6]

Bolton was also representative of a certain kind of Victorian modernity which was expressed through civic pride. The *Annals of Bolton*, written in 1888 by local journalist James Clegg to celebrate the jubilee of the Bolton Corporation, provided a picture of a self-confident and modern town, which could trace its history back to the Romans. The *Annals* presented Bolton as having all the benefits of progress and stability, including 'well-paved and well-lighted streets', a 'handsome and spacious Market Hall', an admirable supply of water, excellent sanitary arrangements and tramways and a 'palatial' Town Hall, erected in 1873 at the enormous cost of £170,000.[7] The Town Hall, by the local architects Bradshaw and Gass, included a classical pediment populated by sculptural figures symbolising Bolton's links to the Empire. These figures, representing the various countries and trades of Britain's imperial partners, stood around a seated female figure representing Bolton itself. The clear message was that Bolton's trade and influence spanned the globe, and that the textile trade was central to the national interest. According to Clegg, the town's less ostentatious public architecture was also something be proud of, since in addition to the Town Hall, it comprised a fine new Gas Offices in the Gothic style, waterworks, gasworks and a Free Library. With these amenities in its possession it was hoped that Bolton would become a byword for 'civic good government, social progress and prosperity'.[8]

Bolton, then, was in many ways a typical Victorian manufacturing town and in others the epitome of civic and imperial modernity. In some respects, the Whitmanites were also characteristically Victorian. They were entirely representative of the late-Victorian meeting of political change with the forces of spiritual, social, personal and cultural reform. This combination was characteristic of many radical and socialist groups in this period, especially across the north of England. In addition, the concern of the College with the future of the working class, the spiritual condition of 'the democracy' and the purity of their own souls was entirely characteristic of social reformers elsewhere. Socialists of the period like Robert Blatchford and Katherine Conway, both of whom came into contact with the College, saw moral, spiritual and cultural reform as an indissoluble unity. Neither were the Bolton Whitmanites alone in their veneration of a prophet of these new times. British socialism at this point was an eclectic mixture of radical, literary and spiritual ideas rather than a solid and coherent party programme. Other small groups of spiritually inclined thinkers formed in Surrey to study the teachings of Tolstoy and in Liverpool to follow those of Ruskin.[9] Carolyn Masel points out that Whitman also had his adherents among religious free-thinkers in Kent.[10] These coteries caught the spiritual idiom of the moment by forming into semi-religious sects.

The most famous of the Whitman/Carpenter-influenced groups of the period was probably C.R. Ashbee's Guild of Handicraft, established in Whitechapel in 1888. Ashbee was in the same Cambridge circle as Carpenter and other Whitmanite intellectuals, such as Roger Fry and Goldsworthy Lowes Dickinson, and was deeply influenced by their advocacy of both a handicraft-based rural simple life which rejected modern industrial society and the need to engage with the needs of working people. For Ashbee, Whitman's poems provided the terms on which the new life of comradeship, artisanal trades and class cooperation would take place. Neither was Ashbee unwilling to propound Carpenter's version of 'homogenic' love and comradely union. In fact he made it central to the formation of his artistic and social thought, the culmination of which was the foundation of the craft colony in rural Gloucestershire in 1902.[11] The spiritual, sectarian and comradely trend in British socialism was also shared by other small but influential groups of reformers, all of whom belong in a similar category to the College and the Guild of Handicraft. In this respect, we might include the College, the Guild and other comradely organisations in the same category as the Men and Women's Club of the 1880s, the Fabians, the Fellowship of the New Life, the Ethical and Labour Church movements, the homophile Order of Chaeronea and other groups which shared a similar holistic approach to reform.

The College was also typical in other ways. Both Joy Dixon and Alex Owen have shown that the use of spirituality as a means to explain and ennoble sexual dissidence and personal radicalism was a common feature of the 1880s and 1890s.[12] This connection was not only a late-Victorian relationship. Andrew Elfenbein has also shown that a cultural correlation between sexual deviance, temperamental genius and the divine had a history dating back to late eighteenth-century romanticism.[13] In spite of this association, Dixon rightly notes that Foucauldian accounts of homosexuality have privileged sexual science above other sources of knowledge and subjectivity. She finds a counterpoint to this historiography in the emphasis placed by both Havelock Ellis and Edward Carpenter on the connection between sexual inversion, spirituality and mysticism. As Dixon points out, Ellis found that some of his subjects for the *Sexual Inversion* section of *Studies in the Psychology of Sex* thought of themselves as 'mystics' with particular gifts of perception. By the 1915 edition of *Sexual Inversion*, Ellis had included an argument based on continental anthropology suggesting that inverts in primitive cultures had a special relationship with the Divine.[14] In addition to employing the insights of continental writers, Ellis was also drawing on the work of Edward Carpenter, who had begun to make a similar connection between the invert and the spirit at the beginning of the 1890s. For Carpenter, homosexuals were an 'intermediate sex' combining the best aspects of male and female temperaments. As a result they were able to develop special spiritual qualities. As Dixon remarks, Carpenter's understanding of homosexuality used a Darwinian idiom to suggest that the invert's particular personality represented a higher stage of evolutionary progress.[15] As I will show below, some of Carpenter's inspiration for this view may have come from his interchange of ideas with the Bolton Whitmanites and with Whitman's American followers.

Whitman's unconventional appeal to both the Eagle Street College and to a large section of the working classes was similarly located in his spirituality, which was combined with an equally popular reverence for the working man. His popularity with British socialists can also be explained partly by their strong affinity with the kind of spiritual, mystical language found in Whitman's verse. Mark Bevir has noted that a similar and powerful strain of romanticism, borrowed from American sources like Emerson and Thoreau, ran through the culture of early socialism in Britain.[16] One of the leading lights of this culture in the north of England was John Trevor, a former Unitarian minister from Manchester who formed the Labour Church in 1891 partly as a protest against the middle-class character of nonconformity in the town. One of the first branches of the Labour Church was established in Bolton in 1892, when a congregationalist chapel, including the minister, threw in its lot with Trevor. The liturgy of the Labour churches, in so far as they had one, was a typically eclectic mixture of nonconformity and more unorthodox sources of spirituality. Whitman's celebration of the common man and his demonstration of the labourer's need for spiritual as well as material sustenance chimed perfectly with the spirit of socialist groups like the Labour Church.

As Bevir notes, ideas with spiritual resonance like theosophy and Tolstoyism were also popular themes in the Labour churches, often in combination with a more orthodox socialism. Yet this kind of thought, like Whitman's poetry, did not merely represent an afterthought to a properly socialist message. Instead, seemingly sectional interests like vegetarianism or anti-vivisection were part of a socialism which was as much about a particular ethos as it was about actual politics. Whitman's contribution to Trevor's thought in particular and to the movement as a whole was also far greater than that of other radical causes which shared platform space with socialism. Rather than being just one among many alternative, 'cranky' radicalisms, Whitman's works and their comradely ethos were at the heart of the movement. His poems were not only frequently used as Labour Church readings, and included in the movement's paper the *Labour Prophet*, but were also seen by Trevor as central to its message. For Trevor and many other socialists, including those indirectly attached to the Eagle Street College, Whitman's writing was in itself a form of religion, and he himself was a sort of living prophet. Whitman, Trevor declared in 1892, 'knows more about that life which to me is Religion than any man living'. He was even 'nearer to God than any man on earth'.[17] Whitman's poetry was 'a volume of my Bible, my Book of Life', a text that helped him in his own 'effort to live'.[18]

By the time Whitman became associated with both socialism and the Eagle Street College in the 1890s, his poetry had a longstanding reputation for immorality. Equally, in socialist circles, Whitman was closely associated with sexual candour, a love of the beauty of nature and the joys of physical intimacy. Whitman's 'smutty' repute among more respectable readers and reviewers partly derived from the 'Children of Adam' section of *Song of Myself*. In 'I Sing the Body Electric', in which the joy of the body and of physicality is celebrated, the beauty of sex is described in typically ecstatic terms, as 'love-flesh swelling and deliciously aching,/Limitless limpid jets of love hot and enormous, quivering jelly of love, white-blow and delirious juice'.[19] Yet, according to John Trevor, the poems expressed not smut, but 'the beauty and pathos of and mystery of life and death and nature'. Even though, as Trevor recognised, most people would be most familiar with Walter Scott's expurgated edition, which had removed most of the poems dealing with sex and the body, Whitman nevertheless forced his readers to an honest contemplation of the corporeal and its beauty. Although Whitman might be dangerous to those who had been raised dishonestly, 'sickly young people, ignorantly introduced to the broad field of life where tares grow apace', the purity and 'bracing morning air' of *Leaves of Grass* or *Song of Myself* was health itself. At least in Whitman sex had been 'honestly faced'. Whitman was simply a natural force, an objective phenomenon which could not be argued with. He was 'such a MAN!' a piece of 'nature humanised', a vital force 'which impresses us as we are impressed by the sun or the sky, or the mountains or the murmuring sea'.[20]

The celebration of comradeship and of the common man which could be found in *Leaves of Grass* and *Song of Myself* also had a strong affinity with an English homoerotic tradition which valued comradeship, youth and manly vigour. This, perhaps, is where Whitman's verse intersected not only with romantic socialism of Ashbee or Carpenter but also with a metropolitan tradition of street encounters and 'trade'. The *Calamus* section of *Leaves of Grass* is replete with imagery of fleeting glances met in a city street, of urban working men and the possibility of gaining their trust and love, and with the evanescent possibility of sexual satisfaction. Whitman himself had many close working-class comrades, the most important of whom was the tram conductor Pete Doyle.[21] Similarly, in an English context, metropolitan aestheticism and a Hellenistic 'Uranian' poetry both celebrated the joys to be found in the company and contemplation of Telegraph boys, working men and athletes. The most striking example of this overlap between a Hellenistic ethos of Platonic spiritual comradeship and a preference for the company of 'lads' can perhaps be found in Wilde himself. According to Montgomery Hyde, his first trial in 1895 turned on the question of whether it was possible to express a disinterested opinion on the beauty of youth.[22] Neither was Wilde alone in his preference for the invigorating company of young working-class men. John Addington Symonds' liking for the company of English soldiers, Swiss peasants and Venetian gondoliers was similarly couched in terms of cross-class comradeship and found a ready justification in the poetry of Whitman. Symonds recalled in his memoirs that Whitman's poems had taught him 'to apprehend the value of fraternity, and to appreciate the working classes'. Whitman's example also showed that relations with men could be taken up 'in a more natural and intelligible manner – more rightly and democratically' than could be done in either the brothel or the street.[23]

The association of Whitman with sexual candour, comradeship and admiration for the working man were themes which appealed directly to the College and Whitman's other English admirers. They also cemented Whitman's place in a homosexual canon. Yet these overtly homoerotic themes were combined with other less controversial but no less appealing ideas. In particular, it was Whitman's spirituality rather than his ethos of homoerotic comradeship which provided a theme of common connection between the Labour Church, early socialism and the Eagle Street College. Even though religion was singled out for its explicit appeal, it was nevertheless connected with comrade love and broader questions of personal desire. Religion, therefore, was one way in which questions of selfhood, comradeship, class and homosexuality could be approached.

WHITMAN, RELIGION AND DESIRE

For Whitman's followers, the ineffable nature of his spirituality was central to the poet's appeal. Whitman propounded an idea which found a telling echo in the post-Darwinian religious sentiment of late-Victorian Britain. Specifically, he insisted upon the oneness of creation, the unity of matter and spirit and the immortality of the soul. Death therefore represented a form of transcendence of the self and its passions. This was an idea which could be readily adapted to articulate a spiritual, timeless love that was elevated above mere personal desire. Just as

Whitman insisted on oneness, immortality and transcendence, post-Darwinian Christianity increasingly relied on an 'immanentist' belief that the presence of the Divine could be discerned almost anywhere, but especially in nature. The Bolton Whitmanites borrowed from both traditions. In particular they looked upon death in Whitman's terms, as a beginning not an end, as a means to transcend the torments of bodily desire and as a sanctification of comrade love.

The 'Master' of the College, J.W. Wallace, epitomised a late-Victorian disenchantment with formal religion and spirituality. He and his friends searched for alternative reassurance that the universe did contain an unseen order and that there was a life beyond death. In this quest they were responding to the widespread crisis of faith induced by scientific materialism. As Mark Bevir and others have noted, one of the principal responses to this post-Darwinian dilemma was not only a search for alternative versions of spirituality like those to be found in Whitman or theosophy, but a revolution in Christian thought. Instead of assuming that God's purpose could be made manifest, as had earlier advocates of evangelical religion, those who followed the insights of scientific materialism propounded a new faith, one which proclaimed that God was immanent in the world.[24] One of the forms that this 'immanentism' took was a new reverence for nature as the working out of a Divine purpose. For the College, Whitman's love of nature represented a similar religious impulse. Whitman also suggested that the soul was immortal and Death should be welcomed as the beginning of a new life. This belief provided the College with an alternative version of the immortality of the soul.

Clearly the College found personal solutions to their own crises of faith and desire in Whitman's poetry. Wallace had begun life as a Presbyterian and a regular church attender, but through his wide reading in the sciences had lost his faith. His readings in philosophy and metaphysics, however, had failed to provide him with an alternative to the immortality of the spirit. Johnston had also gone through the process of losing his faith and, he later recalled, was not far from becoming a sceptical, not to say cynical, man. For Wallace, the death of his mother had turned his thoughts to the possibility of immortality, feelings which he found echoed in *Leaves of Grass*. There, he read in Whitman's *Calamus* lyrics (which most critics have seen as Whitman's most homoerotic writing) a poetry of love and death which confirmed his view that death was merely the gateway to immortality, and that what Wallace called the 'ego' or personality continued after death, merely transformed into a new form of matter.

Such a view relied on an interpretation of scientific reason that was common to late-Victorian attempts to understand the dynamic unconscious and the unseen world of spirituality. Some of these efforts gathered influential adherents, such as the Society for Psychical Research, and took on the method and rhetoric of science to try and show that the personality survived death. The world of the spirit, these researches suggested, as well as the spirit itself, had a quasi-material existence that was accessible to scientific inquiry through the exploration of trance states, hypnotism and automatic writing. Although the College were not active spiritualists or psychical researchers, Wallace concluded in a similar manner that spirit and matter were equivalent entities. Matter was, he concluded, 'a mere film enveloping the soul'. Since spirit and matter were the same, they could be held to have a material existence, and were, according to Wallace, of the same character as the universe itself. Therefore, the soul or spirit was the universe, and all matter was one. An understanding of and sympathy with nature was therefore the closest one could get to an understanding of matter, the universe and the oneness of spirit. Through nature, Wallace suggested, 'we shall slowly come to realize in her myriad colours and forms the many-coloured revelation of one spirit to whom we may speak'.[25] Death was therefore no ending, merely a transformation.

Love was crucial to this religious vision. Whitman's notion of masculine comradeship implied that the transformation wrought by death could only truly be attained by those who felt a perfect love for humanity, a sentiment written into the *Calamus* section of *Leaves of Grass*. Whitman was, Wallace argued, conscious of an 'immortal life' underlying life and death, which was felt most assuredly 'in the presence of those he loved'. Love made us conscious of the Soul, the attributes of which could be attained and expressed by death in a literal sense, but also by the death of 'all purely personal desires and aims, and of all forms of what we call selfishness'. Only in this way, through the triangle of love, death and immortality, could 'the Soul pass into the Universal and Eternal Life in which Love is supreme'.[26]

An effusive love was therefore central to Whitman's religion. In the reading of many of Whitman's British followers, a renewal of faith was intimately linked to the love of comrades. Religion, comradeship, immortality and personal desire were all part of what for the College was a new view of society, each part dependent on the other. The achievement of immortality depended on the possibility of experiencing comrade love, which in turn implied a sympathy with one's fellow man which would drive new forms of political and social organisation. Extravagant expressions of comrade love which might otherwise be seen as problematic and even unnatural were therefore not only licensed, but were imperative to this transcendent religious and social vision.

Whitman himself was the exemplar of the highest spiritual characteristics, and inspired an effort among the College to imitate his sensibility, which was the avatar of a new world. The visits to Whitman undertaken by Wallace and Johnston therefore attained a kind of religious significance. On his return from Camden, Wallace told Johnston that he seemed as though he had experienced a 'spiritual visitation', while Johnston confessed to feeling 'a different man altogether since seeing and conversing with *the Master*' and being 'sanctified and solemnified' by contact with the poet. Whitman was regarded by them as a man of super-perception, who was 'endowed with exceptionally acute senses'.[27] Whitman's doctor, Richard Maurice Bucke, noted that Whitman claimed to 'speak of hearing the grass grow and the trees coming into leaf'.[28] For the starstruck Wallace and Johnston, Whitman's goodness bestowed not only kindness but also a sweetness and light which derived from his ethos of comradeship and which the College friends sought to reproduce in their finer moments. *Leaves of Grass* was assumed to contain an entire approach to life and a set of practical 'teachings', which could be appreciated through the imitation of the poet's life and sensibility.

Loving comradeship was not only a sign of a spiritual personality and the oneness of the universe, but could also have its social and political uses. For Whitman's followers, intense love for one's comrades was therefore not only encouraged in homoerotic terms, but was also necessary to the reformation of the social order. Whitman's loving personality, then, was to be imitated as a spiritual and social duty. Various examples of this sweetness were identified, including 'England's Whitman' himself, Edward Carpenter. But in Bolton it was Wallace who was thought to represent this Whitmanesque quality. He was, for Johnston, the nearest thing to the poet's 'unique spiritual personality' that he knew.[29] Yet Whitman's characteristic personality was not merely a matter of simple reverence. Rather it represented the possibility of comradeship as both a form of subjectivity and, consequently, a radical new social movement that would bridge personal and class differences. According to John Addington Symonds' Whitmanesque poem, 'Love and Death: A Symphony', comrades were imagined as a 'dauntless imperturbable array', 'serried like links of adamant', who would 'make the world one fellowship and plant New Paradise for nations yet to be'. However, for this to take place, this 'true Freemasonry' would have to build temples 'on no earthly coast, but with star-fire on souls and hearts of man!'.[30]

By stressing Whitman's attachment to immortality ('Death or life I am then indifferent, my soul declines to prefer'),[31] Wallace and Johnston were able to reaffirm their religious faith, to try and accommodate it to the findings of science, and to elevate the significance of their comradeship and masculine love. Where critics saw in Whitman's evasive, coded language a vocabulary of homoerotic attachment, his followers read an ethereal, ineffable attachment to death, immortality and the oneness of the universe (or of God) reached only via the love of comrades. This explains why love and its expression was so important to the College, and goes some way to explaining how their effusive idiom of passionate love for one another could exist without the suggestion of pathological desires. By associating love with immortality and faith, comradeship was made all the more powerful and personal desire was transcended.

The template for comradeship within the College and in the wider world was the relationship between Wallace and Johnston. They shared an intense spirituality, with Johnston often cast by his friend only half-jokingly as a subordinate St Paul to his Saviour. Johnston regarded the emulation of Wallace's sweet temperament as he regarded the emulation of Whitman, as a moral duty. The love of comrades, the basis of their belief, required it. 'I love him more and more as a man,' Johnston wrote in 1891, 'strong with heroic strength and gentle and tender and considerate and loving, with all a woman's and a mother's delicate loving soul.'[32] One of Wallace's chief attributes was to have provided Johnston with an alternative faith. For Johnston, Wallace's elucidation of *Leaves of Grass* made him no less than 'my soul's deliverer... the messenger of a new life' and 'a veritable human messiah bringing hope, peace, comfort and salvation from my own sinful self which at one time threatened to engulf my soul in the Slough of Despond'.[33] In addition, there existed 'a curious and mysterious sympathy' between these two great friends which could border on the ethereal. On one occasion Johnston wondered at the coincidence of their low mood and whether it was 'possible that in some mysterious manner I did telepath him and so communicate my melancholy mood to him?'[34] In 1887, Wallace inscribed a copy of John Seeley's *Ecce Homo* with a quote from Whitman's 'To Him That Was Crucified'. The poem begins by pledging 'My spirit to yours dear brother' and ends in the hope that 'the men and women of races, ages to come, *may prove brethren and lovers as we are*'. Johnston's response was no less effusive:

> I accept the book and with it the heart love which prompted the giver to insert that inscription and all that it implies – especially the last six words which to me are inexpressibly precious because I know that he means me to accept them as true. Oh that I were more worthy to be your 'brother and lover.' My dear friend! To be so called by you is a great honour and privilege.[35]

Their intimacy, which, as we shall see, was to be reproduced with certain privileged others, even extended to sharing beds, not a necessity in the large houses owned by both men. In 1901, after a College meeting, 'Wallace stayed all night with me and after the others had gone we had a right good talk together before we went to bed – and after too (for we slept together, my wife being away at Menai Bridge)'.[36]

Their effusive expressions of love perhaps composed part of local as well as imported plebeian and poetic traditions. The literary roots of the College, like those of many other self-improving working men in the region were in the poetry of Robert Burns, in the writings of John Bunyan, Ruskin, Emerson and Matthew Arnold. Eugenio Biagini has pointed out that some of these authors formed part of a popular, Liberal, non-conformist canon which dated back to the 1860s.[37] As Patrick Joyce has shown, an effusive 'cult of the heart' espoused by writers like Emerson, and by his English followers like the Lancashire dialect poet Edwin Waugh, was a significant source of Lancashire's working-class literary culture. The admiration inspired by Emerson in particular, which Joyce sees as 'quasi-religious' and 'almost sexual', might also be seen as a prevision of the influence of Whitman.[38]

The signs of this comradely sensibility were therefore sought by Wallace and Johnston in themselves and in the College. Johnston saw this quality in his friend expressed as a uniqueness 'not to be met with above once a life time', which by itself made 'one think better of the future of the human race'. Mere proximity to Wallace, as to Whitman, 'acts as a spiritual tonic to me', Johnston confided to his diary, 'and I leave him with an elevation of moral resolve and determination to attempt to attain something of the... ideal he seems to set before him'.[39] A certain obscurity, even ineffability, was both the price and the sign of this Whitmanesque mastery. As Johnston put it, Wallace had to be 'studied' and imitated in order for his meaning to be revealed. Yet 'very few of his intimate friends I fear really *know* what a splendid fellow he is', the doctor wrote in his diary, 'and as for knowing him – in the sense of *understanding* him I don't suppose any of us do that'.[40] Wallace himself recognised this fact, apologising to Fred Wild for sending letters which 'puzzle your brains by mystical fandangoes worthy of Old Walt'.[41] Yet, for all its impenetrability, mysticism clearly functioned as one of the modes of loving, masculine intimacy.

Modern critics have seen the association of transcendence, immortality, death and love in *Calamus* as a sign of Whitman's homoerotic desire, which could only be expressed in the most abstract and veiled terms. Eve Kosofsky Sedgwick sees in Whitman's 'phallic erethism – his erectness, his eternally rosy skin, his injection of life and health into scenes of death and wounds' an 'afflatus of phallic worship' coexisting with the dynamics of shame, concealment and exhibition operating in the poems.[42] In a very literal sense, the obscurity of *Leaves of Grass*, and the way in which the College searched it for often contradictory meanings, encouraged an endless debate about what it actually meant. The ineffability of desire expressed in the poems and the collection of hidden meanings therein facilitated readings which allowed the homoerotic content of the poetry to be expressed in indirect ways.

Far from seeing it as openly homoerotic, the College saw *Calamus* as the enigmatic heart of a series of mysteries. Its meaning was typically difficult and reserved, Wallace wrote, quoting Whitman, 'for only "a few," … "only to them that love as I myself am capable of loving," that is with complete self-abandonment'. Only for them, Wallace argued, 'is the full realization of the ineffable raptures and solemn joy of the region which Death discloses'.[43] William Innes, Charles Sixsmith's American correspondent, who thought Edward Carpenter's *Homogenic Love* a 'wonderful' book, had also 'long believed the principal meaning of [Whitman's] work to be hidden and only for the few – very few to understand'.[44] Vivian Pollak has observed that it is the concealment of desire which is the major trope in *Calamus*. Whitman, Pollak argues, uses death as a means to express a kind of 'erotic bereavement', and to suggest unrequited and 'unsatisfied love' for other men.[45]

Wallace similarly read in *Calamus* the association of death and desire. For him, however, *Calamus* suggested the death of selfish passion and the submerging of personal interest in the love of comrades, which itself was the only way to reach immortality. As Whitman put it in *Scented Herbage of My Breast*, a poem which celebrates the association of phallic desire with love and death: 'I am not sure but the high soul of lovers welcomes death most.'[46] In a letter to his cousin on more prosaic matters of finance and business, Wallace advises that the aims of life are to cultivate the self, to 'recognise the perfect One in all others, ignoring all contrary seemings, to cease from personal desires in the trust which comes from knowing that Good alone rules our lives'. To abandon oneself to that purpose was 'the right course for us, and this only'.[47] Abandoning personal desire also enabled individuals to devote their lives to the public good, and hence to assure their immortality, in a peculiarly Victorian fashion. As Johnston pointed out when he invoked Matthew Arnold to support this view, this form of Karmic character-building merged effortlessly with classically Victorian notions of duty and morality. Reading Arnold, Johnston pointed out, showed that 'life is made up of three parts conduct', and that immortality was dependent on conduct in the present. Personal desire and selfishness should be abandoned and life lived '*in and for the sake of others*'.[48]

Calamus, then, had a practical, spiritual application in that it encouraged the love of comrades. For Wallace as for Whitman, the meeting of love and death discerned in *Leaves of Grass* was not only about selflessness and self-cultivation, but was closely associated with the abandonment of desire. This association was echoed in Symonds' poetic symphony 'Love and Death', which Wallace reverently copied into one of his notebooks in 1880. The poem was intended as a Whitmanesque celebration of comradeship in the manner of *Leaves of Grass*, but instead was marked by a fervent celebration of both ancient Greece and the beauty of death. The first movement, 'The Song of Love and Death', in which Love and Death are hailed as 'twin brothers!' chimed exactly with Wallace's reading of *Calamus*. Symonds' poem envisaged a band of comrades uniting the world in fellowship and love, whose true antecedents were the Theban band who had fallen heroically at Thermopylae. These immortal and sexual Athenians would be 'Stirred from their graves to meet our Sacred Host' and 'rising very wan, By death made holy', would acclaim their modern heirs as brothers 'Who achieve what we began'. Symonds embraced this death as the solution to tortured passion. Those 'that sigh for freedom', Symonds wrote, who yearned, 'pent in this prison house of languishing!' should:

> Haste to everlasting fountains; turn your trammels of the flesh to yielding air:
> Your aching hours, your tears that freeze and burn, your dear expense of passionate despair
> Barter for hope unbounded, perfect bliss
> Who swoons for very love, who longs to share
> Two separate souls in one perennial kiss
> To merge the bounds of being.
> To become of twain one sentient shape of blessedness – let him seek Death!
> Therein that tranquil dome where what we were dissolves, what we must be
> Endures regenerate, there the living home of love defies corruptibility. [49]

Death and desire were, for Symonds, inextricably linked. Yet in spite of these veiled and ineffable associations there was also a more overtly homoerotic message in *Calamus*, which was more than problematic for the College and for Whitman's followers. The religious aspect of *Leaves of Grass* allowed homoerotic desire to be spoken of as a transcendent form of immortality and death, but that did not mean that comradeship was entirely free of any association with unnatural desire. On the contrary, Wallace, Johnston, Dixon, Sixsmith and the others were continually exercised or even fascinated by the homoerotic overtones of some of Whitman's work. They reasoned that any such association would damage not only Whitman's literary reputation, but all hopes of promulgating his teachings. However, although Wallace's cosmology of death and desire provided a distracting point of emphasis for students of *Calamus*, other critics were not slow to point out the potentially diseased ethos lurking within comrade love.

The homoerotic content of comrade love was not only the preoccupation of post-Freudian critics. Some of Whitman's contemporaries were prepared to voice their suspicions, albeit in veiled terms. One of Whitman's early reviewers in the *Gentleman's Magazine* noted in 1875 that the poet spoke partly of the 'sick, sick dread of returned friendship, of the comrade's kiss, the arm round the neck'. No such sentiments would avail in Britain, though, for 'he speaks to sticks and stones; the emotion does not exist in us, and the language of his evangel poems appears simply disgusting'.[50] Even in 1894, Edward Carpenter could suggest in his pamphlet *Homogenic Love* (which he gave to Charles Sixsmith) that Whitman 'certainly had the homogenic instinct highly developed'.[51] By 1913, after the advent of sexology, W.C. Rivers could argue that *Leaves of Grass* immediately suggested a 'strong similarity' to 'confessions of homosexual subjects recorded in text-books on the human sex instinct'.[52] One of Whitman's first biographers, Bliss Perry, recognised a similar theme. Even though Perry persistently sought to remove any suspicions about Whitman, he nevertheless fell foul of the poet's circle. In 1906, in an appendix removed from later editions in response to objections from Whitman's executors about the suggestion of homosexuality it aroused, he concluded that 'the truth about him (the innermost truth) escapes from almost every page for those who can read'.[53] In 1925, when the *International Journal of Psychoanalysis* finally got round to noticing Rivers' book, his account of Whitman's 'anomaly' was deemed to be 'obvious at first sight to anyone having any knowledge of homosexuality'.[54]

Yet because of the permissible nature of passionate friendship between men, it was still possible during the 1890s for the College to celebrate both the intensity and the innocence of comradeship. Jeffrey Richards and Steven Seidman have established that the spiritual side of love was a crucial component of Victorian intimacy. As they suggest, the Victorians could, by and large, enjoy and celebrate sex and the body as long as it was distanced from sensuality. As Seidman has argued, the spiritual content of sexual desire performed this role by raising sexuality above the animal and the sensual, and was therefore an indispensable element of marital intercourse.[55] Richards and Alan Sinfield have also shown that manly love, the terms of which were borrowed from evangelical

Christianity, a purified Hellenism and a reverence for an imagined medieval chivalry, was a venerable tradition in nineteenth-century Britain. Traditions of passionate friendship which drew on these sources, Richards suggests, were imported wholesale into the public-school tradition and only began to be morally suspicious in that context in the 1880s.[56]

Comradeship and spiritual love had a wider connotation as well, encompassing both the working-class 'cult of the heart' outlined by Joyce and the intimacies common among new women and feminists. Whereas Lillian Faderman's suggestion that the nineteenth century was a golden age of chaste passionate friendship for women has been challenged, it is nevertheless true that such effusive friendships between women were very common.[57] Spiritual and psychic forms of love were also central to the articulation of feminist accounts of sexuality. As Sheila Jeffreys and Lucy Bland have pointed out, some new women, such as Elizabeth Wolstenhome Elmy and Frances Swiney, envisaged the replacement of bodily intimacy, which might be either physically harmful and lead to marital subordination, with a spiritual 'psychic love'.[58]

In spite of the Victorian tradition of passionate friendship, spiritual and manly love, the early 1890s nevertheless saw a sea change in the interpretation of comradeship because some writers were increasingly willing to test the boundaries of public discourse about homosexuality. Suggestions that comradeship might have a homoerotic content began to be made with a greater insistence. It therefore became imperative to exonerate Whitman from the overt taint of unnatural lust. This became even more pressing following the publication of John Addington Symonds' *Walt Whitman: A Study* in 1893 which suggested that *Calamus* provided the first modern literary justification and defence of homosexual desire. It was clear, Symonds argued, that 'those unenviable mortals who are the inheritors of sexual anomalies, will recognise their own emotion in Whitman's "superb friendship, exalté, previously unknown," which "waits and has been waiting, latent in all men," the "something fierce in me, eligible to burst forth."' Symonds had put this argument to Whitman himself, who had responded with a choleric denial and the assertion that he had fathered six illegitimate children, but this did not settle the matter. 'Had I not the strongest proof in Whitman's private correspondence with myself,' Symonds wrote, 'that he repudiated any such deductions from *Calamus*, I admit that I should have regarded them as justified.'[59] Yet Whitman's letter did not stop Symonds from concluding that 'there are inevitable points of contact between sexual anomaly and his doctrine of comradeship'. The question was whether comradeship could suggest ways in which 'the abnormal instincts may be moralized and raised to higher value', and whether manly intimacy could raise such instincts from the 'filth and mire of brutal appetite'. Symonds, unsurprisingly, concluded that they could, via the agency of a transcendent love. His vision looked beyond personal satisfaction and desire towards social and political virtue. As he had done in his poetic symphony of comrades, Symonds suggested in his study of Whitman that comradeship carried us back to ancient Greece, to 'Plato's Symposium, to Philip gazing on the sacred band of Thebans after the fight at Chaeronea'.[60]

Both Wallace and Johnston corresponded with Symonds on the subject of sexual inversion before the publication of *Walt Whitman: A Study*. Johnston had first contacted Symonds after his visit to Camden, enclosing some photographs of Whitman, to which Symonds warmly responded, taking Johnston's letter 'as a sign that our Master Walt has the power of bringing folk together by a common kinship of kind feeling'. That was the principal meaning of *Calamus*, Symonds suggested, 'the doctrine of Comradeship' which might bring strangers into contact, although he also wondered, like Wallace and William Innes, 'what more than this "Calamus" contains'.[61] There was also correspondence between Symonds and Wallace over the meaning of *Calamus*. Symonds suggested that the 'real drift' of *Calamus* was towards the justification of homosexual feelings and asked Wallace to provide detail of a Bolton man arrested under 'Labouchere's Clause'.[62] He also told Wallace that Whitman's adoring letters to his companion Pete Doyle (some of which Wallace had copied into his notebooks when in Camden) 'As you say... throw a distinct light on what he meant by comradeship, and do more than aught else could to explain Calamus'.[63]

As Eve Kosofsky Sedgwick has noted, masculine intimacy at this date was marked by a historically specific form of homosexual panic.[64] The encroachments of homosexuality into ordinary life which prompted such anxiety meant that for all his interest in the subject of sexual inversion, it was still Johnston's concern to cleanse Whitman's reputation. He thought Symonds' attempt to read *Calamus* as implying the dignity and humanity of homosexual desire 'one of the most damnable [and] atrocious suggestions conceivable' and that 'to speak of "sexual inversion" as being implied seems to me nothing short of a gross insult to Walt himself'. Symonds, he suggested, 'cannot be serious in that odious suggestion!'[65] The true meaning of *Calamus* was surely contained in Symonds' suggestion that it might lead to a 'luminous ideal of a new chivalry based on brotherhood and manly affection'.[66] It was emphatically not the gateway to disease. Johnston approvingly quoted a letter on the subject from Whitman's American acolyte Horace Traubel, who declared in 1887 that Symonds was very wrong. His theory 'argued bad for his comprehension not only of *Leaves of Grass* but of the times in which we live'. Homosexuality had not played any part in history, and 'it certainly would not appear in *Leaves of Grass* where there exists the most solid and substantial avowal of self'. 'Homo Sexuality,' he said, was a 'disease, it is wreck and rot – it is decay and muck,' while Walt was 'health and salvation of purity of growth and beauty – elements vital for upstarting for blossoming for repair.'[67] The extended disavowal of this reading of *Calamus* by Johnston, Wallace and Wentworth Dixon removed the taint of corruption from any association with Whitman. Yet this was not only a form of homosexual panic in the terms outlined by Sedgwick. Excising homoerotic readings of Whitman also had the corresponding and perverse effect of licensing intense friendships by displacing overt homoerotic desire into a distant and abject realm of moral corruption and disease.

In spite of Johnston's violent disavowals of Symonds' reading, the following year he welcomed *Walt Whitman: A Study*. In spite of the fact that it contained the fullest development of Symonds' 'sexual inversion theory' of Whitman, Johnston praised it as 'a fine book'. In keeping with his contradictory attitude to homosexuality, he declared that 'the most cursory examination, shows that it is a thoroughly good one entirely of Symonds and worthy of Walt!' A week later, after a more detailed examination, he wrote in his diary that 'the more I read of it the deeper grows my conviction that in writing it Symonds has done one of the best things of his life' which would do wonders to advance the cause of Whitman in Britain.[68] In addition, Symonds' book was read at College meetings several times in the spring of 1893, although the discussions once again concentrated on his interpretation of Whitman's religion.

Whitman, then, built on existing local traditions of spirituality, self-cultivation and heartfelt love for humanity. The College took these traditions further, using his poems to equip themselves with a thorough philosophy of life, the basis of which was personal connection to, and effusive love for one's comrades. The relevance of Whitman's poetry went beyond spirituality, however, and implied a sense of social mission, which Wallace in particular was keen to take up. This feeling became particularly strong following his life-enhancing visit to Whitman in 1891. Thereafter, Wallace became ever more committed to inventing socialism as a political and spiritual project based on a transcendent comrade love.

The Mission of the College
Wallace's visit to Whitman inspired the 'Master' of Eagle Street to adapt the College and its fellows to a more purposive social role. Viewing his friendship with Whitman as nothing less than a religious experience, Wallace began to talk of 'carrying out the duties of my apostolsy',

responsibilities shared in equal measure by Johnston.[69] Their visits, 'the crown and glory of our whole lives', meant that, as Johnston put it, 'for the Whitman cult in America Bolton is the centre of England'. Will Atkinson hoped that their town might become 'the centre of the world'.[70] This gave the College a predominant place in the emergence of what Wallace clearly hoped would be a religion of Whitman, to rank with the Labour and Ethical Churches. In short, he became ever more determined to spread Whitman's 'teachings' among those to whom it was naturally addressed: the 'democracy'. During the following year, the talk of missions and of a democratic millennium heightened the already intense and passionate atmosphere of the College in ways that were to prove increasingly unpredictable and even disquieting.

The College assumed a role of greater importance in this programme since, for Wallace, it represented a microcosm of the way in which the new society should work. Hearty but serious and open discussion, accompanied by an effusive ethos of love would be the basis of the new democratic social order. However, there were difficulties in embracing labour, chief among which was the fact that the democracy seemed inclined to a socialism which was not always welcome to the College fellows. Johnston had complained that any public affiliation to socialism would not only be bad for his business but also socially devastating. Wallace, however, responded with a messianic call to the new mission which he saw waiting for the College and its members. Divisions about socialism could be healed by reaffirming their comradeship. For what was that but 'the word of Christianity itself'? Each member should, he said, 'dedicate himself to the task of making our College more truly than ever yet 'a band of brothers', a church 'where brothers meet to learn and to communicate the highest wisdom – for the deepest needs of their individual souls and also to learn how best to apply it to the needs of the world outside'. The College should stand 'for a higher ideal' than mere party, 'for aspirations towards a more developed and useful *manhood*, hospitable to ideas and to persons, warmly aiding the right, and forever presenting comradeship and affection to each other'. This, he went on, 'is the basis upon which we may yet do a great work for England!'

That work, Wallace argued, was to suggest a spiritual context for the labour movement by promoting Whitman's teachings among its members. The association of the College with Whitman had marked them out and given them 'an influential status that will increase every year'. It was a position which entailed huge responsibilities towards a democracy 'making rapid strides to power and place in England'. There were many dangers attendant on this process, but the College, by its unique place was 'charged (by profoundest and divine call and sanction) to minimise these dangers and to see to it that the greatest new birth of Time is *indeed* beneficent'. They were, according to Wallace, 'the heaven-appointed preachers to the Democracy of England!' to whom labour leaders would increasingly look for spiritual sustenance. They should make the College into a church which rose above distinction of class and opinion and instead placed comradeship at its heart. 'No call to ancient Israel,' Wallace announced, 'no miraculous guidance of his chosen people, was more authentically Divine than ours!'[71]

In practical terms, this mission meant trying to gain the ear of those influential in the early labour movement. By early 1893, Wallace had succeeded in making contact with Robert Blatchford (editor of the *Clarion*, the most popular socialist newspaper of the time), Keir Hardie and socialist lecturer Katherine Conway, with the latter of whom he was to develop a characteristically intense friendship. In February 1893, the same time that Symonds' 'sexual inversion' theory was causing such a stir in the College, expectations of a homogenic political millennium were raised by Wallace's initial success with ILP leaders. He wrote to key ILP figures, enclosing a copy of *Leaves of Grass*, with hints as to its beneficial contents. The Labour movement, Wallace told Keir Hardie, 'must eventually turn for its gospel and Bible' to *Leaves of Grass*, 'as it must find its supreme prophet in Walt Whitman'. Not only the movement itself, but also Hardie himself would find there 'the deeper need of his spiritual nature' not to mention the 'best incentive and highest cheer for all the circumstance of your public and private life'.[72]

His stated aim was, he confided to Johnston, 'to sweep the whole lot connected with the Labour movement into Whitmanism and my wish is that all these people should find their religion in *Leaves of Grass*'.[73] The signs at this stage were encouraging. Not only did Blatchford and Keir Hardie respond with enthusiasm to Wallace's present of a copy of *Leaves of Grass*, Hardie also visited Bolton and began a correspondence with Wallace. Editorials like that in the *Labour Prophet* of April 1892 boosted the feeling that Whitmanism might, like the Labour and Ethical Churches, foster its own religious organisation. Also at this time Wallace even began to consider standing for parliament as an ILP candidate.[74] One of his lectures on Whitman attracted over 2,000 people to Bolton's Temperance Hall.

The detail of what might have become Wallace's political programme was set out in a speech to an ILP conference in Bolton in May 1894. This outlined an ethical project which stressed the religious necessity of comrade love. In order for a socialist utopia to arrive, the Master argued, it was vital that socialists cultivate their higher selves, so that they were able to love each other as the ethos of comradeship required, and by implication, were ready to establish what was, at heart, a divine order. The cultivation of self of course fitted much more neatly with late-Victorian moral precepts than perhaps Wallace would have liked, but it was this appeal to accepted notions of character which, in typically Whitmanesque fashion, hid much larger concepts of comrade love. The success of socialism, Wallace told the ILP, depended on 'the attraction of our own *personalities*, [on] what we call character'. Socialism required a new form of subjectivity that would allow the 'average man or woman… to shape out and exemplify in ourselves this type of future citizenship'. Wallace's exemplar for this form of being was, unsurprisingly, Walt Whitman. With the development of 'the personal soul' would come 'an equal and universal sympathy and love', the essence of socialism.[75]

Wallace's politics required self-cultivation in order for one's 'higher' senses to emerge. The fact that the self was at the heart of this political and religious vision meant that the College was very sympathetic to new views of consciousness being propagated by the more sober wing of spiritualism and allied psychical and psychological researches. For Wallace, Whitman's special sensibility foreshadowed the possibility of new forms of being which might become a general attribute of humanity. Just as new forms of religion equated death and desire, new ways of understanding consciousness could also provide a way of understanding, experiencing and displacing homoerotic desire. These possibilities were given shape by the association of the College with Dr Richard Maurice Bucke, Whitman's personal physician, whose efforts to theorise new forms of consciousness corresponded perfectly with the emerging utopian spirit of the College.

COSMIC CONSCIOUSNESS AND HOMOSEXUALITY

At the same time as Wallace and Johnston were reaching out to the ILP, they were also entertaining new ideas of consciousness which ran in parallel to their own religious mysticism and heightened the sense of mission and expectation around the College. Their association with Whitman had put them in touch with Dr Bucke, who was beginning to piece together a new understanding of consciousness. His theory proposed that this new level of consciousness – beyond ordinary awareness – was about to come into existence and could already be seen in exceptional men.[76] Bucke came to England in 1891 to visit Edward Carpenter and consult 'England's Whitman' on his theories. Carpenter in turn introduced him to the College where his work was enthusiastically received. As we shall see, cosmic consciousness could function as an explanation of behaviour and thoughts which were out of the ordinary by way of displacing them from ordinary consciousness. It also contained important parallels with homoerotic desire. In spite of its explicitly sexual associations, cosmic consciousness provided professional sanction and scientific theory to justify Wallace's belief in the power of comradeship. Indeed, it confirmed the belief of Wallace and Johnston that comrade love was itself a form of subjectivity, which arose from the cultivation of the 'higher self' and could therefore be attained by people in general. Wallace's belief that, like *Leaves of Grass*, comrade love was initially reserved for a few men whose super-perception enabled them to see the oneness of the universe was also reaffirmed by Dr Bucke. As a result, the importance of cosmic consciousness to the College meant that they were, like some Calvinist elect, both constantly searching for signs of its operation, and willing to see some exceptional forms of behaviour and comradely sentiment as signs of this coming phenomenon. In particular, they were primed to view extravagant expressions of love as the sign of this new awareness and thereby to accept an even greater level of intensity to their friendships. In addition, cosmic consciousness was closely associated with a kind of sexual desire. These desires and hopes focused on an American Whitmanite named Philip Dalmas, who visited Bolton in 1894. His Whitmanesque sweetness and acute sensibilities instantly captivated many of the College. Indeed, his presence inspired the most intense expressions of comrade love that Wallace, Johnston and some others were to experience in the heady period between 1892 and 1895.

Richard Maurice Bucke (1837–1902), the man who introduced these ideas to the College and the circle of Edward Carpenter, occupied an eminent position at the centre of the medical profession. He had trained at McGill Medical School in Montreal and studied in Europe in the early 1860s. On his return to Canada, he took up the post of Superintendent of the asylum for the insane at London, Ontario in 1877. There, he built a reputation as one of Canada's leading alienists and a pioneer of gynaecological operations as a cure for hysteria. In 1882, he became Professor of Mental and Nervous Diseases at Western University, and was elected President of the Psychological Section of the British Medical Association in 1888. Two years later, the year before his visit to Bolton, he was elected President of the American Medico-Psychological Association. He had met Whitman for the first time in 1877 and described the experience (in terms similar to those used by Johnston and Wallace) as 'a sort of spiritual intoxication'.[77]

As S.E.D. Shortt has pointed out, Bucke's work on cosmic consciousness was entirely characteristic of late Victorian attempts to theorise the unconscious mind. Whereas the dominant interpretation of the mind was physiological, and accorded primacy in shaping consciousness to the will, new investigations deriving from varied sources, each of which claimed some degree of scientific authority, suggested that the mind might not be a simply material entity. These explorations of the dynamic unconscious derived from several sources, ranging from spiritualism and psychical research in England, through to the hypnotherapy practised by psychiatric pioneers Charcot and Janet in France on their hysteric patients. Some of these strands of thought, particularly spiritualism and psychical research, shared with the College an attempt to renew the idea of immortality in an age of scientific revolution and loss of faith. By the 1880s, Shortt suggests, the table-rappings of spiritualistic mediums had begun to be dissociated from the more earnest and empirical efforts of the Society for Psychical Research (SPR). The leading researcher of the SPR, Frederic Myers, had also been interested in Whitman. In 1865, as a fellow undergraduate of John Addington Symonds, Myers had introduced his friend to the works of Whitman for the first time. Now, Myers' psychical researches concentrated on the access to the unconscious provided by trance states and automatic writing. Through the study of these he became convinced that there was what he called a 'subliminal self' which acted outside the guidelines of the will. Myers' work culminated in a book, which addressed the very same issue which so preoccupied J.W. Wallace and the College: *Human Personality and Its Survival of Bodily Death.* For Bucke, the work of the SPR showed that telepathy, hypnotism and alternate selves 'really exist'[78] and could be studied empirically. Exceptional forms of consciousness, such as those seen in trance states, or in states of cosmic consciousness, were therefore not alien to the mind, but an integral part of it. The College occupied a similar intellectual milieu to men like Myers and the SPR. Although they lacked his academic connections and authority, they also expressed a keen interest in spiritualism. Johnston in particular was impressed by some aspects of spiritualism, in particular its parallels with Christianity, and commented favourably in his diary on a lecture he witnessed in Bolton in 1892.[79]

Although cosmic consciousness would, according to Bucke, progress according to the laws of natural selection, it was at present restricted to very few men who exhibited acute powers of perception. It could also occur momentarily to others, who included both Bucke himself, J.W. Wallace and Dr Johnston. As Carpenter later pointed out, the experience of cosmic consciousness contained a remarkable affinity with sexual ecstasy. Bucke's own experience of it came after an evening reading and discussing Whitman and other poets. 'At once,' he wrote, 'he found himself wrapped around... by a flame-coloured cloud' which was followed by 'a sense of exultation, of immense joyousness, accompanied or immediately followed by an intellectual illumination quite impossible to describe.' Into his brain 'streamed one momentary lightning flash of the Brahmic Splendor which ever since lightened his life', leaving 'an aftertaste of Heaven'.[80] In that instant:

> he saw and knew that the Cosmos is not dead matter but a living Presence, that the soul of man is immortal, that the universe is so built and ordered that without any peradventure all things work together for the good of each and all, that the foundation principle of the world is what we call love and that the happiness of every one is in the long run absolutely certain.[81]

Wallace, according to Bucke, had experienced the same momentary enlightenment after the death of his mother. From that time he became 'clearly superior to the average man', the proof of which was his status as the 'Master' of Eagle Street. The Fellows had given him their respect and affection because 'they saw clearly in him a superior spiritual nature'.[82]

Cosmic consciousness was, according to the principles of evolution, destined to become a general attribute of humanity. Man had passed through animal awareness, or 'simple consciousness', as far as 'self-consciousness', or awareness of selfhood, and would soon evolve a new 'consciousness of the cosmos, that is, of the life and order of the universe'. The possession of cosmic consciousness almost escaped definition, but was characterised by the enhanced appreciation of the order and oneness of the universe, 'an intellectual enlightenment or illumination' to which was added a 'state of moral exaltation' and an 'indescribable feeling of elevation, elation and joyousness', not to mention 'a quickening of the moral sense'. With these, Bucke suggested, comes 'what may be called a sense of immortality, a consciousness of eternal life'.[83]

The exemplar of cosmic consciousness was, of course, Walt Whitman, who, Bucke suggested, was only able to write the remarkable *Leaves of Grass* after he had experienced his own variety of illumination in which he 'saw the Universe'. Using this new spiritual faculty 'he saw real things... things he could not see before and that we cannot *see*'.[84] However, cosmic consciousness in Bucke's reading also had an unstated but clear association with homosexuality. Whitman's realisation of cosmic consciousness, Bucke told the College in an 1891 lecture, could be read in one of the most homoerotic sections of *Song of Myself*:

> I mind how once we lay such a transparent summer morning
> How you settled your head athwart my hips and gently turn'd over upon me,
> And parted the shirt from my bosom-bone, and plunged your tongue to my bare-stript heart, and reach'd till you felt my beard, and reach'd till you held my feet.

For Bucke, this passage described 'a new power' which 'overshadowed' the poet. It held his feet and beard, 'mastered and controlled him from that time forth'. This new faculty enabled him to see and know things 'that are perfectly hidden from the ordinary mind', which were told only in *Leaves of Grass*.[85] The sexual element in the awakening of cosmic consciousness was not only confined to Bucke's reading of *Song of Myself*. For Edward Carpenter, cosmic consciousness was much more likely to develop in those who possessed a 'homosexual temperament'. Carpenter, with whom Bucke had been consulting prior to his College address, made a specific analogy between sexual ecstasy and cosmic consciousness in his 1892 book based on his travels in India and Ceylon, *From Adam's Peak to Elephanta*. The happiness which such an illumination produced, Carpenter suggested, may be compared 'for its actual force, as a motive of human conduct, with the intensity of the sexual orgasm'. The sexual connotations were clear for other Edwardian critics as well. For W.C. Rivers, the section quoted by Bucke proved a 'prima facie case' of Whitman's homosexuality and was reproduced in his *Walt Whitman's Anomaly* without comment.[86] In spite of the content of the passage, and the clear association which the poem made between homoerotic intimacy and spiritual enlightenment, Johnston thought Bucke's analysis 'a perfect electric illumination of Whitman'.[87]

The power of cosmic consciousness derived not only from its capacity to replicate sexual ecstasy, but also from its apparent conformity to the idea of comradeship. That too was only owned by a few who had cultivated the capacity to love, and who had learned this from a close reading of *Leaves of Grass*, the meaning of which was, in turn, also only available to a few. Accordingly, cosmic consciousness was also an ineffable, unsayable quality of personality which could be met with only in those with special sensual capacities. It is not surprising then, that such men began to be identified in ordinary life as well as in history and literature. In 1893 and 1894, the College, which met frequently at this time (often twice or more a week), was charged with a religious enthusiasm, an awareness of the coming political millennium, and with the search for an apparently new variety of human nature. Into this heady atmosphere in the summer of 1894 stepped a young American composer and singer, Philip Dalmas, who had been introduced to the College by the American Whitman group, and who instantly cast a spell over Wallace, Johnston and some of the others. Dalmas' presence inspired the College fellows to even greater heights of comrade love. He seems to have acted as a focus for their love and their hopes, and to have articulated for them their muted desires.

Dalmas cemented the association between comradeship, cosmic consciousness and the fascination of desire which drove both Wallace and Johnston. Johnston met him for the first time at a College meeting organised in his honour in July 1894, noting in his diary that he was 'a tall, straight-limbed, handsome looking fellow', altogether 'a most striking personality', from whom 'seemed to emanate a spirit of sweetness and tenderness and loving kindness'. From their first meeting, Johnston recalled, 'I felt a curious and irresistible attraction for this gentle-mannered, beautiful-souled man who seemed dowered with the grace of a woman and yet was possessed with the masculinity of a strong man.'[88] Wallace was also enchanted by Dalmas. Soon after their first meeting, Johnston wrote in his diary with an air of disquiet, 'I think I will here record what TS [Thomas Shorrock, a College fellow] said to me about PD and JWW as I sat by his side in the Borough Council one morning.' Dalmas had been staying with Wallace in Adlington, and, according to Shorrock, it was 'extraordinary what an affection' there was between them. Dalmas addressed his host as 'Beloved Wallace', and his music produced rapturous reactions. 'After some of it,' Johnston recorded, 'Wallace threw his arms around Dalmas' neck and sobbed upon his breast like a child.'[89] The two of them, Johnston recalled, '"carry on" like a couple of lovers'[90] and were also sleeping in the same bed. After meeting Dalmas for a second time, Johnston told Wallace that he didn't know whether he was 'on my head or my heels'. Wallace agreed that the state the American aroused was 'either a sweet hell or a perfect place'.[91]

Dalmas also claimed to have the special qualities which Carpenter later associated explicitly with the 'intermediate sex', an assertion which was taken with the appropriate seriousness of those urgently seeking evidence of the immortal spirit in the material world. His cosmic consciousness took the form of an extraordinary sensitivity (what Wallace described as 'wonderfully clear intuitions and perceptions')[92] and a self-declared synaesthetic capacity to hear colours and smell sounds. Synaesthesia was not fully described scientifically until the 1940s, but Dalmas' condition was increasingly visible in late nineteenth-century culture and was even read by sexologists as analogous to sexual inversion. In a wider culture, there was a brief fashion for musical experiments in the 1890s which sought to combine sensations of sound and colour, culminating in the invention of the 'colour-organ' in 1893. Other attempts to reproduce their own synaesthetic experience in the concert hall were also made by Alexander Scriabin and Nikolai Rimsky-Korsakov.[93]

The first properly scientific accounts of synaesthesia also began to appear during the early 1890s, a fact noted by Havelock Ellis. Although it is unlikely that Dalmas knew about the studies from the early 1890s which Ellis cited in *Sexual Inversion* (1897), the tantalising historical coincidence remains that Ellis used synaesthesia to suggest a parallel with homosexuality and later defined it as an explicitly female characteristic. Symonds sought to explain homosexuality as a harmless variation of mental capacity that might be compared to colour-blindness, but for Ellis, 'coloured hearing' was a better comparison. Such an adaptation was not a defect or a 'diseased condition' but rather 'an abnormality of nervous tracks producing new and involuntary combinations'. Just as the synaesthete instinctively reacts to colours as sounds, 'so the invert has his sexual sensations brought into relationship with objects that are normally without sexual appeal'.[94]

More recent studies have commented on the fact that, for synaesthetes like Dalmas, the evidence of the senses is automatically ineffable since it is untranslatable into the language of common experience.[95] It is therefore impossible for the synaesthete to describe his ability or sentiment. Dalmas' synaesthesia thus accorded perfectly with the idiom of the College, its transcendent religion and its attitude to homoerotic attachment. The Fellows went further than usual, however, in suggesting that the American's sensibility provided evidence of an alternate consciousness. It was revealed to them one day after Dalmas had seen a rainbow, which, he claimed, made 'the most beautiful sounds imaginable'. He also claimed to have an astral body, which had visited London and made its sights familiar to him when his corporeal self finally arrived there. There were also literal echoes of Whitman himself in Dalmas, and Johnston even suggested that the poet must have had similarly acute faculties. Dalmas, like Whitman, could 'hear the trees grow up and... the rush of the saps in spring'.[96]

Dalmas' comrade love, as well as his senses, existed on another plane. His letters to Charles Sixsmith ('Charlie my dear and steadfast')[97] perfectly illustrated the connection between immortality, death and a transcendent desire. He spoke of entering his comrade 'with the very inspiration of breath... to dwell forever' beyond time and space.[98] Dalmas promised that immortality, the gateway to love and the soul, could be attained or at least realised in this life. The state of transcendence which allowed love itself to be immortal had already been reached in their relationship, Dalmas suggested. 'Already,' he told Sixsmith, 'I tread with you the unknown and together we transcend time and space to gaze in mute rapture into the world of realities.'[99]

Dalmas also claimed the acute perceptions of the cosmically-conscious invert. In particular he claimed to have had a prevision of the happiness which the College, and in particular Johnston, would bring him. He told Johnston that he had felt his presence before he had met him, and that he was 'drawn to you particularly'. Dalmas told the Doctor, whom he had begun to address as 'the Flower of the North', that 'I would not think of living without you, and in fact could not do so now'. Henceforth, he told Johnston, 'we shall... be always together' beyond life and into immortality.[100] These attitudes, Dalmas confessed to Johnston, meant that people sometimes thought him 'morbid and queer'. They failed to understand him and 'they simply condemn me'. After these revelations, the Doctor recorded, Dalmas 'put his head on my shoulder and almost sobbing said, "And what would it be without you?"'[101]

Part of Dalmas' 'fascination' was the fact that his particular consciousness confirmed the idea that love and super-perception were intimately associated. His sensibility also tended to confirm Dr Bucke's theories. According to one of Charles Sixsmith's American correspondents, 'Dalmas has cosmic consciousness; that grand new sense',[102] while Bucke also found the young American to have 'some extraordinary psychical qualities'.[103] Yet, typically, the attraction of Dalmas was somehow beyond expression. In addition to the literal excisions from Johnston's diary, where he has tried to cross out the most intimate or embarrassing detail, words failed the good doctor and some of the others. Fred Wild thought the American 'an extraordinary fellow' while Will Law, according to Wild, 'adores him and uses words in letters about him that he would not speak'.[104]

Johnston and Dalmas developed a particularly intense friendship, based on their mutual belief in the immortality of the personality and the possibility of cosmic consciousness. At times, their spiritual communion verged on the physical. While out walking together and discussing these matters, Johnston recalled that 'a curious thing happened'. They reached Wallace's house in Adlington, where Dalmas 'threw his arms around me. I did the same to him and we kissed each other-the first time I believe that I ever kissed a man in my life – at least for a very long time'. Dalmas, Johnston recorded, 'has touched something in my heart and it has responded to his touch in a manner which fills me with a strange and indescribable feeling'.[105] Dalmas exerted 'a strange fascination' over Johnston, and had aroused in him 'what no other man ever seems to have done'. 'I feel for him,' Johnston wrote, 'an inexpressible tenderness and affection; my best self "comes to the top" and I feel my heart over flowing with a universal sympathy and filled with a great happiness.'[106] Sixsmith and Wallace too felt this 'peculiar attraction', the latter writing to Johnston that he wished he 'could tell you all I know about Dalmas or translate for you all I have learned from him' and promising him that 'You too at the right moment shall enter into the splendour and joy, which no mortal tongue can express'.[107]

Dalmas represented, for Wallace and Johnston, the possible fulfilment of their beliefs. Yet his visits also encouraged a continual approach and recoil from some of the more awkward aspects of comrade love. Wallace and Johnston could hardly refuse the effusive love the American offered, as it fitted so well with their own worldview. Indeed, they welcomed it as a moment of clarity and intensity. However, after he had gone they went through some attempts at distancing themselves from their own emotion. When the American's brief visit was over, and he and Wallace parted at the station 'like lovers', Dalmas' effusive expressions of love began to appear awkward to Johnston. His letters, in which he addressed the doctor as 'the Flower of the North', appeared to idealise Johnston. These communications, the doctor told Wallace, were 'very embarrassing possessions', which he dared not show to any one as 'they are filled to overflowing with such fervour and affection'. Wallace advised him to 'show them to nobody but me or they may think Dalmas is out of his mind or going that way' and Wallace was sure that he was '*not* a lunatic'. Whereas kisses and embraces had been perfectly acceptable in his company, there was now an effort at distancing themselves, which found a discrepancy between Dalmas' 'sanity' and the fervent expression of love which was his habitual mode of expression. The fact that he was so sane, according to Johnston, made the 'expressions all the more embarrassing' and inexplicable.[108] Yet Dalmas' sentiments could, paradoxically, be explained by his special perception and sense, which again allowed the intensity of his emotions to be displaced into an ineffable realm, to a plane of consciousness which Johnston could make sense of only by incomprehension. Wallace assured him that he would understand Dalmas' love eventually, just as diligent study and the right temperament would elucidate *Leaves of Grass*.[109]

Dalmas' value to the College was in the way he enabled them to see cosmic consciousness and comrade love, however confusingly, working in an individual. It is clear, then, that the peculiar combination of spiritual love of comrades, cosmic consciousness and a Whitmanesque mysticism provided a space in which something akin to homosexual desire could be experienced without being explicitly expressed. The conjunction of these ideas, while not necessarily licensing erotic attachments, could provide the resources out of which a form of homoerotic subjectivity was made. In addition, the contacts of Johnston, Wallace, Dalmas and Sixsmith with Edward Carpenter and his ideas of an 'intermediate sex' who experienced homosexual desire provided further material for their interest in 'sexual inversion'.

Edward Carpenter and the College

Dalmas's characteristics also bore striking similarities to those of the homosexual mystics found in the work of Edward Carpenter. Some of this work must also have been known to the College and have provided an interpretive background to the ideas of Dalmas and Bucke. It is not implausible to think of Carpenter viewing the College, and especially Dalmas, Wallace, Johnston and Sixsmith, as prototypical 'homogenic' or intermediate types. The relationship between Carpenter and the College was also mutually productive in other ways. For Carpenter, the College represented the practical application of the notion of comrade love, while for Wallace and Johnston, Carpenter's ideas provided a further vocabulary for understanding homosexuality.

During the course of the 1890s, Wallace, Johnston, Sixsmith and Dalmas were regular visitors to Carpenter's home at Millthorpe near Sheffield, where they found not only congenial company but also authoritative backing for their own views. In addition, Carpenter provided confidences and information concerning sexual inversion. Johnston in particular appears to have developed an intimacy with the writer which was partly based on a shared interest in homosexuality. In March 1897, Carpenter visited Johnston 'and we had a good talk re "Homo-Sexism" in which he opened his mind to me and told me many strange and curious facts'.[110] In spite of his earlier denunciations of homosexuality in the poetry of Whitman, Johnston was charmed by Carpenter's relationship with George Merrill, whom he described as the 'the most remarkable specimen of "urning"-hood I have ever met'.[111] Wallace too, for all his disavowals of Whitman's homoeroticism, found Carpenter's relationship with his lover George Hukin 'natural' and 'simple'.[112] Not only was Carpenter's personal friendship 'soothing and tranquilising' for Johnston, but their ideas were completely 'harmonious'.[113] After one visit in 1898, during which they again discussed sexual inversion and Havelock Ellis' book on the subject, Johnston returned to Bolton with a 'strange feeling as if I had risen from the dead and were commencing life afresh'.[114] Their discussions during these visits, Johnston wrote, were often 'too intimate to record'.[115]

Carpenter sent a copy of most of his books to Charles Sixsmith, including his 1894 pamphlet *Homogenic Love*. In it he made an explicit association between comrade love and homosexuality in ways which might have been calculated to both describe and appeal to the College. Although comrade love was not necessarily sexual, and therefore could appeal to those who experienced intense feelings for other men, it nevertheless counted as part of a spectrum of homogenic love. According to Carpenter, homogenic types also frequently possessed distinctive mentalities. The physical side of comrade love, he argued, 'from the very nature of the case, can never find expression quite so freely' as heterosexual attachment and therefore developed 'rather more along emotional channels'.[116] Neither was it the case that inverts were degraded either physically or mentally. On the contrary, they tended to be of a 'refined, sensitive nature' and exhibited no physical symptoms of their condition, other than a tendency to 'nervous development'.[117]

These conclusions were clearly reinforced by men like Dalmas and others, who claimed both comrade love and cosmic consciousness. They in turn used Carpenter's ideas in a literal fashion to interpret their own emotions. Through this association Carpenter developed an historical and anthropological basis for the notion that inverts had the potential to develop spiritual qualities and specific forms of consciousness which were not generally found in society. As we have seen, Carpenter's association with Dr Bucke cemented his acceptance of the validity of cosmic consciousness. Also, both men found a parallel between sexual release and the ecstasy of illumination which, however, went unstated in Bucke's work. In spite of Bucke's reluctance to face the sexual elements of cosmic consciousness, Carpenter developed the idea of an alternate consciousness into a theory of the special correspondence between inversion and cosmic consciousness. These ideas were principally developed in three works, *From Adam's Peak to Elephanta* (1892), a 1911 article, 'On the Connection Between Homosexuality and Divination', and in *Intermediate Types Among Primitive Folk* (1914).[118] Like Bucke, Carpenter sought and found scientific support for the existence of a 'secondary' consciousness in the work of psychical researchers like Frederic Myers. For Carpenter, work on trance states focused the attention of Western science on a form of awareness which had long been recognised in Eastern religion and lent foundation to later speculations on the character of homosexuality.

In his 1911 article, Carpenter developed the idea that inverts had, throughout history, been the bearers of special powers. He noted that in a number of early cults and religions, shamans and priests were frequently held to belong to an 'intermediate sex'. From the customs of the Caananites detailed in Kings Chapter 23, to the tribes of the Bering straits and the West African Slave Coast, priests and holy men were associated with gender reversal. Boy priests in Buddhist temples and the *berdaches* of the Illinois all took similar roles, while the 'ancient Scandanavians' regarded 'passive homosexuals' as 'sorcerers'. The fact that inverts mixed both male and female characteristics was the key factor in making them susceptible to divination, Carpenter argued. This 'double life and nature... seems to give them an extraordinary humanity and sympathy together with a remarkable power of dealing with human beings'. The interaction between masculine and feminine fostered a 'mutual illumination of logic and intuition', a mixture of 'action and meditation' which 'may not only raise and increase the power of each of these faculties, but it may give to the mind a new quality, and a new power of perception corresponding to the blending of subject and object'.

It may, in short, lead to the development of 'that third order of perception which has been called cosmic consciousness'.[119]

The holy men Carpenter referred to were 'bisexual' in the sense of possessing both male and female characteristics. As we have seen, both Wallace and Johnston claimed to have experienced moments of a cosmic consciousness which, for Carpenter, was closely associated with inversion. Dalmas appeared to claim that he had attained that state in a more permanent sense. Other fellows applied Carpenter's understanding in an equally literal sense. Will Atkinson, a 'mystic' and spiritualist whom Dr Johnston thought had 'so much in common with myself that I marvel at the duplication of my own nature and mentality in him', thought of himself in ways which were similar to the self-perception of Philip Dalmas. Indeed, according to Fred Wild they were alike in many ways and possessed a mutual 'sympathy'.[120] Johnston related in 1907 that three years previously Atkinson had undergone 'a remarkable physical change' similar to the awakening of cosmic consciousness, since which time 'he has had many remarkable experiences and powers'. He was 'gifted with remarkable powers of insight – far ahead of anything I am conscious of myself' and claimed to have a '"psychical body" which leaves his physical body during sleep'. In addition to this he stated he was 'bi-sexual' in the sense of being 'psychically and physically both male and female'. Not only that, but Atkinson claimed to experience 'the sexual orgasm constantly within himself' and averred that 'semen is injected into his blood and that he has known it come out through his nostrils[,] his eyes and his mouth!' Whitman must have been the same, Atkinson had suggested, in order to have written *Leaves of Grass*, since in its mystical lyrics he had found literal echoes of his own experiences.[121]

Johnston was sympathetic to Atkinson's story not only because Dalmas and Carpenter had familiarised him with the idea that sexual inversion was accompanied by acute perception, but also because he himself habitually sought evidence of his own rebirth. He finally claimed to have experienced a brief cosmic consciousness in 1901. Although, he recorded in his diary, he had appreciated the teachings of Whitman and Dr Bucke, he had until the time of his 'aurora' failed to 'realize it as a personal possession and to recognize its... vitality as a fact in and factor of soul life'. The illumination came to him as he walked in Rivington with Wallace, reading J.W. Lloyd's *Dawn Thoughts*. As Wallace's words sank in, 'there flashed through me a consciousness of their truth... and glorious illuminating thought seemed to suffuse my entire being with a heavenly refulgence'. At that moment 'was revealed to me in a flash the Great fact of the Unity and the spirituality of the Universe'. Such thoughts 'dazed me... as with a mighty presence, filling me with a joy untellably great'. Cosmic consciousness was not only a religious awakening and a form of quasi-sexual ecstasy, but signified the mark of election to a newly evolving mode of being which was closely associated with inversion. It may even be regarded as a conversion experience akin to a more stringent version of coming out. In any case, given the closeness of his connection to Carpenter, Johnston can hardly fail to have realised the resonance of his own experience of cosmic illumination.

As Johnston's account of his illumination demonstrates, the value of the evidence left by the College lies in the way it illustrates the intellectual interchange which informed the search for what might be termed a homosexual mentality. In Carpenter's case this had little to do with metropolitan subcultures and everything to do with spirituality. While Carpenter was concerned to associate one area of experience with homosexual men, he also suggested that because of their 'intermediate' status, they existed along a spectrum of masculine attachment. The College therefore showed homogenic love to be a spectrum of desires and interests which were not necessarily physical, but which shared a common mentality or consciousness. For Carpenter, as for Johnston and Wallace, homogenic love was primarily a question of sensibility rather than of congenital 'orientation'.

Although in retrospect it appeared to Wallace that the moment of comrade love and cosmic consciousness had been brief and fleeting, the idea that homosexuality could be equated with an acute temperament or special sensibility remained. Neither were Carpenter and Whitman irrelevant to a subsequent British tradition of homosexual self-formation. Historians have tended to assume that both Carpenter's utopianism and Whitman's ethos of comradeship became largely irrelevant during the 'Wilde Century' that followed 1900, when sexual science and effeminacy came to dominate the representation of homosexuality. But at least at the beginning of the twentieth century, Carpenter and Whitman were still prominent figures in a homosexual canon. Elsewhere, I have explored the fact that Whitman appears alongside Carpenter and Wilde as a regular reference point in early 'lonely hearts' advertisements written by homosexual men.[122] An ethos of 'friends' and comrades also informed the short-lived 'magazine of friendship', the *Quorum*, which sought to bring together enlightened opinion on homosexuality. The association of religious mysticism and transcendent sensibility was also expressed in the more overtly Whitmanite interwar Irish periodical *Calamus: The Quarterly Journal of the Order of the Great Companions*. Moreover, words connoting acute perception which derived in part from this Whitman/Carpenter tradition such as 'artistic' and 'musical' were also key terms of homosexual self-description until well into the twentieth century.

Probably the most fully developed version of Carpenter's views on the 'intermediate sex' and its relation to evolution and perception was expressed in A.T. Fitzroy's pacifist novel of 1918, *Despised and Rejected*. The Carpenterian sensibility of the protagonist, and the idea that a higher form of being might evolve from sexual inversion, are both strong themes in the novel. The upper-class Dennis Blackwood is a classic example of a feminine temperament fostering special talents, in his case for music. Once at school, he discovers by chance that he can play the piano without instruction, and that he had found chords 'that began to release, bit by bit, some of the music that was imprisoned in my head'.[123] But Fitzroy's set-piece speech in favour of the invert is given to another bohemian character, who forcefully argues that men like Dennis 'who stand midway between the extremes of the two sexes', are the epitome of a higher type of personality and as such represent the 'advance guard of a more enlightened civilisation'. The evolutionary principle, which so excited the followers of Whitman and appeared to be personified in men like Philip Dalmas, is fully present in Fitzroy's account of the invert. Her novel shows that the unspeakable quality of homosexual desire, when combined with the spiritual and evolutionary idiom which developed in the culture of British socialism and in apparently unlikely places in the north of England, had clearly fostered a durable tradition which associated comradeship, homosexuality and higher consciousness. *Despised and Rejected* is replete with a millennialism that might have come directly from Carpenter himself. From intermediate types, the conscientious objector Barnaby exclaims, 'a new humanity is being evolved'. Stunted and imperfect versions of the invert might be produced who simply sought the gratification of their desires, but such imperfection was simply the result of a natural process of evolution. In spite of the suffering of these lower types, he declares, there nevertheless:

> will arise something great – something God-given: the human soul complete in itself, perfectly balanced, not limited by the psychological bounds of one sex, but combining the power and the intellect of the one with the subtlety and intuition of the other; a dual nature, possessing the extended range, the attributes of both sides.[124]

It is clear that at certain moments during the last two decades of the nineteenth century it became easier to describe and denounce same-sex desire in public. These moments, in the form of public scandal, became more frequent during these decades as the unspeakable nature of homosexual desire was challenged by homophile writers like Symonds and Carpenter. Terminology became more precise in certain quarters and an entire genre of sexological science was devoted to explicitly detailing what had previously been simply 'abominable'.

The fascination of the Eagle Street College lies in the fact that it forms part of the same cultural moment as these other, metropolitan moments of clarity. It began life in 1885, when it was still possible to celebrate the poetic beauty of Greek athletes without accusations of indecency and to insist on the innocence of comrade love, and it declined just as these rich vocabularies of evasion became increasingly difficult to animate. For the College, Whitman was an avatar of comradeship and the oneness of the Universe, whereas for some of their contemporaries he was simply and incontestably a homosexual. The College existed at the overlap of both these ways of knowing. Even in their own lives, Wallace, Johnston and Sixsmith enacted the peculiar English drama of attraction and repulsion from the fascination of homosexual desire. At certain moments in the 1890s and 1900s, they became intensely interested in sexual inversion, only to deny it later and dissociate themselves from the more pathological implications of comrade love. In order to do this, they employed other practices of dissociation, principally through the ideas of cosmic consciousness and spirituality. In a personal sense, it was still possible to separate any interest in sexual inversion from one's public life and, like Johnston, participate fully in civic culture. However, the acknowledgement and recognition of same-sex desire required a more elaborate set of terms. Comrade love and sexual inversion were incorporated into the psyche using the idea of cosmic consciousness and the transcendent, immortal love which was spoken of by men like Dalmas. On this mainly spiritual plane an intense love, an 'inexpressible tenderness' or a 'peculiar attraction' for another man could exist and be ennobled. The vagaries of the spirit and the 'psychical body' could also explain individual inversion, as in the case of Will Atkinson. In broader terms, the assertion of Edward Carpenter that inverts possessed special powers gave authority to the self-conception of men like Dalmas, Johnston and, to a lesser extent, Wallace. For Carpenter, the College, in its intense but seemingly non-physical homogenic love, may have represented the promise of his ideas in action.

The College represented both the limitations upon, and the opportunities available to those men outside of metropolitan literary or bohemian cultures who were both attracted and repelled by the prospect of homosexual desire. The experience of the College in the years between 1891 and 1895 showed how same-sex desire could be rationalised in the lives of 'ordinary' men, and how it could inform utopian vistas of selfhood and consciousness. Looking back on this cultural moment in 1904, Wallace perhaps realised the overreaching nature of his vision. 'At one time,' he recalled, 'the College seemed to occupy a very exalted position.' But it had proved 'too much for us'. All that remained was comradeship, a glimmer of hope for another moment when the world would be truly ready for the message of *Leaves of Grass*, a future in which 'selfishness will be replaced by love'.[125]

Conclusion

From the beginning of the nineteenth century to the Wolfenden Report and on to Section 28, the Thatcher government's attempt to deligitimise homosexuality by preventing anyone discussing it in schools, homosexuality has been commonly linked with issues of secrecy and privacy. Although this problematic issue of disclosure is still with us, it was during the nineteenth century that it became particularly intense. The development of legal and police practice, and the habits of representation which developed within the criminal process and out of practical necessity and moral scruple, structured the way in which homosexuality was encountered and spoken of long after 1900.

However, the unspeakable status of homosexuality in nineteenth-century society did not censor. It produced paradoxical opportunities not only for representation, but also for self-making. That is not to suggest that the language of the law *caused* the particular form of late-Victorian subjectivity that I have described. Instead it is to observe their affinity, to argue that both belonged in the same mental universe. This was a universe created by the overlapping demands of various nineteenth-century institutions, ideas and forms. In an obvious sense, the unspeakable quality of homosexuality came about because of the illegality of male homosexuality and the theoretically pervasive extent of the law. In a less obvious fashion, this illegality determined new ways of defining public and private and helped to institutionalise these interpretations. Silence about sodomy in this context also had an explicit public function.

In particular, it sought to supplement the criminal process by enforcing the boundaries of privacy and hence policing the private sphere in a way that was politically and legally problematic for the state and its agencies. The contradictory status of privacy, in that it was both theoretically subject to the law and in practice a relative space of impunity, mirrored the contradictory ways in which homosexuality could be spoken of. The institutionalisation of the 'open secrecy' of sodomy in legal and police practice in turn produced a particular form of representation, which both identified and denied the existence of the 'unnatural crime'.

This formation of secrecy responded to specific nineteenth-century imperatives. In particular, the press were caught between the necessity of reporting the operations of public bodies and restricting access to obscene materials. In addition, the need to encourage and maintain the civility of the public world required that the world of the street and the blackmailer be kept apart from the legitimate and respectable public realm. These restrictions created the contours of a public discourse which could directly and openly describe the nameless crime. However, the process by which homosexuality became illegal was seen, in itself, to actively endanger the order of masculine public life. Prosecuting sodomites produced the activities of the blackmailer, which in turn focused attention on the precarious nature of reputation and character. The legal process was open to abuse, but so were the instruments of public knowledge themselves. The scandals of the 1880s showed that the press, and even the government itself, was ultimately not above using the techniques of the blackmailer to disrupt public life and slander opponents. In addition, naming the crime, investigating its locations, its origins and nature, along with identifying a context for its explanation, were paradoxical consequences of the criminal process. Sodomy was not always a secret, even an open one, for the Victorians. It had an unpredictable, unruly and continuous presence in nineteenth-century society and required monitoring, controlling and distancing. The subjectivities I have described took part in the same dynamic process of identification and denial, of approach and recoil. Wallace, Johnston, Carpenter, Symonds and the others illustrate the various ways in which the namelessness of homoerotic desire could provide perverse opportunities for its expression. Secrecy and negation, then, had their uses, as modes of both power and resistance.

Notes

Introduction to the Paperback Edition

1. Adultery and fornication had long been punished by church courts with fines and religious penance. Adultery had been made a capital crime by the Commonwealth in 1650, but this law was not enforced. By the early eighteenth century, church courts in Britain had lost their jurisdiction over sexual immorality, and by the 1730s, civil or religious prosecutions for adultery had ceased. See David Turner, *Fashioning Adultery: Gender, Sex and Civility in England, 1660–1740* (Cambridge, 2002), pp. 4–5; For the wider story of such privatizing of morality, see Roger Chartier, (ed.), *A History of Private Life*, vol. III, *Passions of the Renaissance* (Cambridge, MA, 1989).

2. For example, see Louis Crompton, *Homosexuality and Civilization* (New York, 2003).

3. For a fuller discussion of this case see H.G. Cocks, 'Safeguarding Civility: Sodomy, Class, and the Limits of Moral Reform in Early 19th Century England', *Past and Present*, 190 (February 2006), pp. 121–46.

4. *Lancaster Gazette*, 20 Aug 1806, 3.

5. John Borron to Earl Spencer, 20 Sep 1806, British Library Add. Mss. 75899, Althorp Papers, vol. dc.

6. Lord Sefton to Thomas Earle, 18 Jan 1807, Althorp Papers, vol. dc.

7. *Voluntary Examination of Thomas Rix*, 15 Sep 1806, Althorp Papers, vol. dc.

8. Lord Ellenborough to Earl Spencer 12 Sep 1806, Althorp Papers, vol. dc.

9. Richard Gwillym to Earl Spencer, 21 Jan 1807, Althorp Papers, vol. dc.

10. Marcel Proust, *Sodom and Gomorrah* (trans. C.K. Scott Moncrieff and Terence Kilmartin, revised by D.J. Enright, London, 2000), pp. 37–8: 'For,

no sooner had they arrived there [in Sodom] than the Sodomites would leave the town…would take wives, keep mistresses in other cities where they would find, incidentally, every diversion that appealed to them. They would repair to Sodom only on days of supreme necessity, when their own town was empty, at those seasons when hunger drives the wolf from the woods. In other words, everything would go on very much as it does today in London, Berlin, Rome, Petrograd or Paris.'

11. Matt Houlbrook, *Queer London: Perils and Pleasures in the Gay Metropolis, 1918–1957* (Chicago, 2005); George Chauncey, *Gay New York: Gender, Urban Culture, and the Making of the Gay Male World, 1890–1940* (New York, 1994). See also Patrick Higgins, *Heterosexual Dictatorship: Male Homosexuality in Post War Britain* (London, 1994).

12. On this see Dan Healey, *Homosexual Desire in Revolutionary Russia* (Chicago, 2001); Jeffrey Merrick and Bryant T. Ragan, (eds.) *Homosexuality in Modern France* (New York, 1996); James D. Steakley, *The Homosexual Emancipation Movement in Germany* (New York, 1975); Houlbrook, *Queer London*, intro, ch. 7; H.G. Cocks, 'Homosexuality in Europe, 1914–2004', in Jay Winter and John Merriman, (eds.), *Encyclopaedia of Europe: 1914–2004* (New York, 2006).

13. For the argument that the eighteenth century molly represented the modern form of homosexuality see Randolph Trumbach, 'Modern Sodomy, 1700–1800: The Origins of Homosexuality', in Matt Cook, (ed.), *A Gay History of Britain* (London, 2007), pp.77–106; Trumbach, *Sex and the Gender Revolution Vol. 1, Heterosexuality and the Third Gender in Enlightenment London* (Chicago, 1998).

14. David Halperin, *How to do the History of Homosexuality* (Chicago, 2002), p. 107.

15. On the apparent acceptability of homosexual relationships, subject in most cases to the privileges and alibis of class, and the fact of living outside England, see Sharon Marcus, *Between Women: Friendship, Desire and Marriage in Victorian England* (Oxford, 2007); Martha Vicinus, *Intimate Friends: Women Who Loved Women 1778–1928* (Chicago, 2004); Sheila Rowbotham, *Edward Carpenter* (London, 2008); Graham Robb, *Strangers*, in which Robb suggests that the nineteenth century was a golden age of same sex desire for men, and that being in an unhappy marriage was worse than being a homosexual in the nineteenth century. Being unhappily married may have been a life sentence, but was never a capital crime.

16. See below, p. 90 for a discussion, and also H.G. Cocks, 'Homosexuality Between Men in Britain Since the Eighteenth Century', *History Compass* 5 (March 2007); 'Secrets, Crimes and Diseases', in Matt Cook, (ed.), *A Gay History of Britain* (London 2007), pp. 107–44.

17. Thomas Laqueur, *Solitary Sex: A Cultural History of Masturbation* (New York, 2003), introduction, ch. 2.

Introduction

1. Douglas' phrase first appeared in his poem 'Two Loves', *Chameleon* (December 1894). On its appearance at Wilde's trial, see Richard Ellman, *Oscar Wilde* (London, 1987), pp. 421–5 and 435. E.M. Forster, *Maurice* (London, 1971), p. 145; John Addington Symonds, *A problem in modern ethics* (London, 1891), reproduced in part in H. Ellis, *Sexual Inversion* (London, 1897), p. 3.

2. See, for instance, Rictor Norton, *The Myth of the Modern Homosexual: Queer History and the Search for Cultural Unity* (London, 1997); D. Allen, Review of David Halperin, Saint Foucault, *Journal of Homosexuality*, 34, 1 (1997), pp. 87–92.

3. Michel Foucault, *The History of Sexuality, Volume One: An Introduction*, trans. Robert Hurley (London, 1979), p. 9.

4. William Cohen, *Sex Scandal: The Private Parts of Victorian Fiction* (Durham NC, 1996), p. 3.

5. Eve Kosofsky Sedgwick, *Epistemology of the Closet* (London, 1991), p. 73. See also George Chauncey, *Gay New York: The Making of the Gay Male World, 1890–1940* (London, 1995); Michael P. Brown, *Closet Space: Geographies of Metaphor from the Body to the Globe* (London, 2000).

6. Ed Cohen, *Talk on the Wilde Side: Towards a Genealogy of a Discourse on Male Sexualities* (New York, 1993).

7. Christopher Lane, *The Burdens of Intimacy: Psychoanalysis and Victorian Masculinity* (Chicago, 1999).

8. D.A. Miller, *The Novel and the Police* (Berkeley, 1985), p. 206; Alan Sinfield, *The Wilde Century: Oscar Wilde, Effeminacy and the Queer Moment* (London, 1994), pp. 15–16.

9. James Eli Adams, *Dandies and Desert Saints: Styles of Victorian Manhood* (Ithaca, 1995), pp. 105–6.

10. John Kucich, *The Power of Lies: Transgression in Victorian Fiction* (Ithaca, 1994), p. 34.

11. A.D. Harvey, 'Prosecutions for Sodomy at the Beginning of the Nineteenth Century', *Historical Journal* 21, 47 (1978), pp. 939–949; Arthur Gilbert, 'Social Deviance and Disaster during the Napoleonic Wars', *Albion* 9, 2 (1977); Gilbert, 'The "Africaine" Court Martial: A Study of Buggery in the British Navy', *Journal of Homosexuality* 1, 1 (Fall 1974), pp. 111–122; Gilbert, 'Buggery and the British Navy 1700–1861', *Journal of Social History* 10 (1976–77), pp. 72–98; Louis Crompton, *Byron and Greek Love: Homophobia in Georgian England* (London, 1985); Mary McIntosh, 'The Homosexual Role', *Social Problems* 16, 2 (Fall, 1968) pp. 182–192; Randolph Trumbach, *Sex and the Gender Revolution, vol 1: Heterosexuality and the Third Gender in Enlightenment London* (Chicago, 1998).

12. See, for example, Chris White (ed.), *Nineteenth Century Writings on Homosexuality* (London, 1999).

13. Judith Walkowitz, *City of Dreadful Delight: Narratives of Sexual Danger in Late Victorian London* (London, 1992), chapters 3 and 4.

14. Leslie J. Moran, *The Homosexual(ity) of Law* (London, 1996), p. 2; Peter Bartlett, 'Silence and Sodomy: The Creation of Homosexual Identity in Law', *Modern Law Review* 61, 1 (January 1998), pp. 102–113; Bartlett, 'Sodomites in the Pillory in Eighteenth Century London', *Social and Legal Studies* 6, 4 (1997), pp. 553–572.
15. Moran, *Homosexual(ity) of Law*, p. 9.
16. On existing famous trials see Neil Bartlett, *Who Was That Man?: A Present For Mr Oscar Wilde* (London, 1987); Charles Upchurch, 'Forgetting the Unthinkable: Cross-Dressers and British Society in the Case of the Queen vs Boulton and Others', *Gender and History* 12, 1 (2000), pp. 127–157.

Chapter One

1. James Smith to Fred Larner, Letter A, 3 September 1858, PRO ASSI 6/25.
2. James Smith to Fred Larner, Letter C, 12 September 1858, PRO ASSI 6/25.
3. Deposition of Rebecca Larner (undated) 1858, PRO ASSI 6/25.
4. Hansard, Third Series, CCCXLI, 28 February 1890, cols 1534, 1535. See also his comments made after the trial of Oscar Wilde, *Truth*, 30 May 1895.
5. Randolph Trumbach, 'The Birth of the Queen: Sodomy and the Emergence of Gender Equality in Modern Europe 1660–1750', in George Chauncey, Martin Duberman and Martha Vicinus (eds), *Hidden From History: Reclaiming the Gay and Lesbian Past* (New York, 1989), pp. 129–140.
6. Randolph Trumbach, *Sex and the Gender Revolution: Heterosexuality and the Third Gender in Enlightenment London* (Chicago, 1998), pp. 3–8; Katharine Binhammer, 'The Sex Panic of the 1790s', *Journal of the History of Sexuality* 6, 3 (1996), pp. 409–435; Thomas Laqueur, *Making Sex, from the Greeks to Freud* (Cambridge, MA, 1990); Dror Wahrman, 'Percy's Prologue: From Gender Play to Gender Panic in 18th Century England', *Past & Present* 159 (1998), pp. 113–160.
7. Louise Jackson, *Child Sexual Abuse in Victorian England* (London, 2000), p. 7.
8. These were the classifications adopted by judicial statistics in Parliamentary Papers.
9. Parliamentary Papers, Judicial Statistics, various volumes.
10. Parliamentary Papers, Judicial Statistics, various volumes.
11. Sodomy remained a capital offence until 1861, although no one was executed after 1835. Before 1861, transportation for life replaced the capital penalty when prisoners were reprieved.
12. For which see chapter two below.
13. Anthony Simpson, 'Masculinity and Control: The Prosecution of Sex Offences in Eighteenth Century London' (Ph.D., University of Michigan, 1984), p. 482.
14. Calendar of Prisoners, 1756–1822, Corporation of London Record Office (CLRO).
15. Ibid.

16. In 1844, there were 166 committals in England and Wales. Parliamentary Papers (PP), Judicial Statistics, 1845 [651] XXXVII.1.

17. PRO, Central Criminal Court (CCC) indictments for January to September (no sodomitic crimes were tried after that date, or in April) 1840, PRO CRIM 4/133 January; 4/135 February; 4/137 March; May 4/142; June 4/144; July 4/146; August, 4/148; September 4/150. Hampshire Spring Assizes 1869, PRO ASSI 25/48/7, Summer 1869, 25/48/14; Summer 1870, PRO ASSI 25/48/34; Winter 1870, PRO ASSI 25/48/36.

18. Jackson, *Child Sexual Abuse*, pp. 18–22.

19. Anthony Simpson reaches the same conclusion from an examination of Old Bailey indictments between 1750 and 1830. See on this Simpson, 'Masculinity and Control', pp. 434–5.

20. CCC Misdemeanours, 1836 PRO CRIM 4.

21. *Report of the Proceedings at the Several Police Offices*, 8 May 1830, PRO HO 62/5.

22. See, for instance, indictment against William Patey and William Houston, CCC Misdemeanours, 4 April 1836, bill 287, PRO CRIM 4/35.

23. Howard Taylor, 'Rationing Crime: The Political Economy of Criminal Statistics since the 1850s', *Economic History Review* LI, 3 (1998), pp. 569–590.

24. Offences Against the Person Act, 1828, s. 17; See also case law: R *v* Reekspear (1832); R *v* Cozins (1834), cited in J.W. Cecil Turner (ed.), *Russell On Crime* (1819, repr. London, 1964), p. 736.

25. Offences Against the Person Act 1861, ss. 62–64, PP 1861 (18) III.627.

26. Cohen, *Talk on the Wilde Side*, p. 119.

27. PP 1845 [651] XXXVII.1: 1888 C. 5553 CVIII.1.

28. Alan Bray, *Homosexuality in Renaissance England* (London, 1982); Tim Hitchcock, *English Sexualities 1700–1800* (London, 1997).

29. Sir Edward Coke, *The Third Part of the Institutes of the Laws of England. Concerning High Treason, and other Pleas of the Crown, and Criminal Causes* (London, 1642), p. 59: 'So as there must be penetratio, that is res in re, either with mankind, or with beast, but the least penetration maketh it carnall knowledge.'

30. R *v* Hill (1781), cited in debate on the Offences Against the Person bill, Hansard New Series, IX, 5 May 1828, cols 350–60. See also R *v* Reed, Henry Gouldburn to Home Office, 17 April 1811, HO 47/46; Hyde, *The Other Love*, p. 90.

31. Cecil Turner (ed.), *Russell on Crime*, p. 735.

32. R *v* Jacobs (1817), cited in Cecil Turner (ed.), *Russell on Crime*, p. 736.

33. J.M. Beattie, *Crime and the Courts in England 1660–1800* (Oxford, 1986), p. 459.

34. See, for example, bill of indictment against John Lights, PRO ASSI 25/39/6.

35. On the nature of acts being criminalised, see also Simpson, 'Masculinity and Control', p. 469.

36. *The Times*, 29 May 1847.

37. CLRO, Calendar of Indictments 1821–1834.

38. Indictment, CCC Misdemeanours, 16 September 1839, PRO CRIM 4/124. See also *The Times*, 21 May 1830.

39. Indictment, CCC Misdemeanours, 5 July 1841, PRO CRIM 4/175.

40. Charges against Martin Kirwan and Gustavus Cornwall, *The Times*, 25 July 1884; 31 July 1884.

41. See chapter two below.

42. For the genealogy of this process see Douglas Hay, 'Controlling the English Prosecutor', *Osgood Hall Law Journal* 21 (1993), pp. 165–186. The case law relates to R *v* Attwood and R *v* Hervey and Fordham, *Annual Register*, 49 (1807), pp. 356–7, in which the judge commented that a conviction on the evidence of an accomplice was unsafe. See also Simpson, 'Masculinity and Control', p. 53; H.G. Cocks, 'Making the Sodomite Speak: Voices of the Accused in English Sodomy Trials, c.1800–1898', *Gender and History*, 18, 1 (April 2006): 87–107; Cocks, 'Safeguarding Civility: Sodomy, Class, and the Limits of Moral Reform in Early 19th Century England', *Past and Present*, 190 (February 2006), pp. 121–146.

43. James Smith to the Home Secretary, July 1890, PRO HO 144/20/58480.

44. James Smith, First Petition to the Home Secretary, April 1877, PRO HO 144/20/58480.

45. *The Times*, 17 August 1842.

46. Quoted in H. Montgomery Hyde, *The Cleveland Street Scandal* (London, 1976), p. 18.

47. Indictment, CCC Misdemeanours, 11 May 1857, PRO CRIM 4/576; CCC Proceedings, 11 May 1857, PRO PCOM 1/73, p. 90.

48. Edward Cox (ed.), *Reports of Cases of Criminal Law Argued and Determined in all the Courts in England and Ireland*, 31 vols (London, 1843–1940), vol. 1: 1843–46 (London, 1846).

49. *The Times*, 12 April 1852.

50. Cox, *Reports of Cases* vol XI, 1869–71 (London, 1871), p. 661.

51. Hesney Wedgwood to Lord Russell (not dated), November 1835, PRO HO 17/120 Xv 13.

52. *The Times*, 20 November 1851.

53. Peel to Solicitor General, 24 July 1822, Law Officers' Letter Books, PRO HO 49/7, pp. 201–2.

54. Hobhouse to Maule, 1 December 1825, Law Officers' Letter Books, PRO HO 49/7. For other soldiers prosecuted by the government see Maule to Hobhouse, 5 September 1822, Law Officer's Letter Books, PRO HO 49/7, p. 206; Hobhouse to Maule, 10 August 1819, Law Officer's Letter Books PRO HO 49/7, p. 119.

55. M.J.D. Roberts, 'The Society for the Suppression of Vice and its Early Critics, 1802–1812', *Historical Journal* 26, 1 (1983), pp. 159–176; Roberts, 'Making Victorian Morals? The Society for the Suppression of Vice and its Critics, 1802–1886', *Historical Studies* 21, 83 (October, 1981), pp. 157–173.

See also Alan Hunt, *Governing Morals: A Social History of Moral Regulation* (Cambridge, 1999), chapter 1.

56. On the prosecution societies, see for example David Phillips, '"Good men to Associate and Bad Men to Conspire": Associations for the Prosecution of Felons in England 1760–1860', in Douglas Hay and Francis Snyder (eds), *Policing and Prosecution in Britain 1750–1850* (Oxford, 1991), pp. 113–170.

57. Roberts, 'The Society for the Suppression of Vice', p. 170. For the opposite view, see Louis Crompton, *Byron and Greek Love: Homophobia in Georgian England* (London, 1985), p. 62.

58. Calendar of Prisoners, 1756–1822, CLRO.

59. *Report From the Select Committee on the Police of the Metropolis*, 11 July 1828, PP (533) VI, p. 73.

60. Valentine Jackson, *Remarkable Trials at the Lancashire Assizes, Held August 1806 At Lancaster Before Sir Robert Graham, Knight* (London, 1806), p. 63. Cocks, 'Safeguarding Civility'.

61. Jackson, 'Remarkable Trials', p. 36.

62. For Goode's case and petition, see PRO HO 19/114 Wq-Ws. Nicolls' execution is described in *The Times*, 13 August 1833. For a similar celebrated case of betrayal by a sexual partner, see Anon., *The Trial of David Robertson of the Jerusalem Hotel, Charles-street, Covent-Garden, late of the Standard Tavern, Leicester-Fields, for an Unnatural Crime...* (London, 1806).

63. *The Times*, 29 November 1832. Beauclerk cut his own throat in prison rather than face trial. Goode was prosecuted on the evidence of a servant in his lodging house in March 1834.

64. Statement of Richard Hardy, 26 March 1834, PRO HO 17/47 Part 2 Gt 39.

65. S.N. Brewster to Lord John Russell, 8 August 1836, PRO HO 17/110 Vw 34.

66. These conclusions will be discussed fully in chapter two.

67. Beattie, *Crime and the Courts in England*, p. 193.

68. Peter King, 'Decision Makers and Decision Making in the English Criminal Law, 1750–1800', *Historical Journal* 27, 1 (1984), pp. 25–58.

69. PRO CRIM indictments for 1844. Various files.

70. Sir Richard Birnie, quoted in *The Times*, 23 August 1825.

71. Douglas Hay, 'Using the Criminal Law, 1750–1850: Policing, Private Prosecution and the State', in Hay and Snyder (eds), *Policing and Prosecution*, pp. 3–54, p. 41.

72. Petition of Arthur Garton to the King (not dated, 1834), PRO HO 17/100 Part 1 St 37.

73. Petition of George Dawson Lowndes to the Marquis of Normanby, 5 March 1841, PRO HO 18/43/33.

74. Mr Phillips (chairman of the Surrey Sessions) to the Home Office, 10 March 1834; Deposition of Elizabeth Taylor (undated, 1834), PRO HO 19/114 Wq-Ws.

75. Petition of John Avis (undated, 1829), PRO HO 47/75.
76. Trial notes of judge in R *v* Andrews, 22 March 1844, PRO HO 18/142/1.
77. Deposition of Elizabeth Taylor (undated, 1834), PRO HO 19/114 Wq-Ws.
78. Deposition of Robert Scrimmiger, 28 March 1843, PRO HO 18/110/8.
79. Justice Patterson to Lord John Russell, 26 August 1835, PRO HO 17/95 Rv 9.
80. Anon., *Don Leon: A Poem by the Late Lord Byron...* (London, 1866), p. 17.

Chapter Two

1. Elaine Reynolds, *Before the Bobbies: The Night Watch and Metropolitan Police Reform in London* (Basingstoke, 1998), chapters 5 and 6.
2. Ruth Paley, '"An Imperfect, Inadequate and Wretched System"? Policing London before Peel', *Criminal Justice History* X (1989), pp. 95–130.
3. Reynolds, *Before the Bobbies*, chapters 7 and 8.
4. On this, see *Report From the Select Committee on the Cause of the Increase in the Number of Commitments and Convictions in London and Middlesex and the State of the Police*, PP 1828 (533) VI. 1.
5. Parliamentary Papers, Judicial Statistics, various volumes, 1822–1878.
6. On the limitations of urban crime statistics, see Rob Sindall, 'The Criminal Statistics of Nineteenth Century Cities: A New Approach', *Urban History Yearbook* (1986), pp. 28–36.
7. On this, see Robert Storch, 'Police Control of Street Prostitution in Victorian London: A Study of the Contexts of Police Action', in D.H. Bayley (ed.), *Police and Society* (London, 1977), pp. 49–73. For the difficulties the police experienced in raiding and prosecuting disorderly houses and the (female) prostitutes within, see the case of the notorious brothel madam Kate Franks, *Police Report, 'C' Division, by James Pay, Inspector* (1863, not dated). PRO HO 45/9511/17216.
8. Vagrancy Act 1824 s. 3, PP 1824 (332) III.177. See also Penelope J. Corfield, 'Walking the City Streets: The Urban Odyssey in Eighteenth Century England', *Journal of Urban History*, 16, 2 (February 1990), pp. 132–174; M.J.D Roberts, 'Public and Private in Early Nineteenth Century London: The Vagrancy Act of 1822 and its enforcement', *Social History* 13 (October 1988), pp. 273–294.
9. See, for instance, *Daily Reports from the Several Police Offices*, 18 June 1830, PRO HO 62/5 and 6. In 1856, for example, 32,008 people were charged under the Vagrant Act in England and Wales. PP, 1857–58 [2407] LVII.383.
10. *The Times*, 19 April 1869.
11. *The Times*, 16 August 1825.
12. *The Times*, 2 September 1825.
13. *The Times*, 12 April 1830.
14. *The Bishop! Particulars of the Charge Against the Hon Percy Jocelyn...* (London, 1822), quoted in Rictor Norton, *Mother Clap's Molly House: The Gay Subculture in England 1700–1830* (London, 1992), p. 220.

15. 'An Advocate of Police Reform' to Robert Peel, 27 May 1827, PRO HO 44/ 18 ff. 426–7.
16. *The Yokel's Preceptor, or More Sprees in London!...* (London, 1850), quoted in Pisanus Fraxi (Henry Spencer Ashbee), *Bibliography of Prohibited Books (Index Librorum Prohibitorum: Bio-Biblio-Icono-graphical and Critical Notes on Curious, Uncommon and Erotic Books)* (1871, repr. New York, 1962) p. 405.
17. *The Times*, 30 July 1864.
18. *The Times*, 11 June 1866.
19. *The Times*, 20 April 1883; Central South London Free Church Council to the Home Office, 25 October 1912, PRO MEPO 2/5815.
20. Report of Supt. Walker as to the State of Hyde Park after the Gates are Closed at Night, 19 July 1864, PRO HO 45/7618/2.
21. Sir Richard Mayne to J.G. Baring MP, 25 July 1864, PRO HO 45/7618/2.
22. Figures taken from CCC indictments, various PRO CRIM classmarks for 1828, 1830, 1836, 1840 and 1844.
23. For this case, see above, Chapter 1.
24. Stephenson to Howard Liddell, 8 February 1877, PRO HO 144/20/ 58480.
25. George Long to Home Office, 3 April 1848, PRO HO 45/2275.
26. Note by S.G. Phillips, PRO HO 45/2275. Original emphasis.
27. Comments [by Sir George Grey?] on letter from George Long [magistrate at the Marylebone office] to Home Office, PRO HO 45/2275. See also comments on scandal by Justice Talfourd, PRO HO 18/346/48.
28. For example, David Philipps notes a refusal rate of 7.4 per cent for all crimes between 1835 and 1860 in the West Midlands. David Philipps, *Crime and Authority in Victorian England: The Black Country, 1835–1850* (London, 1977), p. 103.
29. Old Bailey indictment files, CLRO SFP 106–108; Old Bailey indictment files CLRO SFP 319–326.
30. I am indebted to Douglas Hay and Ruth Paley for a discussion of the nature of indictments and witnesses.
31. CCC Misdemeanours/felonies 1836 PRO CRIM 4/29–47; CCC Misdemeanours/Felonies 1844 PRO CRIM 4/240–259.
32. Hay and Snyder, 'Using the Criminal Law 1750–1850', in Hay and Snyder (eds), *Policing and Prosecution*, pp. 39–41.
33. *Royal Commission on the Criminal Law, Third Report*, 1837, PP 1837 [79] XXXI.1; Evidence of John Hughes Preston, in *Report From the Select Committee on Public Prosecutors*, 9 August 1855, PP, 1854–55 (481) XII.I, p. 98; both quoted in Hay and Snyder, 'Using the Criminal Law', pp. 42–43.
34. *Report From the Select Committee on Public Prosecutors*, 9 August 1855, p. 98. The police were said to conspire with 'low attorneys' to get up cases and inflate the expenses of investigation.
35. Hansard, Third series, col. 1651 (1855), quoted in Hay and Snyder, 'Using the Criminal Law', p. 42.

36. *Report From the Select Committee on Public Prosecutors*, p. 186, quoted in Hay and Snyder, 'Using the Criminal Law', p. 43.

37. *The Times*, 20 April 1830.

38. *The Times*, 26 April 1830. The policing of the Parks had been a problem since at least 1808, when the Home Secretary ordered that Hyde and St James's Park should be locked at night in order to prevent 'scandalous practices'. Lord Hawkesbury to Lord Sydney, 8 November 1808, PRO HO 79/1/66. See also A.D. Harvey, 'Prosecutions for Sodomy at the Beginning of the Nineteenth Century', *Historical Journal* 21 (1978), pp. 939–949.

39. *The Times*, 21 May 1830.

40. Statement of John Tierney, R *v* Bankes, Brief for the Prosecution, PRO TS 11/897, 1841.

41. *The Times*, 13 March 1833.

42. CCC Misdemeanours, 5 February 1844, PRO CRIM 4/242; 8 April 1844, CRIM 4/247; 1 February 1836, CRIM 4/31; 4 April 1836, CRIM 4/35; 13 June 1836, CRIM 4/39.

43. Notes on Statement of William Bennett, PRO TS 11/897.

44. Statement of William Hard, PRO TS 11/897.

45. *The Times*, 23 October 1884. Glynn had committed two previous offences. He was convicted in September 1880 of 'attempting an abominable crime', in March 1884 of 'personating a Police Constable' and finally convicted of extortion in October 1884, for which he received life imprisonment. See the submission for his release under licence, gaol reports, etc. October 1904, PRO HO 144/529/A37983.

46. Alfred Swaine Taylor, *Medical Jurisprudence* (7th edition, London, 1861), p. 714. For cases in which individual officers were prosecuted for extortion see *The Times*, 18 April 1850, and CCC indictment against PC Charles Thresher for malicious prosecution and perjury in an indecent assault case, CCC indictment 17 June 1839 PRO CRIM 4/118, and 12 August 1839, PRO CRIM 4/122.

47. Stefan Petrow, *Policing Morals: The Metropolitan Police and the Home Office 1870–1914* (Oxford, 1994), p. 129.

48. Ibid.

49. Munro to Home Office, 18 February 1889, quoted in Petrow, *Policing Morals*, p. 135.

50. Memo by Lushington, 26 March 1888, quoted in Petrow, *Policing Morals*, p. 150.

51. *Star*, 15 January 1890.

52. Duke of Newcastle to Home Office, 1 March 1826, PRO HO 44/16 ff. 19. On the case of Benjamin Candler, the Duke's valet, and the men hanged with him, William Arden and John Doughty, see *The Times*, 14 November 1822; 17 March 1823; 31 March 1823.

53. *Second Report on the State of the Police of the Metropolis*, 1816 PP [1817] (484) VII.321, p. 392.

54. *The Times*, 25 August 1825; 22 September 1825.

55. For other raids on molly houses, see *The Times*, 10 July 1827; 19 April 1830.

56. See Phyllis Grosskurth (ed.), *The Memoirs of John Addington Symonds* (New York, 1984), pp. 253–254, in which Symonds visits a male brothel 'near the Regent's Park barracks' in February 1877.

57. Sir Edmund Henderson to Sir Richard Airey, 19 February 1875, Commissioner's Letter Books, 1867–1891, PRO MEPO 1/48.

58. Private cuttings collection of William Bell Macdonald, 'Various Trials Cut From Newspapers' (not dated), quoted in Thomas Boyle, *Black Swine in the Sewers of Hampstead: Beneath the Surface of Victorian Sensationalism* (New York, 1989), p. 11.

59. *Morning Chronicle*, 1 August 1854.

60. *Morning Chronicle*, 1, 2 August 1854.

61. *Manchester Evening News*, 30 September 1880.

62. Ibid.

63. *Illustrated Police News*, 2 October 1880.

64. Ibid.

65. *Manchester Evening News*, 30 September 1880.

66. *Manchester Evening News*, 1 October 1880.

67. *Manchester Evening News*, 30 September 1880.

Chapter Three

1. Morris Kaplan, 'Did My Lord Gomorrah Smile? Homosexuality, Class, and Prostitution in the Cleveland Street Affair', in Nancy Erber and George Robb (eds), *Disorder in the Court: Trials and Sexual Conflict at the Turn of the Century* (New York, 1999), pp. 78–99.

2. For an extended discussion of this, see Moran, *Homosexual(ity) of Law*, chapter 3.

3. Sir William Blackstone, *Commentaries on the Laws of England* (London, 1767), pp. 215–6.

4. Patrick Colquhoun, *A Treatise on the Police of the Metropolis...* (London, 1795), p. 46.

5. *Buckinghamshire County Chronicle*, 12 July 1873.

6. Jeremy Bentham, 'Of Publicity', quoted in David Vincent, *The Culture of Secrecy: Britain, 1832–1998* (Oxford, 1998), p. 3.

7. *The Times*, 30 May 1870.

8. Evidence of John Greenwood, Clerkenwell Magistrate, *Report From the Select Committee of the House of Lords Appointed to Consider the Law of Defamation and Libel*, PP 1843 (513) V.259 p. 134.

9. Jean-Marie Goulemot, *Forbidden Texts: Erotic Literature and its Readers in Eighteenth Century France* (Cambridge, 1994); Robert Darnton, *The Forbidden Bestsellers of Pre-Revolutionary France* (New York, 1995); Darnton, 'First Steps Towards a History of Reading', in *The Kiss of Lamourette: Reflections in Cultural History* (London, 1990), pp. 154–190; also Lynn Hunt (ed.), *The*

Invention of Pornography: Obscenity and the Origins of Modernity, 1500–1800 (New York, 1996). See also trials for obscene libel, Court of King's Bench, Proceedings, PRO KB 28/428/22, quoted in Donald Thomas, *A Long Time Burning: The History of Literary Censorship in England* (London, 1969), pp. 192, 194.

10. Walter Kendrick, *The Secret Museum: Pornography in Modern Culture* (New York, 1987), p. 65.

11. Iain McCalman, *Radical Underworld: Prophets, Revolutionaries and Pornographers in London* (Oxford, 1998); Lynda Nead, *Victorian Babylon: People, Streets and Images in Nineteenth Century London* (New Haven, 2000).

12. *Report of The Society for the Suppression of Vice* (London, 1825), PRO HO 44/8. Prichard to Peel, 6 May 1828, PRO HO 44/8 ff. 113–142.

13. Quoted in Christopher Kent, 'The Editor and the Law', in Joel Weiner (ed.), *Innovators and Preachers: The Role of the Editor in Victorian England* (London, 1985), pp. 99–119, p. 108.

14. Ibid., p. 110.

15. *Edinburgh Review* (March 1824), quoted in Ian Burney, 'Making Room at the Public Bar: Coroner's Inquests, Medical Knowledge and the Politics of the Constitution in Early Nineteenth Century England', in James Vernon (ed.), *Rereading the Constitution: New Narratives in the Political History of England's Long Nineteenth Century* (Cambridge, 1996), pp. 123–153, p. 139.

16. *The Times*, 7 August 1884.

17. *The Times*, 8 June 1833.

18. *The Age*, 16 June 1833.

19. *The Times*, 30 March 1833.

20. *The Times*, 29 April 1833.

21. Evidence of Lord Brougham, *Report From the Select Committee of the House of Lords Appointed to Consider the Law of Defamation and Libel*, p. 24.

22. Evidence of John Black, *Report From the Select Committee of the House of Lords Appointed to Consider the Law of Defamation and Libel*, p. 122.

23. Petition of George Lowndes to Marquis of Normanby, 5 March 1841, PRO HO 18/43/33.

24. A.L. Goodhart and H.G. Hanbury (eds), Sir William Holdsworth, *A History of the English Law*, 9 vols (London, 1965), vol IX, p. 191–2.

25. Larceny Act 1827, PP, 1826–27 (390) I.137.

26. Act for Extending the Provisions of the Law Respecting Threatening Letters and Accusing Parties with a view to Extort Money, PP, 1847 (480) IV 167.

27. Indictment, CCC Felonies, 5 July 1841, CRIM 4/175. Original emphasis.

28. J.J. Buxton to Lord Russell, 23 April 1837, PRO HO 17/75 Part 2 Nx 8.

29. Frederick Cox to Lord Melbourne, 15 March 1834, PRO HO 17/114 Ws 11.

30. Anon, *Don Leon* (*c*.1866), quoted in Andrew Elfenbein, *Romantic Genius: The Prehistory of a Homosexual Role* (New York, 1999), p. 70.

31. T.E. Baker to Home Office, 20 May 1830, PRO HO 44/20 ff. 205–207.

32. Hesney Wedgwood to Home Office (n.d), November 1835, PRO HO 17/120 Xv13.
33. John Addington Symonds to Edmund Gosse, 23 February 1891, in Herbert. M. Schueller and Robert Peters (eds), *The Letters of John Addington Symonds*, 3 vols (Detroit, 1969), Vol. III, p. 554–5.
34. Percy Fitzgerald, *Chronicles of Bow Street Police Office* (London, 1888), p. 214.
35. Bankes's committal hearing in 1833 was said to have attracted 2,000 people. *The Times*, 8 June 1833.
36. *The Times*, 14 March 1827.
37. *The Times*, 21 August 1830.
38. Aled Jones, *Powers of the Press: Newspapers, Power and the Public in Nineteenth Century England* (Aldershot, 1996), p. 33.
39 Walter Bagehot, 'Charles Dickens', in Norman St John Stevas (ed.), *Collected Works*, 3 vols (London, 1965), vol. 2, p. 87.
40. Walter Benjamin, 'On Some Motifs in Baudelaire', in Hannah Arendt (ed.), *Illuminations* (London, 1992), pp. 152–196, p. 155.
41. Anne Humphreys, 'Generic Strands and Urban Twists: The Victorian Mysteries Novel', *Victorian Studies* 34 (Summer 1991), pp. 455–472; Walkowitz, *City of Dreadful Delight*.
42. Walkowitz, *City*, chapters 3 and 4.
43. Walkowitz, *City*, p. 84.
44. Parliamentary Papers, Judicial Statistics, various volumes.
45.vJ. Edward Chamberlain and Sander Gilman (eds), *Degeneration: The Dark Side of Progress* (New York, 1985); Daniel Pick, *Faces of Degeneration: A European Disorder, c. 1848–1918* (Cambridge, 1989). See also Matt Cook, 'The Inverted City: London and the Constitution of Homosexuality, 1885–1914' (Ph.D, University of London, 2000).
46. See, for example, Randolph Trumbach, 'The Birth of the Queen: Sodomy and the Emergence of Gender Equality in Modern Europe 1660–1750', in George Chauncey, Martin Duberman and Martha Vicinus (eds), *Hidden From History: Reclaiming the Gay and Lesbian Past* (New York, 1989), pp. 129–140.
47. *Morning Chronicle*, 10 January 1851.
48. CCC Proceedings, 13 April 1850, CRIM 10/31. Original emphasis.
49. Statement of Jack Saul PRO DPP 1/95/4, also quoted in Kaplan, 'Did 'My Lord Gomorrah Smile?', p. 90.
50. Matthew Sweet, *Inventing the Victorians* (London, 2001), p. 196.
51. Indictment for libel, CCC Misdemeanours, 19 August 1850, PRO CRIM 4/408. Allen was later found insane. See CCC Proceedings, 24 August 1850, PRO PCOM 1/60, p. 538.
52. Quoted in Lewis Chester, David Leitch and Colin Simpson, *The Cleveland Street Affair* (Boston, 1976), p. 131.
53. Henry Wood to James Ware, 14 July 1857, Indictment, CCC Felonies, 17 August 1857, PRO CRIM 4/581.

54. Report of Inspector Edward Drew and Supt. T. Moore, 1 March 1901, PRO HO 144/173/A43930.

55. Report of James Munro, 24 July 1886, PRO HO 144/173/A43930.

56. Comments of Mr Rawlinson, Marylebone magistrate, *The Times*, 16 February 1843; 'An Advocate of Police Reform' to the Home Office, 27 May 1827, PRO HO 44/18 (ff. 426–427).

57. Sedgwick, *Epistemology of the Closet*, pp. 44–48.

58. Terry Castle, *Masquerade and Civilisation: The Carnivalesque in Eighteenth Century English Culture and Fiction* (London, 1986), p. 4.

59. Ibid., p. 102.

60. James Vernon, '"For Some Queer Reason": The Trials and Tribulations of Colonel Barker's Masquerade in Interwar Britain', *Signs* 26, 1(2000), pp. 37–62; Marjorie Garber, *Vested Interests: Cross Dressing and Cultural Anxiety* (London, 1992).

61. Garber, *Vested Interests*, p. 10.

62. Ibid., p. 11.

63. Vernon, '"For Some Queer Reason"', p. 38.

64. Walter Benjamin, *Charles Baudelaire: A Lyric Poet in the Era of High Capitalism* (London, 1983). See also, for example, Simon Gunn, *The Public Culture of the Victorian Middle Class: Ritual and Authority and the English Industrial City 1840–1914* (Manchester, 2000); Walkowitz, *City of Dreadful Delight* (London, 1994); Dana Brand, *The Spectator and the City in Nineteenth Century American Literature* (Cambridge, 1991); Keith Tester, *The Fl%oneur* (London, 1994).

65. G.W.M. Reynolds, *The Mysteries of London*, 6 vols (London, 1846), Chapter XXII, quoted in Trefor Thomas (ed.), *Reynolds' Mysteries of London* (Keele, 1996), p. 46.

66. See, for example, 'Manchester Swells', [Manchester] *City Lantern* II (9 February 1876), p. 160; also p 287, 291; 'Manchester Ladies', *City Lantern* III (29 December 1876), p. 106, Manchester Central Library, Local Studies Section. I am indebted to Chris Otter for a discussion of these matters and for alerting me to these sources.

67. Richard Sennett, *The Fall of Public Man* (Cambridge, 1974); Gunn, *Public Culture*; Elizabeth Wilson, *Adorned in Dreams: Fashion and Modernity* (London, 1985).

68. Gunn, *Public Culture*, p. 66.

69. Police Report, 'K' Division, 1 April 1858, PRO HO 6628/9.

70. Gunn, *Public Culture*, p. 69.

71. Richard Maxwell, *The Mysteries of Paris and London* (Charlottesville, 1992), p. 162.

72. G.W.M. Reynolds, *The Mysteries of London*, 6 vols (London 1846), vol. 2 p. 4.

73. Reynolds, *Mysteries of London*, Epilogue to vol. 1, quoted in Thomas (ed.), *Reynolds' Mysteries*, p. 197.

74. George Augustus Sala, 'The Key to the Street', in Sala, *Gaslight and Daylight with some London Scenes they Shine Upon* (London, 1859), p. 5.

75. Diaries of Arthur Munby, 4 June 1863, Trinity College Cambridge, pp. 209–212.

76. Munby Diaries, 15 January 1860.

77. Munby Diaries, 23 July 1862.

78. Munby Diaries, 10 April 1863.

79. Munby Diaries, 13 April 1864, quoted in Hudson, *Munby: Man of Two Worlds*, p. 188.

80. See Peter Farrer, *In Female Disguise: An Anthology of English and American Short Stories and Literary Passages* (Garston, 1992); Farrer, *Borrowed Plumes: A Selection of Letters From Edwardian Newspapers* (Garston, 1978).

81. Peter Bailey, 'Conspiracies of Meaning: Music Hall and the Knowingness of Popular Culture', *Past and Present*, 144 (August 1994), pp. 138–170.

82. See Camilla Townsend, '"I Am the Woman for Spirit": A Working Woman's Gender Transgression in Victorian London', *Victorian Studies* 36 (Spring 1993), pp. 293–314. See also cases of cross-dressing women, Anne Jane Thornton, *The Times*, 11 February 1835; 'The Woman Husband', *The Times*, 18 April 1838; Sarah Blaymires, *The Times*, 19 June 1861; Mlle De La Tour, *Lloyd's Weekly London Newspaper*, 15 June 1862; Rose Brown, *The Times*, 30 August 1871.

83. Upchurch, 'Forgetting the Unthinkable'.

84. *Lloyd's Weekly London Newspaper*, 22 March 1846; also *The Times*, 17 March 1846.

85. *Illustrated Police News*, 2 October 1880.

86. *The Times*, 17 March 1846.

87. *Lloyd's Weekly London Newspaper*, March 22 1846.

88. *Lloyd's Weekly London Newspaper*, 29 September 1850. For Scott's indictment, see CCC Misdemeanours, 21 October 1850, PRO CRIM 4/413.

89. *Morning Chronicle*, 2 August 1854.

90. *Lloyd's Weekly London Newspaper*, 22 March 1846.

91. *Lloyd's Weekly London Newspaper*, 12 July 1863. Bracketed remarks in original.

92. Briefs for the Prisoner (not dated), attached to Petition of Henry Harrison, August 1852, PRO HO 18/346/48.

93. *The Times*, 27 June 1835. See also 'George Robinson', *The Times*, 24 July 1845, who was 'known in court as the illegitimate son of a distinguished royal personage (deceased)'; 'John Fawcett', whose 'real name did not transpire', *The Times*, 26 October 1847.

94. Evidence of John Greenwood, *Report From the Select Committee of the House of Lords Appointed to Consider the Law of Defamation and Libel*, 1843, p. 134.

95. *The Times*, 5 February 1846.

96. *The Times*, 9 February 1846.

97. *The Times*, 15 February 1843.

98. *Morning Chronicle*, 14 and 16 February 1843; see also *The Times*, 15 February 1843; *Lloyd's Weekly London News*, 19 February 1843.

99. *Morning Chronicle*, 14 February 1843.

100. This was the term used in the headlines in the *Illustrated Police News*, 20 May 1871.

101. Evidence of Detective William Chamberlain, in Queen *v* Boulton and others before the Lord Chief Justice, PRO DPP 4/6, p. 100. The trial transcript is paginated on the right hand page only. I have given these numbers in all footnotes.

102. *Weekly Dispatch*, 1 May 1870.

103. William Roughhead, *Bad Companions* (New York, 1931).

104. Hyde, *The Other Love*, p. 96.

105. For accounts of the trial, see Fitzgerald, *Chronicles of Bow Street*; Roughhead, *Bad Companions*; Hyde, *Other Love*; Weeks, *Sex, Politics and Society*; Bartlett, *Who Was That Man?*; Laurence Senelick, 'Boys and Girls Together: The Subcultural Origins of Glamour Drag in Nineteenth Century England', in Lesley Ferris (ed.), *Crossing the Stage: Controversies in Cross Dressing* (London, 1994), pp. 80–95.

106. Sinfield, *Wilde Century*, p. 7.

107. Henry Matthews, *Queen v Boulton...*, p. 581.

108. Henry Parry, *Queen v Boulton...*, p. 535.

109. *Queen v Boulton...*, p. 971.

110. *Queen v Boulton...*, p. 972. Also, Mr. Parry observed in his opening, 'I am told... that a thrill of horror ran through the jury box when all these [Boulton and Park's] dresses appeared upon the floor of the court.' *Queen v Boulton...*, pp. 537–8.

111. *The Times*, 14 June 1870.

112. Anon., *The Lives of Boulton and Park* (London, 1870), p. 5.

113. *Queen v Boulton...*, p. 100.

114. *Illustrated Police News*, 28 May 1870.

115. *Illustrated Police News*, 14 May 1870.

116. *Queen v Boulton...*, p. 623.

117. Sinfield, *Wilde Century*, p. 67.

118. Stefan Collini, *Public Moralists: Political Thought and Intellectual Life in Britain 1850–1930* (Oxford, 1991), p. 96.

119. Adams, *Dandies and Desert Saints*, chapters 1 and 5.

120. Samuel Smiles, *Life and Labour* (London, 1887), p. 34, quoted in Abraham Smythe Palmer, *The Perfect Gentleman: His Character Delineated in a Series of Extracts from Writers Ancient and Modern...* (London, 1892), p. 215.

121. W.R. Browne, 'The English Gentleman', *National Review* (April 1886) 261–271, p. 261.

122. Fisk to Boulton, *Queen v Boulton...*, pp. 97–98, quoted in Cohen, *Sex Scandal*, p. 112.

123. Anon., *The Lives of Boulton and Park*, p. 8.

124. Fitzgerald, *Chronicles of Bow Street*, pp. 320–1.

125. *Queen v Boulton...*, pp. 985–6.

126. *Queen v Boulton...*, p. 999.

127. *Illustrated Police News*, 20 May 1871.

Chapter Four

1. Cohen, *Sex Scandal*, p. 14.

2. Evidence of William Hilliard, CCC Proceedings, 28 October 1846, PRO CRIM 10/24, p. 863.

3. Anon., *A Doleful Dirge on the Wicked Men Condemned to Suffer at Lincoln Gallows by the Lord Judge the Right Honourable Sir James Allen Park, at the Lincoln Assizes in March 1823*, BL, 1889. d.3, p. 168.

4. Anon., *The Execution of Charles Clutton.*

5. Hesney Wedgwood to Lord John Russell (not dated) November 1835. PRO HO 17/120 Xv 13.

6. William Acton, *The Functions and Disorders of the Reproductive Organs* (London, 1865), p. 219.

7. Collini, *Public Moralists*, pp. 96–97. See also Nathan Roberts, 'Investigating character in England, c.1890–1914' (Ph.D. dissertation, University of Manchester, 2002).

8. *The Times*, 18 November 1842. For this case, see also Petition of Patrick Leigh Strachan to Sir James Graham, 28 February 1844, PRO HO 18/134/2.

9. Douglas Hay, 'Prosecution and Power: Malicious Prosecution in the English Courts 1750–1850', in Hay and Synder (eds), *Policing and Prosecution in Britain*, pp. 343–396, p. 383.

10. John Seymour was tried at the Salisbury Assizes by a jury 'consisting of gentlemen of the highest respectability'. *Salisbury and Winchester Journal*, 17 March 1828.

11. Evidence of William Erle, *Report From the Select Committee on the Law and Practice relating to the Summoning, Attendance and Remuneration of Special and Common Juries*, 8 July 1867, PP 1867 (425) IX. 597, p. 1.

12. On special juries, see Jeremy Bentham, *Elements of the Art of Packing, As Applied to Special Juries, Particularly in Cases of Libel Law* (London, 1821), pp. 32–3. Bentham argued that, at least in libel cases, it was possible for court officials to pack the jury with those whose verdict could be relied upon. This was a result of the fact that very few of those who were qualified as special jurors actually served, preferring to be fined instead, and this created a group of around 400 men who served over and over again and even made their living in this way. These men were known as 'guinea men' or 'guinea pigs'. See also James Oldham, 'The Origins of the Special Jury', *University of Chicago Law Review*, 50 (Winter 1983), pp. 137–210.

13. Petition of Patrick Leigh Strachan, PRO HO 18/134/2.

14. Evidence of George Gillet Potter Esq. *Report From the Select Committee... on Special and Common Juries*, pp. 39–40.

15. Michael Davitt, *Leaves From a Prison Diary, Or Lectures to a 'Solitary' Audience* (London, 1885), p. 128.

16. Ibid., pp. 131–2.

17. McCalman, *Radical Underworld*, chapter 2. See also Polly Morris, 'Defamation and Sexual Reputation in Somerset 1733–1850' (Ph.D. dissertation, Warwick University, 1985).

18. Official report on Davenport Sedley, quoted in McCalman, *Radical Underworld*, p. 35.
19. McCalman, *Radical Underworld*, p. 41.
20. Henry Hunt, *The Memoirs of Henry Hunt, Written by Himself*, 3 vols (London, 1820, repr. London, 1967) vol. 3, p. 583. I am indebted to Matthew McCormack for this reference and a discussion of related matters.
21. See McCalman, *Radical Underworld*, pp. 34–5. *The Age*, 30 June 1830, noted that 'nauseous and abominable libels against him… have been repeated so often as to pass in the minds of the vulgar as truths'.
22. On this, see John Belchem, *Orator Hunt: Henry Hunt and English Working Class Radicalism* (Oxford, 1985), p. 196. See also Daniel French, *French versus Cobbett* (London, 1829); also the case of Robert Passingham, *Cowdroy's Manchester Gazette*, 2 March 1805. See also the long-running dispute over money between the impecunious Sir Thomas Champneys and Nathaniel Messiter, *The Times*, 28 July 1820, 16 August 1822.
23. Theodore Norton, *The Duke of Cumberland, And A Word, By the Way, of Cant and Slander* (London, 1832).
24. *Crim. Con. Gazette*, 25 August 1838.
25. Charles Westmacott, quoted in Donald J. Gray, 'Early Victorian Scandalous Journalism: Renton Nicholson's *The Town* (1837–42)', in Joanne Shattock and Michael Wolff (eds), *The Victorian Periodical Press: Samplings and Soundings* (Leicester, 1982), pp. 317–349, pp. 325–6. Gray maintains that Barnard Gregory, the editor of *The Satirist*, extorted money from his readers by threatening to print their sexual indiscretions. For this see p. 34.
26. Evidence of Stanley Lees Giffard, *Report From the Select Committee of the House of Lords Appointed to Consider the Law of Defamation and Libel*, 1843, p. 52.
27. Evidence of Lord Brougham to *Select Committee on the Law of Libel and Slander*, 4 June 1834, quoted in Appendix to *Report From the Select Committee of the House of Lords Appointed to Consider the Law of Defamation and Libel*, 1843, p. 24.
28. See, for instance, their report of the execution of Captain Beauclerk, *Poor Man's Guardian*, 10 August 1833.
29. *The Times*, 29 September 1835. The *Crim. Con. Gazette* argued that 'these miscreants' were 'addicted to the propensities they would impute to the guiltless'. *Crim. Con. Gazette*, 19 January 1839.
30. 'An Advocate of Police Reform' to Robert Peel, 27 May 1827, PRO HO 4418 ff. 426–427.
31. Simpson, 'Masculinity and Control', chapter IX.
32. Simpson, 'Masculinity and Control', p. 553.
33. W.H.D. Winder, 'The Development of Blackmail', *Modern Law Review*, 5 (July 1941), pp. 21–50.
34. R *v* Hickman, quoted in Mike Hepworth, *Blackmail: Publicity and Secrecy in Everyday Life* (London, 1975) p. 13.

35. R *v* Hickman, quoted in Winder, 'The Development of Blackmail', p. 26. The same result was given in R *v* Knewland (1796), in which the fear of the results of such an accusation was deemed 'equal to the fear of losing life itself'. Quoted in Winder, 'Development', p. 26.

36. Threatening Letters Act, PP 1823 (437) I. 55. See also Simpson, 'Masculinity and Control', chapter IX for a discussion of this legislation.

37. Larceny Act, PP 1826–7 (390) I. 137, s. 7.

38. An Act for extending the provision of the law respecting threatening letters, and accusing parties with a view to extort money, PP, 1847 (480) IV. 167; CCC Proceedings, 13 April 1850, PRO CRIM 10/31, p. 700.

39. This was ruled on in the case of R *v* Cracknell and Walker: 'On the trial of an indictment for threatening to accuse of an infamous crime in order to extort money, the guilt or innocence of the party is quite immaterial.' Cox, *Reports*, vol X (1864–67), p. 408.

40. Hepworth, *Blackmail*, p. 15.

41. Alexander Welsh, *George Eliot and Blackmail* (Cambridge, MA, 1985).

42. Lord Ellenborough's decision in R *v* Southerton, 1805, quoted in Welsh, *George Eliot and Blackmail*, p. 83.

43. Welsh, *George Eliot and Blackmail*, p. 83.

44. Ibid., p. 81.

45. Ibid., p. 80.

46. Frederick Cox (Chaplain of Buckinghamshire County Gaol) to Lord Denman, 10 March 1834, PRO HO 17/114 Ws 11.

47. *The Times*, 2 August 1825.

48. *The Times*, 14 September 1853.

49. Cox, *Reports of Cases*, vol X, 1864–67, p. 160.

50. *The Peculiar and Unprecedented Case of Thomas Skinner who Lately Received his Majesty's Free Pardon… After Being Condemned to Death for the Crime of Beastiality* (London, 1821).

51. Stefan Collini calculates, making all due allowances for economic variables, that to obtain the rough equivalent of today's prices it is necessary to multiply 1850 prices by 30, *Public Moralists*, p. 35. The case of the banker appears in *The Times*, 5 June 1862, 4, 5 August 1862.

52. See, for example, E.P. Thompson, *The Making of the English Working Class* (London, 1963), p. 620; Eric Hobsbawm, *Captain Swing* (Harmondsworth, 1973), pp. 73–4. E.P. Thompson, "The Crime of Anonymity", in Douglas Hay, Peter Linebaugh and John G. Rule, (eds.), *Albion's Fatal Tree: Crime and Society in Eighteenth Century England*, (London 1975), pp 255–308.

53. *The Times*, 16 April 1825.

54. Petition of John Whatoff to Sir James Graham, 2 April 1842, PRO HO 18/78/45. See also *The Times* 22 March 1842.

55. Letters to Thomas Welsh (24 March 1857) and William Allingham, indictment, CCC Felonies, 11 May 1857, PRO CRIM 4/575. See also CCC Proceedings, 14 May 1857, PRO PCOM 1/73. See also *The Times*, 16, 23 April 1857; 18 June 1857; *Reynolds' Newspaper*, 19 April 1857, 21 June 1857.

56. *The Times*, 31 July 1885.

57. All descriptions of status and occupation in quotes are taken from newspaper sources.

58. *Morning Chronicle*, 15 April 1850. See also *The Times*, 14 March 1850;15 April 1850. For the trial of the gang, see CCC Proceedings 13 April 1851, PRO CRIM 10/31, pp. 699–711. The police said at the committal hearing that 'the whole of the prisoners were well known as the associates and accomplices of a gang of men who lived by extorting money from timid people by similar means' and that the Bow Street magistrate had received 'a great number of anonymous letters from persons who appear to have been victimized by the gang of miscreants with whom the prisoners are associated'. One of them, John Sullivan, was in the habit of dressing in the uniform of a cavalry soldier in order to encourage advances. *The Times*, 14 March 1850.

59. Nead, *Victorian Babylon*, pp. 161–189.

60. *The Times*, 11 April 1843.

61. *The Times*, 11 April 1843.

62. *The Times*, 1 July 1843.

63. *The Times*, 19 November 1867.

64. *The Times*, 23 March 1871.

65. PP 1839, XXXVIII. 241. Between 1835 and 1890 there were 249 committals for the offence of 'sending threatening letters to extort money' and 121 for 'obtaining property by threats to accuse of unnatural crimes'. See Parliamentary Papers, Judicial Statistics, various volumes.

66. Woolrych, *History and Present Results*, p. 151, quoted in Simpson, 'Masculinity and Control', p. 569. If Woolrych's estimate was even remotely accurate, the levels of extortion it suggests are astonishing. In 1821 there were 9,678 committals nationally for simple larceny, larceny from the person, threatening letters, and robbery on the highway and other places. There were other offences listed as types of robbery, but even without those categories, 20 per cent of this total (1,924) would be a very large figure. PP 1826–27 XIX. 183.

67. *The Times*, 22 September 1866. Cracknell and Walker had done some painting and decorating for a Dr Henry Juler and after a dispute over the cost of materials and his refusal to give them a character, they accused him of having committed an indecent assault on them. He initially agreed to pay them, but told the police, who hid behind a curtain at the meeting which Juler had arranged with his accusers. The officer, on hearing the terms of the threat repeated, leapt out and arrested the two men.

68. *The Times*, 21 December 1838.

69. *Crim. Con. Gazette*, 19 January 1839. The editorial offered the advice that extortionists must be met with firmness and resolution. 'Negotiations with these miscreants... betray a timidity by which innocence ought never to be influenced, to the emboldening of its accusers... Grapple with the ruffian at once, seize the villain by the throat at every risk, and deliver him up to justice, say we.' This advice was offered (perhaps tongue in cheek for its own victims)

'for the guidance of persons who by possibility may hereafter be placed in so awkward a predicament'.

70. *The Times*, 21 April 1866.
71. *Reynolds' Newspaper*, 21 June 1863, also *The Times*, 12 June 1863.
72. Hay, 'Prosecution and Power'.
73. On this, see Goodhart and Hanbury (eds), *History of the English Criminal Law*, vol. XV, p. 501.
74. *The Satirist*, 20 May 1848.
75. W.C. Humphreys, *Observations on the Inutility of Grand Juries* (London, 1842), p.1. See also the similar arguments of Peter Laurie in *An Enquiry Into the Uses and Abuses of Grand Juries* (London, 1832).
76. Humphreys, *Observations*, p. 8, quoted in Hay, 'Prosecution and Power', p. 381.
77. Humphreys, *Observations*, p. 8.
78. Evidence of Lord Brougham, *Report From the Select Committee of the House of Lords Appointed to Consider the Law of Defamation and Libel*, 1843, p 6.
79. Hay, 'Prosecution and Power', p 351.
80. *The Times*, 29 October 1846.
81. *Weekly Dispatch*, 15 August 1847.
82. CCC Proceedings, 13 April 1850, PRO CRIM 10/31, pp. 699–711. Original emphasis: slang terms were usually given in italics.
83. On the Woolwich affair, see *Reynolds' Newspaper*, 13 October 1850; *The Times*, 11, 12, 15, 16 October 1850.
84. Sir John Eardley-Wilmot to Earl Grey, 30 October 1846, PP 1847 (262) (400) XXXVIII513, 527. See also Ronald Hyam, *Empire and Sexuality: The British Experience* (Manchester, 1990), p. 26. For the debate on the case see *The Times*, 9 June 1847.
85. Robert Hughes, *The Fatal Shore: A History of the Transportation of Convicts to Australia, 1787–1868* (London, 1987), p. 538.
86. *The Times*, 16 September 1856.
87. *Manchester Guardian*, 17 September 1856.
88. Lucy Brown, *Victorian News and Newspapers* (Oxford, 1985), pp. 275–6.
89. T.P. O'Connor, 'The New Journalism', *New Review* I (1889), pp. 429–30, quoted in Gary Weber, 'Henry Labouchere, *Truth* and the New Journalism of Late Victorian Britain', *Victorian Periodicals Review* (Spring 1993), pp. 36–43, p. 39.
90. Dellamorra, *Masculine Desire*, p. 202.
91. Weber, 'Henry Labouchere', p. 41; Joseph Hatton, *Journalistic London* (London, 1882), p. 104, quoted in Weber, 'Henry Labouchere', p. 41.
92. J.O. Baylen, 'Politics and the "New Journalism": Lord Esher's Use of the *Pall Mall Gazette*', *Victorian Periodicals Review* 20, 4 (1987), pp. 126–141.
93. W.T. Stead, 'Government by Journalism', *Contemporary Review*, 49 (May 1886), quoted in Raymond L. Shults, *Crusader in Babylon: W.T. Stead and the Pall Mall Gazette* (Lincoln, 1972), p. 206.

94. William O'Brien, *Evening Memories: Being A Continuation of Recollections by the Same Author* (Dublin, 1920), p. 14.

95. *United Ireland*, 25 August 1883.

96. *United Ireland*, 20 October 1883.

97. French was alleged to be unfit to plead because of this debility. See *The Times*, 20 August 1884; *The Times*, 1 November 1884.

98. *United Ireland*, 10 May 1884.

99. O'Brien, *Evening Memories*, p. 22.

100. Hansard, Third Series, Vol. CCCXXXVIII, 17 June 1884, cols 679–722.

101. *Pall Mall Gazette*, 21 August 1884.

102. Hansard, Third Series, Vol. CCLXXVIII, 17 June 1884, col 694.

103. *Pall Mall Gazette*, 26 August 1884.

104. *United Ireland*, 24 May 1884.

105. Spencer to Gladstone, 26 August 1884 (Gladstone Papers, BL, Add. MS 4431, ff.77–81, 179–86; Trevelyan to Gladstone, 26 July 1884 (Add. MS 44335, ff.168–9), quoted in Sally Warwick-Haller, *William O'Brien and the Irish Land War* (Dublin, 1990), p. 73.

106. William Nash was convicted in September 1884 of trying to extort money from his own father and brother under threats. Mr Nash senior was a Limerick JP. Similar letters were sent to the Lord Chancellor and the Catholic Bishop of Limerick. See *The Times*, 5 August 1884, 24 September 1884.

107. *The Times*, 10 September 1884, p. 9.

108. *The Times*, 25 July 1884, p. 9. Despite its denunciations of the Irish, *The Times* did cover the trials in exhaustive detail, though not quite as comprehensively as *United Ireland*. See *The Times*, 1, 3, 4, 5, 7, 10, 12, 16, 17, 19, 20, 24, 25, 26, 29, 30, 31 July; 4, 5, 7, 14, 20, 25 August; 9 September; 29 October; 1 November 1884.

109. For Stead's coverage, see *Pall Mall Gazette* 8, 15, 19, 20, 21, 25, 26, 29 August; 23, 24 September 1884. The *Illustrated Police News* devoted two front pages to the scandals, 26, 30 July 1884.

110. *United Ireland*, 19 July 1884.

111. *United Ireland*, 30 August 1884.

112. Resolution of Matthew Harris, *The Times*, 10 July 1884.

113. *Dublin Evening Telegraph*, quoted in *United Ireland*, 5 July 1884. At the beginning of Cornwall's libel trial the judge expressed his opinion that it would be better if the case were held behind closed doors, while French's first committal hearing was held *in camera*. The magistrate in that case argued that such a proceeding was 'a course which every right-minded person in the community will approve'. Publicity was not only likely to encourage immorality, but it prevented the names of those who might be innocent from being named in the public press in connection with the case. The police had a list of around 30 people whose names had been mentioned in the course of the inquiry and 'many of these move in respectable society, and a very heavy responsibility would rest upon the authorities if either justice were baffled or injustice done by any publicity respecting them'. *The Times*, 7 August 1884.

114. *Freeman's Journal*, quoted in *United Ireland*, 12 July 1884.
115. On this, see Hyde, *Cleveland Street Scandal*, p. 95. Hyde effectively agrees with the account of Richard Webster, the Attorney-General, in the debate on the scandal. For this see Hansard, Third Series, Vol. CCCXLI, 28 February 1890, cols 1564–6.
116. *Reynolds' Newspaper*, 19 January 1890.
117. Hamilton Cuffe to W.H. Smith, 21 March 1890, PRO DPP 1/95/6. On the Home Office, see Jill Pellew, *The Home Office 1848–1914: From Clerks to Bureaucrats* (London, 1982).
118. Stephenson to Munro, 20 July 1889, PRO DPP 1/95/1.
119. Stephenson to Matthews, 17 August 1889, PRO DPP 1/95/1.
120. Munro to Home Office, 22 July 1889, PRO HO 144/477/x24427A.
121. Stephenson to Matthews, 31 August 1889, PRO DPP 1/95/1.
122. Webster's comments on Saul's statement, 3 February 1890, PRO DPP 1/ 95/4. *The Times* agreed that 'The result of the prosecution instituted by Lord Euston [the defeat of the *North London Press*] showed beyond all doubt that the law officers were fully justified in declining to institute further prosecutions upon evidence which appeared in the witness box to be not only tainted in its origin, but absolutely untrustworthy from beginning to end.' The Attorney General's answers to Labouchere in the debate on 28 February were conclusive and showed that the law officers acted from a dispassionate view 'of what was for the public interest and was capable of being established in a court of justice'. *The Times*, 1 March 1890.
123. *The Times*, 17 January 1890.
124. *Reynolds' Newspaper*, 29 September 1889.
125. *Referee*, 24 November 1889.
126. *St Stephen's Review*, 9 November 1889.
127. *St Stephen's Review*, 9 November 1889.
128. *North London Press*, 21 December 1889.
129. *The Times*, 20 December 1889.
130. *North London Press*, 23 November 1889.
131. *The Times*, 1 March 1890.
132. *Star*, 1 March 1890.
133. Kaplan, 'Did "My Lord Gomorrah" Smile', p. 92.
134. *The Times*, 20 December 1889.
135. *The Hawk*, 28 January 1890.
136. *The Times*, 1 March 1890.
137. *Truth*, 8 May 1879, quoted in Weber, 'Henry Labouchere', p. 39.
138. See, for example, Josephine Butler, *An Address Delivered at Croyden, July 3 1871* (Manchester, 1871), p. 3; Thomas Biggs, *The Proposed Extension of the Contagious Diseases Acts in its Moral and Economic Aspects* (London, 1870).
139. *Globe*, 3 March 1890. Original emphasis.

Chapter Five

1. See, for instance, Susan Sontag, 'Notes on Camp', in *A Susan Sontag Reader* (London, 1982), pp. 105–120; David Bergman (ed.), *Camp Grounds: Style and Homosexuality* (Amherst, 1993); Moe Meyer (ed.), *The Politics and Poetics of Camp* (London, 1994).
2. J.W. Wallace and John Johnston, *Visits to Walt Whitman* (London, 1917), p. 18.
3. Ibid., p. 19.
4. *The Song of the Eagle Street College. Dedicated to 'The Masther' and the other Philosophers* (1889), Johnston Papers, Bolton Library ZJO 5/1.
5. G.N. Barnes, *From Workshop to War Cabinet* (London, 1924), p. 42, quoted in Stephen Yeo, 'A New Life: The Religion of Socialism in Britain, 1883–1896', *History Workshop Journal*, 4 (1977), pp. 5–56, p. 31.
6. John K. Walton, *A Social History of Lancashire*, 1558–1939 (Manchester, 1987), p. 303.
7. James Clegg, *Annals of Bolton: History, Chronology, Politics* (Bolton, 1888), p. 708.
8. Ibid., p. 36.
9. See, on this, Yeo, 'A New Life'; Jonathan Mendilow, *The Romantic Tradition in British Political Thought* (London, 1986), pp. 198–235; K.S. Inglis, 'The Labour Church Movement', *International Review of Social History* 3, 3 (1958), pp. 445–460; Mark Bevir, 'British Socialism and American Romanticism', *English Historical Review* 110, 438 (1995), pp. 878–901; Bevir, 'The Labour Church Movement, 1891–1902', *Journal of British Studies* 38 (April 1999), pp. 217–245.
10. Carolyn Masel, 'Poet of Comrades: Walt Whitman and the Bolton Whitman Fellowship', in Janet Beer and Bridget Bennett (eds), *International Episodes: Anglo-American Exchanges, 1885–1900* (forthcoming, Manchester, 2002).
11. On this, see Fiona MacCarthy, *The Simple Life: C.R. Ashbee in the Cotswolds* (London, 1981), p. 23; Alan Crawford, *C.R. Ashbee: Architect, Designer and Romantic Socialist* (New Haven, 1985).
12. Joy Dixon, *Divine Feminine: Theosophy and Feminism in England* (Baltimore, 2001); Alex Owen, *The Darkened Room: Women, Power and Spiritualism in Late Nineteenth Century England* (London, 1989).
13. Elfenbein, *Romantic Genius*, chapter 1.
14. Joy Dixon, 'Sexology and the Occult: Sexuality and Subjectivity in Theosophy's New Age', *Journal of the History of Sexuality* 7, 3 (1997), pp. 409–433, p. 412.
15. Ibid., p. 413.
16. Bevir, 'British Socialism', p. 878.
17. *Labour Prophet*, April 1892, p. 28.
18. *Labour Prophet*, February 1895, p. 1.
19. Walt Whitman, 'I Sing the Body Electric', in Francis Murphy (ed.), *Walt Whitman: The Complete Poems* (London, 1996), p. 131.
20. *Labour Prophet*, April 1892, p. 28; *Labour Prophet*, March 1896, p. 40.

21. See, for example, Gary Schmidgall, *Walt Whitman: A Gay Life* (New York, 1997), chapter 2; Robert K. Martin, *The Homosexual Tradition in American Poetry* (Austin, 1979).

22. H. Montgomery Hyde, *Famous Trials: Oscar Wilde* (Harmondsworth, 1962), pp. 133–4.

23. Grosskurth (ed.), *The Memoirs of John Addington Symonds*, p. 191.

24. Bevir, 'The Labour Church Movement', p. 221. See also Frank Miller Turner, *Between Science and Religion: The Reaction to Scientific Naturalism in Late Victorian England* (New Haven, 1974).

25. J.W. Wallace, 'The "Calamus" Poems in "Leaves of Grass"' (Address to College, 2 July 1920), J.W. Wallace Collection, John Rylands University Library Manchester, Deansgate (JRULM), Eng MS 1186/8/5/1, p. 2.

26. Ibid.

27. Diaries of John Johnston, 28 June 1887, Bolton Library Whitman Fellowship Collection, ZJO 1/1.

28. Wallace and Johnston, *Visits to Walt Whitman*, p. 58.

29. Johnston Diaries, 28 June 1890.

30. John Addington Symonds, *Love and Death: A Symphony. To the Prophet Poet of Democracy Religion Love This Verse a Feeble Echo of his Song is Dedicated August 1880*. For Wallace's copy see Wallace Papers, Bolton Library ZWN 6/2/2.

31. Walt Whitman, 'Scented Herbage of My Breast', in Murphy (ed.), *Walt Whitman, The Complete Poems*, p. 147.

32. Johnston Diaries, 28 October 1891.

33. Johnston Diaries, 20 December 1887.

34. Johnston Diaries, 29 June 1891.

35. Johnston Diaries, 20 December 1887. Original emphasis.

36. Johnston Diaries, 5 October 1901.

37. Eugenio Biagini, *Liberty, Retrenchment and Reform: Popular Liberalism in the Age of Gladstone* (Cambridge, 1992).

38. Patrick Joyce, *Democratic Subjects: The Self and the Social in Nineteenth Century England* (Cambridge, 1994), p. 48.

39. Johnston Diaries, 6 December 1887.

40. Johnston Diaries, 6 June 1887.

41. J.W. Wallace to Fred Wild, April 1887, quoted in Johnston Diaries, 9 June 1889.

42. Eve Kosofsky Sedgwick, *Between Men: English Literature and Male Homosocial Desire* (New York, 1992), p. 205.

43. J.W. Wallace, 'The "Calamus" Poems in "Leaves of Grass"'.

44. William Innes to Sixsmith, 4 December 1893, Sixsmith Collection, JRULM Deansgate, Eng MS 1170/2/1/1/2.

45. Vivian R. Pollak, 'Death as Repression, Repression as Death: A Reading of Whitman's "Calamus" Poems', in Geoffrey Sill (ed.), *Walt Whitman of Mickle Street: A Centennial Collection* (Knoxville, 1994), pp. 179–193, p. 187.

46. Walt Whitman, 'Scented Herbage of My Breast', in Murphy (ed.), *Walt Whitman, The Complete Poems*, p. 147.

47. J.W. Wallace to Jim Wallace, 8 August 1901, Wallace Collection, JRULM Deansgate, Eng MS 1186/2/5/2.

48. Johnston Diaries, 10 October 1889, original emphasis.

49. John Addington Symonds, *Love and Death: A Symphony. To the Prophet Poet of Democracy Religion Love This Verse a Feeble Echo of his Song is Dedicated August 1880*. Wallace Papers, Bolton Library, ZWN 6/2/2.

50. Quoted in W.C. Rivers, *Walt Whitman's Anomaly* (London, 1913).

51. Edward Carpenter, *Homogenic Love* (Manchester, 1894).

52. Rivers, *Walt Whitman's Anomaly*, p. 1.

53. Quoted in Rivers, *Walt Whitman's Anomaly*, p. 3.

54. *International Journal of Psychoanalysis* 6 (January 1925), Part 1, p. 85.

55. Seidman, 'The Power of Desire and the Danger of Pleasure: Victorian Sexuality Reconsidered', *Journal of Social History* 24, 1 (1990), pp. 47–67, p. 49.

56. Jeffrey Richards, '"Passing the Love of Women": Manly Love and Victorian Society', in J.A. Mangan and James Walvin (eds), *Manliness and Morality: Middle Class Masculinity in Britain and America, 1800–1940* (New York, 1987), pp. 92–122, p. 111; Sinfield, *Wilde Century*, chapter 3.

57. Lillian Faderman, *Surpassing the Love of Men: Romantic Friendship and Love Between Women From the Renaissance to the Present* (London, 1985); Lisa Moore, '"Something More Tender Still than Friendship": Romantic Friendship in Early 19th Century England', *Feminist Studies* 18, 3 (1992), pp. 499–520; Jill Liddington, *Land, Gender and Authority: The Anne Lister Diaries and Other Writings, 1833–36* (London, 1998).

58. Lucy Bland, *Banishing the Beast: English Feminism and Sexual Morality, 1885–1914* (2nd edition, London, 2002), Chapters 5 and 6; Sheila Jeffreys, *The Spinster and Her Enemies: Feminism and Sexuality, 1880–1930* (London, 1985), Chapter 7.

59. John Addington Symonds, *Walt Whitman: A Study* (London, 1893), p. 93.

60. Ibid., p. 96.

61. John Addington Symonds to John Johnston, 12 January 1891, Wallace Collection, JRULM Deansgate, Eng MS 1186/3/1/1.

62. Symonds to Wallace, 19 December 1892, quoted in Herbert M. Schueller and Robert C. Peters (eds), *The Letters of John Addington Symonds* 3 vols (Detroit, 1969), Vol. III, p. 792.

63. Symonds to Wallace, 17 February 1893, quoted in Schueller and Peters (eds), *Letters*, Vol. III, pp. 819–20.

64. Sedgwick, *Between Men*, coda.

65. Johnston Diaries, 25 December 1892.

66. Symonds to Johnston, 12 January 1891, quoted in Schueller and Peters (eds), *Letters*, p. 792.

67. Johnston Diaries, December 1892.

68. Johnston Diaries, 27 April 1893.

69. Quoted in Johnston Diaries, 28 February 1893.
70. Johnston Diaries, 16 October 1892.
71. J.W. Wallace, *Address to the College*, 6 January 1893, Sixsmith Collection, JRULM Deansgate, Eng MS 1331/1/7/3/2.
72. J.W. Wallace to Keir Hardie, quoted in Johnston Diaries, 14 February 1893.
73. Johnston Diaries, 6 February 1893.
74. Johnston Diaries, Vol. 26, 18 March 1893.
75. J.W. Wallace, *Paper Read Before an ILP Conference at Bolton*, 26 May 1894, Bolton Library, ZWN 6/2/23.
76. On Bucke see Lorna Weir, 'Cosmic Consciousness and the Love of Comrades: Contacts Between R.M. Bucke and Edward Carpenter', *Journal of Canadian Studies* 30, 2 (Summer 1995), pp. 39–57; S.E.D. Shortt, *Victorian Lunacy: Richard M. Bucke and the Practice of Late Nineteenth-Century Psychiatry* (Cambridge, 1986); Artem Lozynsky (ed.), *Richard Maurice Bucke, Medical Mystic: Some Letters of Dr. Bucke to Walt Whitman and his Friends* (Detroit, 1977).
77. R.M. Bucke, *Cosmic Consciousness: A Study in the Evolution of the Human Mind* (2nd edition, New York, 1901), preface.
78. R.M. Bucke, 'Mental Evolution in Man', address to the BMA, quoted in Shortt, *Victorian Lunacy*, p. 122.
79. Johnston Diaries, 26 June 1892.
80. *Proceedings and Transactions of the Royal Society of Canada*, Series II, Vol. 12, pp. 159–196, quoted in R.M. Bucke, *Cosmic Consciousness*, preface.
81. Bucke, *Cosmic Consciousness*, p. 9.
82. Ibid., p. 333.
83. Ibid., p. 3.
84. Report of College Meeting held to Honour Dr. Bucke, 24 August 1891, Bolton Library, ZWN 2/2.
85. Ibid.
86. Rivers, *Walt Whitman's Anomaly*, pp. 14–15.
87. Report of College Meeting held to Honour Dr. Bucke, 24 August 1891, Bolton Library ZWN 2/2.
88. Johnston Diaries, 21 July 1894.
89. Johnston Diaries, 21 July 1894. Johnston crossed out most of this sentence.
90. Johnston Diaries, 22 July 1894.
91. This last sentence was crossed out by Johnston.
92. J.W. Wallace, quoted in Johnston Diaries, 27 September 1894.
93. See, on this, Richard Cytowic, *The Man Who Tasted Shapes* (New York, 1993); C.S. Myers, 'A Case of Synaesthesia', *British Journal of Psychology* 6 (1914), pp. 228–232; Cretien van Campen, 'Synaesthesia and Artistic Experimentation', *Psyche*, 3, 6 (November 1997), <www.psyche.cs.monash.edu.au>, February 2001.
94. Havelock Ellis, *Studies in the Psychology of Sex, Volume II, Sexual Inversion* (London, 1897, repr. New York, 1936), p. 318. See also Ellis, *Man and*

Woman: A Study of Human Secondary Sexual Characteristics (6th edition, London, 1930), p. 184, where he argues that women are predisposed towards colour hearing because they have a greater 'nervous irritability' than men.

95. See Cytowic, *The Man Who Tasted Shapes*, p. 119.
96. Philip Dalmas, quoted in Johnston Diaries, 22 July 1894.
97. Dalmas to Sixsmith, 28 August 1894, Sixsmith Collection, JRULM Deansgate, Eng MS 1170/2/1/4/1.
98. Dalmas to Sixsmith, 12 April [1896?] Sixsmith Collection, JRULM Deansgate, Eng MS 1170/2/1/4/4.
99. Dalmas to Sixsmith, 28 August 1894, Sixsmith Collection, JRULM Deansgate, Eng MS 1170/2/1/4/1.
100. Johnston Diaries, 23 July 1894.
101. Johnston Diaries, 30 July 1894.
102. William Innes to Charles Sixsmith, n.d, 1892, Sixsmith Collection, JRULM Deansgate, Eng MS 1170/2/1/1/7.
103. Dr Bucke to J.W. Wallace, 16 July 1893, Whitman Correspondence, Bolton Library ZWN 9/98.
104. Johnston Diaries, 22 July 1894.
105. Johnston Diaries, 23 July 1894.
106. Johnston Diaries, 3 August 1894.
107. Johnston Diaries, 23 July 1894.
108. Johnston Diaries, 27 September 1894.
109. Ibid.
110. Johnston Diaries, 30 March 1897.
111. Johnston Diaries, 2 August 1899.
112. J.W. Wallace, *Notes of a Visit to Edward Carpenter*, 13–15 August 1892, Wallace Papers, Bolton Library ZWN 6/2/11.
113. Johnston Diaries, 18 January 1901.
114. Johnston Diaries, 11 August 1898.
115. Johnston Diaries, 11–12 November 1906.
116. Carpenter, *Homogenic Love*, p. 39.
117. Ibid., p. 20.
118. Edward Carpenter, 'On the Connexion Between Homosexuality and Divination, and the Importance of the Intermediate Sexes Generally in Early Civilisations', *Revue D'Ethnographie et de Sociologie* (1911), p. 311, Sixsmith Collection, Eng MS 1331/2/1/44. Carpenter, *From Adam's Peak to Elephanta*; Carpenter, *Intermediate Types Among Primitive Folk: A Study in Social Evolution* (London, 1914).
119. Edward Carpenter, 'On the Connexion Between Homosexuality and Divination'. See also Joy Dixon's discussion of *Intermediate Types*; Dixon, 'Sexology and the Occult', pp. 413–4.
120. Johnston Diaries, 22 July 1894.
121. Johnston Diaries, 8 September 1907.

122. '"Sporty" Girls and "Artistic" Boys: Friendship, Illicit Sex and the British "Companionship" Advertisement 1913–28', *Journal of the History of Sexuality* (forthcoming, 2002).

123. A.T. Fitzroy, *Despised and Rejected* (London, 1918), p. 84.

124. Ibid., p. 350.

125. J.W. Wallace, quoted in Johnston Diaries, 22 April 1904.

Select Bibliography

1. UNPUBLISHED PRIMARY SOURCES

Indictment Files: Assizes
(All PRO Kew unless stated)
Hampshire
ASSI 25/37–45
Northern Circuit
ASSI 12/3
Midland Circuit
ASSI 12/2
Devon
ASSI 25/24–46
Lancashire
PL 26/170, 171 and 173
ASSI 51/30–32
Kent
ASSI 35/274, 276, 291–2, 302

Indictment Files: Central Criminal Court
(All PRO CRIM files unless stated)
4/2, 9, 21, 23 and 29
4/29, 31, 33, 35, 37, 39, 43, 47, 49, 51
4/55
4/110, 112, 114, 116, 118, 120, 122, 124, 126, 128
4/133, 135, 137, 142, 144, 146, 148, 150
4/163, 167, 169, 171, 173, 175, 177, 179

4/396
4/575, 576, 581

Indictment Files: Old Bailey (Corporation of London Record Office)

Index to London Indictments, 1756–92; Calendar of Indictments, 1793–1822; Indictment files SFP 106–108; 319–326; 354–366

Depositions

PRO Kew, ASSI 45/38/2/128; 45/38/1/101; 45/39/2/37; 45/40/2/176; 45/39/2/25; 36/9; 6/24

Case Papers

PRO Kew, CRIM 4/1/2/20; HO 144/159/A41311; HO 144/29/71577; HO 144/173/A43930; HO 144/30/73134; HO 144/8/21080; HO 144/20/58480; HO 144/529/A37983; HO 144/216/A41934

Proceedings (Central Criminal Court)

PRO Kew, CRIM 10/9, 14, 20, 24, 29, 31, 32
PCOM 1/73

Petitions (All PRO HO files)

Register of Criminal Petitions HO 19/5, 6, 7, 8, 9, 10, 12

Andrews	18/141/1
Avis	47/175
Baigent	19/7 Cx 43
Booth	17/95 Rv 9
Boughton	19/7 Ww 13
Bramley	18/170/13
Braznell	18/347/26
Brown	18/154/56
Brown	18/1/31
Brunsdon	18/101/24
Callaway	19/7 Hw 18
Capel	17/114 Ws 11
Carter	18/167/22
Clare	18/367/1
Claxton	19/7 Rx 32
Coldham	19/7 Zx 37
Collings	19/7 Zx 32
Cook	19/7 Cw 57
Coulson	18/335/8
Cozins	17/119 Part 2 Xs 6
Crane	18/51/42
Davies	18/104/13
Davis	18/139/15
Davison	18/182/20

Denham	18/141/32
Diamond	18/33/25
Dilkes	18/86/42
Dodd	18/171/33
Dodsworth	18/3/25
Evans	19/7 Ex14
Fain	17/100 St 6
Fielding	18/181/23
Froom	18/76/36
Garton	17/100 Part 1 St 37
Gibson	17/47 Part 2 Gt 39
Goode	19/114 Wq-Ws
Gook	17/29 Cz 24
Green	18/141/40
Guppy	18/323/51
Hall	17/100 Sw 43
Harley	19/6/Wv 25
Harris	18/107/53
Harrison	18/346/48
Hawen	18/20/45
Haydon	18/158/23
Heatley	18/119/32
Heywood	19/6 Zs 13
Hood	19/6 Tv 21
Howe	18/158/46
Inwood	17/105 Tv 27
Jones	19/6 Wv 37
Joyce	18/183/13
Keeble	19/6 Vp 26
Kelly	19/6 Ss 50
Lane	17/110 Vw 34
Litson	18/70/37
Long	17/75 Part 2 Nx 8
Lowen	18/35/49
Lowndes	18/43/33
McMahon	19/6 Np 22
Mannings	19/6 Lv 38
Menington	18/329/9
Metcalfe	18/361/16
Mill	19/6 Iv 14
Millard	18/110/8
Mills	19/6 Yp 16
Morley	18/93/43
Morse	19/6 Np 13
Nettleton	119/18/A20
Newman	18/131/43

Nicholls	17/111 Vz3
Nicholls	18/110/33
Noakes	18/175/33
Ogilvie	18/152/8
Pardington	17/126 Yx 27
Parker	18/151/25
Peace	18/184/63
Peden	18/161/22
Peveril	17/60 Kt 3
Pikesley	18/10/3
Poulson	18/3/32
Pratt	17/120 xV 13
Pritchard	17/100 Part 2 Sw 43
Reason	19/7 Nw 18
Rodgers	17/129 Part 2 zs 22
Sandaman	18/336/11
Savage	18/323/63
Senior	18/162/47
Sharp	18/89/33
Simpson	18/122/34
Smith	19/6 Ep 39
Southworth	18/343/26
St John	19/6 Ov 19
Strachan	18/134/2
Taylor	18/88/25
Turner	18/56/30
Turner	19/7 Cx 43
Varcoe	18/362/6
Wallace	17/47 Part 2 Gt 27
Webster	18/114/49
Westley	19/6 Zv 50
Williams	19/6 Vv11
Woollard	19/7 Lx 21
Wright	18/359/33

Police Reports

HO 45/7618/1–5; HO 45/6628/9; HO 45/9511/17216; MEPO 3/1; MEPO 1/48

Home Office Files

HO 44/8; HO 44/18 ; HO 44/16; HO 44/20 ; HO 45/2275; HO 47/46; HO 47/75; HO 49/7; HO 119/18; DPP 4/6; DPP 1/95/1–7

Magistrates Court Records

HO 62/5 and 6; HO 62/17 and 18; Hammersmith Police Court Registers 1878 (Greater London Record Office) PS WLN/A1/2; WLN/A1/3; WLN/A/1/4

Personal Papers

Diaries of Arthur Munby (Trinity College Cambridge)
Diaries and papers of John Johnston (Bolton Library)
Bolton Whitman Fellowship collection (Bolton Library)
Charles Sixsmith collection (John Rylands University Library Manchester, Deansgate)
J.W. Wallace collection (John Rylands University Library Manchester, Deansgate)

2. PUBLISHED PRIMARY SOURCES

Books

Acton, William, *The Functions and Disorders of the Reproductive Organs* (London, 1857)

Anon., *Satan's Harvest Home: or the Present State of Whorecraft, Adultery Fornication, Procuring, Pimping, Sodomy and the Game at Flatts...* (London, 1749)

————, *The Complete Juryman: Or, a Compendium of the Laws Relating to Jurors* (Dublin, 1774)

————, *The Trial of David Robertson... for an Unnatural Crime* (London, 1806)

————, *A Doleful Dirge on the Wicked Men Condemned to Suffer at Lincoln Gallows by the Lord Judge the Right Honourable Sir James Allen Park, at the Lincoln Assizes in March 1823* (1824) [British Library 1889.d.3, p.168]

————, *The Execution of Charles Clutton, Who was Executed on the New Drop at Northampton on Friday August 13th 1824 for Sodomy* (1824). [British Library 1889.d.3, p.196]

————, *Hints to the Public and to the Legislature on the Prevalence of Vice and on the Dangerous Effects of Seduction* (London, 1811)

————, *The Last Dying Words, Behaviour and Confession of D.J. Myers Who Was Executed at Peterborough on Monday the 4th of May, for an Unnatural Crime* (1812) [British Library 1889.d.3. p. 214]

————, *The Trial and Conviction of John Church, the Surrey Tabernacle Preacher, for an Abominable Offence; including the whole of the evidence;* (London, 1817)

————, *The Peculiar and Unprecedented Case of Thomas Skinner who lately Received his Majesty's free pardon...after being condemned to death for the crime of Bestiality* (London, 1821)

————, *The English Gentleman: His Principles, His Feelings, His Manners, His Pursuits* (London, 1849)

————, *Men in Petticoats* (London, 1870)

————, *The Lives of Boulton and Park: Extraordinary Revelations* (London, 1870)

Ashbee, Henry Spencer, *Bibliography of Prohibited Books (Index Librorum Prohibitorum: Bio-Biblio-Icono-graphical and Critical Notes on Curious Uncommon and Erotic Books, by Pisanus Fraxi)* (repr. New York, 1962)

Ballantine, William, *Some Experiences of a Barrister's Life* (London, 1883)

Bentham, Jeremy, *The Elements of the Art of Packing, As Applied to Special Juries, Particularly in cases of Libel Law* (London, 1821)

Blackstone, William, *Commentaries on the Laws of England, by William Blackstone Solicitor-General to Her Majesty*, 4 vols (Oxford, 1769)

Bucke, R.M., *Cosmic Consciousness: A Study in the Evolution of the Human Mind* (2nd edition, New York, 1901)

Burke, P., *The Criminal Law and its Sentences, in Treasons, Felonies and Misdemeanours* (London, 1842)

Byron [pseud.], *Don Leon: A Poem by the Late Lord Byron... And Forming Part of the Private Journal of his Lordship* (London, 1866)

Caminada, Jerome, *Twenty-Five Years of Detective Life By Jerome Caminada, Chief Inspector of the Manchester Police with Illustrations of Some Noted Places and Faces* (Manchester, 1895)

Carpenter, Edward, *Homogenic Love and its Place in a Free Society* (Manchester, 1894)

————, *Sex Love and its Place in a Free Society* (Manchester, 1894)

————, *Iolaus: An Anthology of Friendship* (Manchester, 1902)

————, *The Intermediate Sex: A Study of Some Transitional Types of Men and Women* (London, 1908)

————, *My Days and Dreams, Being Autobiographical Notes* (London, 1916)

————, *Intermediate Types Among Primitive Folk: A Study in Evolution* (London, 1914)

Clegg, James, *Annals of Bolton: History, Chronology, Politics* (Bolton, 1888)

Coke, Sir Edward, *The Institutes of the Laws of England*, 3 vols (London, 1642)

Colquhoun, Patrick, *A Treatise on the Police of the Metropolis* (London, 1795)

Commons, House of, *Report from the Select Committee on the State of the Nightly Watch and Police in the Metropolis*, 1812, PP (127) II. 95

————, *Second Report from the Select Committee on the State of the Police of the Metropolis*, 1816, PP, 1817 (484) VII.321

————, *Report from the Select Committee on the Criminal Laws July 1819, Appointed to Consider so Much of the Criminal Laws as Relates to Capital Punishments in Felonies...* 1819 PP (585) VIII.1

————, *Report From the Select Committee on Existing Laws Relating to Vagrants*, 1821 PP 1821 (543) IV. 121

————, *Report from the Select Committee on the Cause of the Increase in the Number of Commitments and Convictions in London and Middlesex and the State of the Police*, 1828 PP (533) VI. 1

————, *Report on the Police of the Metropolis and the State of Crime*, 1834 PP (600) XVI.1

————, *Report From the Select Committee on Public Prosecutors*, 1855, PP 1854–55 (481) XII.1

————, *Report of the Select Committee on the Law and Practice Relating to the Summoning, Attendance and Remuneration of Special and Common Juries*, 1867, PP 1867 (425) IX.597

————, *Report From the Select Committee of the House of Lords Appointed to Consider the Law of Defamation and Libel*, PP 1843 (513) V.259

Cox, Edward W., *Reports of Cases of Criminal Law Argued and Determined in All the Courts in England and Ireland*, 31 vols (London, 1843–1940)

Davitt, Michael, *Leaves From a Prison Diary, Or Lectures to a 'Solitary' Audience* (London, 1885)

Ellis, Henry Havelock, *Studies in the Psychology of Sex*, 3 vols (1897, New York, 1936)

Fenner, Ball, *Raising the Veil, or Scenes in the Courts... Embellished with Portraits of Police, Court Officers etc.* (London, 1856)

Fitzgerald, Percy, *Chronicles of Bow Street Police Office With an Account of the Magistrates, 'Runners' and Police and A Selection of the Most Interesting Cases* (London, 1888)

Fitzroy, A. T., *Despised and Rejected* (London, 1918)

Frost, John, *The Horrors of Convict Life* (1856, repr. Hobart, 1973)

Grabbett, J., *A Treatise on the Criminal Law* (Dublin, 1843)

Greenwood, James, *The Seven Curses of London* (London, 1869)

Hale, Matthew, *Pleas of the Crown, A Methodical Summary* (London, 1678)

———, *Historia Placitorum Coronae· The History of the Pleas of the Crown* (London, 1736)

Hawkins, William, *A Treatise of the Pleas of the Crown* (London, 1716)

Hodder, George, *Sketches of Life and Character, Taken at the Police Court, Bow Street, etc.* (London, 1845)

Holloway, Robert, *The Vere Street Coterie or the Phoenix of Sodom* (London, 1813)

Humphreys, W. C., *Observations on the Inutility of Grand Juries, and Suggestions for their Abolition* (London, 1842)

Hunt, Henry, *Memoirs of Henry Hunt Esq, Written by Himself*, 3 vols (1820–22, repr. London, 1967)

Jackson, Valentine, *Remarkable Trials at the Lancashire Assizes, Held August 1806 At Lancaster Before Sir Robert Graham, Knight* (London, 1806)

Laurie, Peter, *An Enquiry into the Use and Abuse of Grand Juries* (London, 1832)

Law Journal, *The Law Journal Reports for the Year 1861... New Series* (London, 1865)

Magistrate, A, *Metropolitan Police Court Jottings, by a Magistrate* (London, 1882)

O'Brien, William, *Evening Memories: Being a Continuation of Recollections by the same Author* (Dublin, 1920)

Peake, Thomas, *A Compendium of the Law of Evidence* (London, 1822)

Pickering, William, *On the Principles of Criminal Law* (London, 1846)

Poe, Edgar Allan, *Selected Tales* (London, 1994)

Reynolds, G.W.M., *The Mysteries of London*, 6 vols (London, 1846–9)

Rivers, W.C., *Walt Whitman's Anomaly* (London, 1913)

Russell, William Oldnall, and Ryan, Edward, *Crown Cases Reserved for Consideration... 1799–1824* (London, 1825)

Ryan, Michael, *Prostitution in London* (London, 1839)

Sala, George Augustus, *Gaslight and Daylight with Some London Scenes they Shine Upon* (London, 1859)

———, *Looking at Life; or Thoughts and Things* (London, 1860)

Smythe Palmer, Abraham, *The Perfect Gentleman: His Character Delineated In a Series of Extracts from Writers Ancient and Modern Selected by Rev A. Smythe Palmer* (London, 1892)

————, *The Ideal of a Gentleman, or a Mirror for Gentlefolk* (London, 1908)

Stephen, James Fitzjames, *A Digest of the Criminal Law (Indictable Offences)* (London, 1877)

Swaine Taylor, Alfred, *Medical Jurisprudence* (London, 1861)

Symonds, John Addington, *A Problem in Greek Ethics* (London, 1883)

————, *A problem in modern ethics: being an inquiry into the phenomenon of sexual inversion addressed especially to medical psychologists and jurists* (London, 1891)

————, *Walt Whitman: A Study* (London, 1893)

Taylor, Herbert, *The Statesman* (Cambridge, 1836)

Wallace, J. W. and Johnston, J. *Visits to Walt Whitman* (London, 1917)

Walter, *My Secret Life*, 11 vols (Amsterdam, 1889)

Wight, John, *Mornings at Bow Street* (London, 1838)

Woolrych, Humphrey W., *The History and Present Results of the Present Capital Punishments in England to which are added full tables of Convictions, Executions etc.* (London, 1832)

————, *A Practical Treatise on Misdemeanours* (London, 1842)

Articles

Browne, W.R., 'The English Gentleman', *National Review* (April 1886), pp. 261–271

Dickens, Charles, 'A Detective Police Party', *Household Words*, I (27 July 1850), pp. 409–414

Carpenter, Edward, 'On the Connexion Between Homosexuality and Divination, and the Importance of the Intermediate Sexes Generally in Early Civilisations', *Revue D'Ethnographie et de Sociologie* (1911)

Pitt-Taylor, James, 'Defects of Criminal Procedure', *Law Magazine*, 34/64 (1844), pp. 244–247

Sala, George Augustus, 'The Key to the Street', *Household Words*, 17 (6 September 1851), pp. 553–576

Newspapers

Age
Bristol Gazette and Public Advertiser
Buckinghamshire County Chronicle
Cowdroy's Manchester Gazette
Crim. Con. Gazette
Daily News
Glasgow Evening News and Star
Glasgow Weekly Mail
Illustrated Police News
Illustrated Times
John Bull

Labour Prophet
Lloyd's Weekly London Newspaper
Manchester and Salford Advertiser
Manchester Evening News
Morning Chronicle
North London Press
Pall Mall Gazette
Paul Pry
Referee
Reynolds' Weekly Newspaper
Salisbury and Winchester Journal
Satirist
St. James's Gazette
St. Stephen's Review
Star
The Times
Truth
United Ireland
Weekly Budget
Weekly Dispatch
Western Luminary and Family Newspaper
Western Times
Wheeler's Manchester Chronicle

2. SECONDARY SOURCES

Books

Abelove, Henry, Halperin, David, and Barale, Michele Aina (eds), *The Gay and Lesbian Studies Reader* (New York, 1993)

Ackroyd, Peter, *Dressing Up: Transvestism and Drag, The History of an Obsession* (London, 1979)

Adams, James Eli, *Dandies and Desert Saints: Styles of Victorian Manhood* (Ithaca, 1995)

Arendt, Hannah (ed.), *Illuminations* (London, 1992)

Aronson, Theo, *Prince Eddy and the Homosexual Underworld* (London, 1995)

Ascoli, David, *The Origins and Development of the Metropolitan Police 1829–1879* (London, 1979)

Auerbach, Nina, *Private Theatricals: The Lives of the Victorians* (Cambridge, MA, 1990)

Bailey, Victor (ed.), *Policing and Punishment in Nineteenth Century Britain* (London, 1981)

Bartlett, Neil, *Who Was That Man? A Present for Mr. Oscar Wilde* (London, 1987).

Beattie, J. M., *Crime and the Courts in England 1660–1800* (Oxford, 1986)

Belchem, John, *Orator Hunt: Henry Hunt and English Working Class Radicalism* (Oxford, 1985)

Biagini, Eugenio, *Liberty, Retrenchment and Reform: Popular Liberalism in the Age of Gladstone, 1860–1880* (Cambridge, 1992)

————, *Citizenship and Community: Liberals, Radicals and Collective Identities in the British Isles, 1865–1931* (Cambridge, 1996)

Bland, Lucy, *Banishing the Beast: English Feminism and Sexual Morality 1885–1914* (London, 1995)

Boyce, George, Curran, James, and Wingate, Pauline, *Newspaper History from the Seventeenth Century to the Present Day* (London, 1978)

Boyd White, James, *Heracles' Bow: Essays on the Rhetoric and Poetics of the Law* (Madison, 1985)

Boyle, Thomas, *Black Swine in the Sewers of Hampstead: Beneath the Surface of Victorian Sensationalism* (New York, 1989)

Bradley, Ian, *The Call to Seriousness: The Evangelical Impact on the Victorians* (London, 1976)

Brake, Laurel, *Subjugated Knowledges: Journalism, Gender and Literature in the Nineteenth Century* (London, 1994)

Brake, Laurel, Jones, Aled, and Madden, Lionel, *Investigating Victorian Journalism* (London, 1990)

Brand, Dana, *The Spectator and the City in Nineteenth Century American Literature* (Cambridge, 1991)

Bratton, J. (ed.), *Music Hall: Performance and Style* (Milton Keynes, 1986)

Bray, Alan, *Homosexuality in Renaissance England* (London, 1982)

Bristow, Edward J., *Vice and Vigilance: Purity Movements in Britain Since 1700* (Dublin, 1977)

Brown, F. K., *Fathers of the Victorians: The Age of Wilberforce* (Cambridge, 1961)

Brown, Lucy, *Victorian News and Newspapers* (Cambridge, 1985)

Bullough, Vern, and Bullough, Bonnie, *Cross Dressing, Sex and Gender* (Philadelphia, 1993)

Burchell, Graham, Gordon, Colin, and Miller, Paul, *The Foucault Effect: Studies in Governmentality* (Hemel Hempstead, 1991)

Butler, Judith, *Gender Trouble: Feminism and The Subversion of Identity* (London, 1990)

————, *Bodies That Matter: On the Discursive Limits of 'Sex'* (New York, 1993)

Castle, Terry, *Masquerade and Civilization: The Carnivalesque in Eighteenth-Century English Culture and Fiction* (London, 1986)

————, *The Apparitional Lesbian: Female Homosexuality and Modern Culture* (New York, 1993)

Charvet, Patrick E., *Baudelaire: Selected Writings on Art and Artists* (Harmondsworth, 1972)

Chauncey, George, Duberman, Martin, and Vicinus, Martha (eds), *Hidden From History: Reclaiming the Gay and Lesbian Past* (London, 1991)

Chauncey, George, *Gay New York: The Making of the Gay Male World 1890–1940* (London, 1995)

Cecil Turner, J. W. (ed.), *Russell on Crime* (London, 1986)

Chester, Lewis, Leitch, David, and Simpson, Colin, *The Cleveland Street Affair* (Boston, 1976)

Clark, Anna, *Women's Silence, Men's Violence: Sexual Assault in England, 1770–1845* (London, 1987)

————, *The Struggle for the Breeches: Gender and the Making of the British Working Class* (New Haven, 1995)

Cocks, Raymond, *The Foundations of the Modern Bar* (London, 1983)

Cohen, Ed, *Talk on the Wilde Side: Towards a Genealogy of a Discourse on Male Sexualities* (New York, 1993)

Collini, Stefan, *Public Moralists: Political Thought and Intellectual Life in Britain 1850–1930* (Oxford, 1991)

Conley, Carolyn A., *The Unwritten Law: Criminal Justice in Victorian Kent* (Oxford, 1991)

Critchley, T. A., *A History of the Police in England and Wales* (London, 1978)

Crompton, Louis, *Byron and Greek Love: Homophobia in Georgian England* (London, 1985)

Crossick, Geoffrey, *An Artisan Elite in Victorian Society* (London, 1978)

Curtin, Michael, *Propriety and Position: A Study of Victorian Manners* (New York, 1987)

Curtis, L. P., *Coercion and Conciliation in Ireland 1880–1892* (Princeton, 1963)

Cytowic, Richard, *The Man Who Tasted Shapes* (New York, 1993)

Darnton, Robert, *The Forbidden Best-Sellers of Pre-Revolutionary France* (New York, 1995)

————, *The Kiss of Lamourette: Reflections in Cultural History* (London, 1990)

Davenport-Hines, Richard, *Sex, Death and Punishment: Attitudes to Sex and Sexuality in Britain Since the Renaissance* (London, 1990)

Davis, Tracy, *Actresses as Working Women: Their Social Identity in Victorian Culture* (New York, 1991)

Dellamora, Richard (ed.), *Victorian Sexual Dissidence* (Chicago, 1999)

————, *Masculine Desire: The Sexual Politics of Victorian Aestheticism* (Chapel Hill, 1990)

Digest, *The Digest: Annotated British, Commonwealth and European Cases*, 51 vols (London, 1993)

Dollimore, Jonathan, *Sexual Dissidence: Augustine to Wilde, Freud to Foucault* (Oxford, 1991)

Dowling, Linda, *Hellenism and Homosexuality in Victorian Oxford* (Ithaca, 1994)

Dyos, H.J., Cannadine, David, and Reeder David (eds), *Exploring the Urban Past: Essays in Urban History by H.J. Dyos* (Cambridge, 1982)

Dyos, H.J., and Wolff, Michael, *The Victorian City: Images and Realities* (London, 1973)

Ekins, Richard, and King, Dave (eds), *Blending Genders: Social Aspects of Cross Dressing and Sex Changing* (New York, 1996)

Elfenbein, Andrew, *Romantic Genius: The Prehistory of A Homosexual Role* (New York, 1999)

Ellman, Richard, *Oscar Wilde* (London, 1987)

Emsley, Clive, *Policing and Its Context* (London, 1983)

————, *The English Police: A Political and Social History* (London, 1991)

Epstein Nord, Deborah, *Walking the Victorian Streets: Women, Representation and the City* (Ithaca, 1995)

Faderman, Lillian, *Surpassing the Love of Men: Romantic Friendship and Love between Women from the Renaissance to the Present* (London, 1985)

————, *Scotch Verdict: Miss Pirie and Miss Woods v. Dame Cumming Gordon* (New York, 1993)

Farrer, Peter, *Borrowed Plumes: A Selection of Letters From Edwardian Newspapers* (Garston, 1978)

————, *In Female Disguise: An Anthology of English and American Short Stories and Literary Passages* (Garston, 1992)

Feldman, David and Steadman Jones, Gareth, *Metropolis London: Histories and Representations Since 1800* (London, 1989)

Foldy, Michael S., *Oscar Wilde: Deviance, Morality and Late Victorian Society* (New Haven, 1997)

Forster, E.M., *Maurice* (London, 1971)

Foucault, Michel, *Discipline and Punish: The Birth of the Prison* (London, 1978)

————, *The History of Sexuality*, 3 vols (London, 1979–86)

Freedman, Estelle, et al (eds), *The Lesbian Issue: Essays From Signs* (Chicago, 1985)

Fuss, Diana (ed.), *Essentially Speaking* (New York, 1992)

————, *Inside Out: Lesbian Theories, Gay Theories* (New York, 1991)

Gagnier, Regenia, *Idylls of the Marketplace: Oscar Wilde and the Victorian Public* (Aldershot, 1986)

Gallagher, Catherine, and Laqueur, Thomas, *The Making of the Modern Body: Sexuality and Society in the Nineteenth Century* (Berkeley, 1987)

Garber, Marjorie, *Vested Interests: Cross Dressing and Cultural Anxiety* (London, 1992)

Gatrell, V. A. C., Lenman, Bruce, and Parker, Geoffrey (eds), *Crime and the Law: The Social History of Crime in Western Europe since 1500* (London, 1980)

Gatrell, V. A. C., *The Hanging Tree: Execution and the English People 1770–1868* (Oxford, 1994)

Gilmour, Robin, *The Idea of the Gentleman in the Victorian Novel* (London, 1981)

Goldberg, Jonathan, *Sodometries. Renaissance Texts, Modern Sexualities* (New York, 1992)

———— (ed.), *Reclaiming Sodom* (New York, 1993)

Goodich, M., *The Unmentionable Vice: Homosexuality in the Later Medieval Period* (Santa Barbara, 1979)

Goulemot, Jean-Marie, *Forbidden Texts: Erotic Literature and Its Readers in Eighteenth Century France* (Cambridge, 1995)

Green, Thomas A., *Verdict According to Conscience: Perspectives on the English Criminal Trial Jury 1200–1800* (Chicago, 1985)

Greenberg, David, *The Construction of Homosexuality* (Chicago, 1988)

Grosskurth, Phyllis, *John Addington Symonds: A Biography* (London, 1964)

———— (ed.), *The Memoirs of John Addington Symonds* (New York, 1984)

Gunn, Simon, *The Public Culture of the Victorian Middle Class* (Manchester, 2000)

Haley, Bruce, *The Healthy Body and Victorian Culture* (Cambridge, MA, 1978)

Hallam, Paul, *The Book of Sodom* (London, 1993)

Halperin, David, *One Hundred Years of Homosexuality* (New York, 1990)

Hay, Douglas, and Snyder, Francis (eds), *Policing and Prosecution in Britain 1750–1850* (Oxford, 1989)

Hepworth, Mike, *Blackmail: Publicity and Secrecy in Everyday Life* (London, 1975)

Herdt, Gilbert (ed.), *Third Sex, Third Gender: Beyond Sexual Dimorphism in Culture and History* (New York, 1994)

Hudson, Derek, *Munby: Man of Two Worlds. The Life and Diaries of Arthur J. Munby 1828–1910* (Cambridge, 1972)

Humphreys, Anne, *Travels into the Poor Man's Country* (Athens, 1977)

Hunt, Lynn (ed.), *The Invention of Pornography: Obscenity and the Origins of Modernity, 1500–1800* (New York, 1996)

Jones, Aled, *Powers of the Press: Newspapers, Power and the Public in Nineteenth Century England* (Aldershot, 1996)

Joyce, Patrick, *Democratic Subjects: The Self and the Social in Nineteenth Century England* (Cambridge, 1994)

Kee, Robert, *The Laurel and the Ivy: The Story of Charles Stuart Parnell and Irish Nationalism* (London, 1993)

Kendrick, Walter, *The Secret Museum: Pornography in Modern Culture* (New York, 1987)

Kingsley Kent, Susan, *Sex and Suffrage in Britain 1860–1914* (London, 1990)

Kosofsky Sedgwick, Eve, *Between Men: English Literature and Male Homosocial Desire* (New York, 1985)

————, *Epistemology of the Closet* (London, 1991)

Kucich, John, *The Power of Lies: Transgression in Victorian Fiction* (Ithaca, 1994)

Lane, Christopher, *The Burdens of Intimacy: Psychoanalysis and Victorian Masculinity* (Chicago, 1999)

Laqueur, Thomas, *Making Sex, from the Greeks to Freud* (Cambridge, MA, 1990)

Lee, Alan J., *The Origins of the Popular Press in England 1855–1914* (London, 1976)

Letwin, Shirley R., *The Gentleman in Trollope: Individuality and Moral Conduct* (London, 1982)

Loving, Jerome, *Walt Whitman: The Song of Himself* (Berkeley, 1999)

Lyons, F.S., *Parnell* (London, 1977)

Mangan, J.A., and Walvin, James (eds), *Manliness and Morality: Middle Class Masculinity in Britain and America, 1800–1940* (Manchester, 1987)

Martin, Robert K., *The Homosexual Tradition in American Poetry* (Austin, 1979)

Mason, Michael, *The Making of Victorian Sexual Attitudes* (Oxford, 1994)

————, *The Making of Victorian Sexuality* (Oxford, 1994)

Mason, Paul, *The English Gentleman: The Rise and Fall of an Ideal* (London, 1993)

Maxwell, Richard C., *The Mysteries of Paris and London* (Charlottesville, 1992)

McCalman, Iain, *Radical Underworld: Prophets, Revolutionaries and Pornographers in London 1795–1840* (Cambridge, 1988)

McCormick, Ian, *Secret Sexualities: A Sourcebook of 17th and 18th Century Writing* (London, 1997)

Mclaren, Angus, *The Trials of Masculinity: Policing Sexual Boundaries 1870–1930* (Chicago, 1997)

Mcnay, Lois, *Foucault: A Critical Introduction* (Oxford, 1994)

Miller, Andrew, and Adams, James Eli, *Sexualities in Victorian Britain* (Bloomington, 1996)

Miller, D. A., *The Novel and the Police* (Berkeley, 1988)

Moers, Elen, *The Dandy, Brummell to Beerbohm* (New York, 1960)

Montgomery Hyde, H., *Famous Trials: Oscar Wilde* (London, 1948)

————, *The Other Love: An Historical and Contemporary Survey of Homosexuality in Britain* (London, 1970)

————, *The Cleveland Street Scandal* (London, 1976)

Moran, Leslie J., *The Homosexual(ity) of Law* (London, 1996)

Morris, R.J. (ed.), *Class, Power and Social Structure in Nineteenth Century Towns* (Leicester, 1986)

————, *Class, Sect and Party: The Making of the British Middle Class, Leeds, 1820–1850* (Manchester, 1990)

Mort, Frank, *Dangerous Sexualities: Medico-Moral Politics in England Since 1830* (London, 1987)

Murphy, Francis (ed.), *Walt Whitman, The Complete Poems* (London, 1996)

Nead, Lynda, *Myths of Sexuality: Representations of Women in Victorian Britain* (Oxford, 1988)

————, *Victorian Babylon: People, Streets and Images in Nineteenth Century London* (New Haven, 2000)

Norton, Rictor, *Mother Clap's Molly House: The Gay Subculture in England 1700–1830* (London, 1992)

————, *The Myth of the Modern Homosexual: Queer History and the Search for Cultural Unity* (London, 1997)

O'Day, Alan, *The English Face of Irish Nationalism: Parnellite Involvement in British Politics 1880–1886* (Dublin, 1977)

Olsen, Donald J., *The Growth of Victorian London* (London, 1976)

Pearson, Hesketh, *Labby: The Life and Character of Henry Labouchere* (London, 1936)

Pellew, Jill, *The Home Office 1848–1914: From Clerks to Bureaucrats* (London, 1982)

Petrow, Stefan, *Policing Morals: The Metropolitan Police and the Home Office 1870–1914* (Oxford, 1994)

Plummer, Ken (ed.), *The Making of the Modern Homosexual* (London, 1981)

———— (ed.), *Modern Homosexualities: Fragments of Lesbian and Gay Experience* (London, 1992)

Radzinowicz, Sir Leon, and Hood, Robert, *A History of English Criminal Law and its Administration from 1750*, 3 vols (London, 1956)

Roughead, William, *Bad Companions* (New York, 1931)

Rowbotham, Sheila and Weeks, Jeffrey, *Socialism and the New Life: The Personal and Sexual Politics of Edward Carpenter and Havelock Ellis* (London, 1977)

Sainty, J. V., *Home Office Officials 1782–1870* (London, 1975)

Schmidgall, Gary, *Walt Whitman: A Gay Life* (New York, 1997)

Schueller, Herbert M., and Peters, Robert C. (eds), *The Letters of John Addington Symonds*, 3 vols (Detroit, 1969)

Senelick, Laurence, *Gender in Performance: The Presentation of Difference in the Performing Arts* (Hanover, 1992)

Sennett, Richard, *The Fall of Public Man* (Cambridge, 1974)

Shattock, Joanne, and Wolff, Michael (eds), *The Victorian Periodical Press: Samplings and Soundings* (Leicester, 1982)

Shortt, S. E. D., *Victorian Lunacy: Richard M. Bucke and the Practice of Late Nineteenth-Century Psychiatry* (Cambridge, 1986)

Showalter, Elaine, *Sexual Anarchy: Gender and Culture at the Fin de Siecle* (London, 1992)

Shults, R. L., *Crusader in Babylon: W. T. Stead and the Pall Mall Gazette* (Lincoln, 1972)

Sinfield, Alan, *Cultural Politics: Queer Reading* (London, 1994)

————, *Faultlines: Cultural Materialism and the Politics of Dissident Reading* (Berkeley, 1992)

————, *Out on Stage: Lesbian and Gay Theatre in the Twentieth Century* (London, 1999)

————, *The Wilde Century: Effeminacy Oscar Wilde and the Queer Moment* (New York, 1994)

Sparrow, John (ed.), *Leaves From a Victorian Diary, by Edward Leeves* (London, 1985)

Stallybrass, Peter, and White, Allon, *The Politics and Poetics of Transgression* (Ithaca, 1986)

Stanley, Liz (ed.), *The Diaries of Hannah Cullwick, Victorian Maidservant* (London, 1984)

Steadman Jones, Gareth, *Outcast London: A Study in the Relationship Between Classes in Victorian Society* (Oxford, 1971)

Tester, Keith, *The Flâneur* (London, 1994)

Thomas, Donald, *A Long Time Burning: The History of Literary Censorship in England* (London, 1969)

Thomas, Trefor (ed.), *Reynolds' Mysteries of London* (Keele, 1996)

Thorold, A.L., *The Life of Henry Labouchere* (London, 1913)

Trodd, Anthea, *Domestic Crime in the Victorian Novel* (London, 1989)

Trumbach, Randolph, *The Rise of the Egalitarian Family: Aristocratic Kinship and Domestic Relations in Eighteenth Century England* (New York, 1978)

————, *Sodomy Trials, Seven Documents* (New York, 1986)

Tsuzuki, Chushichi, *Edward Carpenter, 1844–1929: Prophet of Human Fellowship* (Cambridge, 1980)

Vernon, James (ed.), *Re-reading the Constitution: New Narratives in the Political History of England's Long Nineteenth Century* (Cambridge, 1996)

Waldron, J., *Maamtrasna: The Murders and the Mystery* (Dublin, 1992)

Walkowitz, Judith R., *City of Dreadful Delight: Narratives of Sexual Danger in Late Victorian London* (London, 1994)

————, *Prostitution and Victorian Society: Women, Class and the State* (Cambridge, 1980)

Warner, Michael (ed.), *Fear of a Queer Planet: Queer Politics and Social Theory* (Minneapolis, 1993)

Warwick-Haller, Sally, *William O'Brien and the Irish Land War* (Dublin, 1990)

Weeks, Jeffrey, *Coming Out, Homosexual Politics from the Nineteenth Century to the Present* (London, 1977)

————, *Sex, Politics and Society: The Regulation of Sexuality in Britain Since 1800* (London, 1981)

Weeks, Jeffrey, Altman, Denis, Vance, Carol, and Vicinus, Martha (eds), *Homosexuality, Which Homosexuality? Conference Papers from the International Scientific Conference on Lesbian and Gay Studies, Free University of Amsterdam, December 1987* (London, 1989)

Welsh, Alexander, *George Eliot and Blackmail* (Cambridge, MA, 1985)

Wheelwright, Julie, *Amazons and Military Maids: Women Who Dressed as Men in the Pursuit of Life, Liberty and Happiness* (London, 1989)

Whitbread, Helena, *I Know my Own Heart: The Diaries of Anne Lister* (London, 1988)

————, *No Priest But Love: Excerpts from the Diaries of Anne Lister 1824–1826* (Otley, 1992)

Chris White (ed.), *Nineteenth Century Writings on Homosexuality: A Sourcebook* (London, 1999)

Wiener, Joel (ed.), *Innovators and Preachers: The Role of the Editor in Victorian England* (London, 1985)

————, *Papers for the Millions: The New Journalism in Britain, 1850–1914* (New York, 1988)

Wiener, Martin, *Reconstructing the Criminal: Culture, Law and Policy in England 1830–1914* (Cambridge, 1994)

Articles

Aston, Elaine, 'Male Impersonation in the Music Hall: The Case of Vesta Tilley', *New Theatre Quarterly* 4 (August 1988), pp. 247–257

Bailey, Peter, '"Will the Real Bill Banks Please Stand Up?" Towards a Role Analysis of mid-Victorian Working Class Respectability', *Journal of Social History* 12 (1979), pp. 336–353

————, 'Champagne Charlie: Performance and Ideology in the Music Hall Song', in J.S. Bratton (ed.), *Music Hall: Performance and Style* (Milton Keynes, 1986), pp. 49–69

————, 'Conspiracies of Meaning: Music Hall and the Knowingness of Popular Culture', *Past and Present* 144 (August 1994), pp. 138–170

Baylen, J.O., 'Politics and the "New Journalism": Lord Esher's Use of the *Pall Mall Gazette*', *Victorian Periodicals Review* 20, 4 (1987), pp. 126–141

Beattie, J.M., 'Scales of Justice: Defence Counsel and the English Criminal Trial in the 18th and 19th Century', *Law and History Review* 9, 2 (1991), pp. 221–267

Benjamin, Walter, 'On Some Motifs in Baudelaire', in Hannah Arendt (ed.), *Illuminations* (London, 1992), pp. 152–196

Berridge, Virginia, 'Popular Sundays and mid-Victorian Society', in George Boyce, James Curran and Pauline Wingate (eds), *Newspaper History from the 17th Century to the Present Day* (London, 1978), pp. 247–64

Bevir, Mark, 'British Socialism and American Romanticism', *English Historical Review* 110, 438 (1995), pp. 878–901

————, 'The Labour Church Movement, 1891–1902', *Journal of British Studies* 38 (April 1999), pp. 217–245

Binhammer, Katharine, 'The Sex Panic of the 1790s', *Journal of the History of Sexuality* 6, 3 (1996), pp. 409–435

Boswell, John, 'Revolutions, Universals and Sexual Categories', in George Chauncey, Martin Duberman and Martha Vicinus (eds), *Hidden From History: Reclaiming the Gay and Lesbian Past* (London, 1991), pp. 17–37

Brake, Laurel, 'Gendered Space and the British Press', in Michael Harris, and Tom O'Malley (eds), *Studies in Newspaper and Periodical History 1995 Annual* (London, 1997), pp. 99–110

Brantlinger, Patrick, 'What is Sensational about the 'Sensation' Novel?', *Nineteenth Century Fiction* 37 (1982), pp. 1–28

Brown, Lucy, 'The Treatment of News in mid-Victorian Newspapers', *Transactions of the Royal Historical Society* xxvii (1977), pp. 23–41

Burck-Morss, Susan, 'Benjamin's Passagen-Werk', *New German Critique*, 29 (1983), pp. 211–240

————, 'The *Flâneur*, the Sandwichman and the Whore: The Politics of Loitering', *New German Critique* 39 (1986), pp. 99–139

Burney, Ian, 'Making Room at the Public Bar: Coroners' Inquests, Medical Knowledge and the Politics of the Constitution in Early Nineteenth Century England', in James Vernon (ed.), *Re-reading the Constitution: New Narratives in the Political History of England's Long Nineteenth Century* (Oxford, 1996), pp. 123–53

Butler, Judith, 'Critically Queer', *GLQ: A Journal of Lesbian and Gay Studies* 1, 1 (1994), pp. 17–32

Castle, Terry, 'The Culture of Travesty: Sexuality and Masquerade in Eighteenth Century England', in G.S. Rousseau and Roy Porter (eds), *Sexual Underworlds of the Enlightenment* (Manchester, 1987), pp. 156–180

Chauncey, George, 'From Sexual Inversion to Homosexuality: Medicine and the Changing Conceptualisation of Female Deviance', *Salmagundi* (Fall 1982–Winter 1983), pp. 114–146

Childers, Joseph W., 'Observation and Representation: Mr Chadwick Writes the Poor', *Victorian Studies* 37, 3 (Spring 1994), pp. 405–432

Cohen, Ed, 'Legislating the Norm: From Sodomy to Gross Indecency', *South Atlantic Quarterly* 88, 1 (Winter 1989), pp. 181–218

Collini, Stefan, 'The Idea of Character in Victorian Political Thought', *Transactions of the Royal Historical Society* xxxv (1985), pp. 29–55

Conley, Carolyn A., 'Rape and Justice in Victorian England', *Victorian Studies* 29, 4 (Summer 1986), pp. 519–536

Cordery, Simon, 'Friendly Societies and the Discourse of Respectability in Britain 1825–1875', *Journal of British Studies* 34 (January 1995), pp. 35–58

Corfield, Penelope, 'Walking the City Streets: The Urban Odyssey in Eighteenth Century England', *Journal of Urban History* 16, 2 (February 1990), pp. 132–174

Cott, Nancy, 'Passionlessness: An Interpretation of Victorian Sexual Ideology, 1790–1850', *Signs* 4 (1978), pp. 219–236

Crompton, Louis, 'Gay Studies: From the French Revolution to Oscar Wilde', *Nineteenth Century Contexts* 11, 1 (1987), pp. 23–32

Crossick, Geoffrey, 'From Gentlemen to the Residuum: Languages of Social Description in Victorian Britain', in P.J. Corfield (ed.), *Language, History and Class* (Oxford, 1991), pp. 150–178

Curtis, T. C., and Speck, W. A., 'The Societies for the Reformation of Manners: A Case Study in the Theory and Practice of Moral Reform', *Literature and History* 3 (March 1976), pp. 45–64

Darnton, Robert, 'First Steps Towards a History of Reading', in Robert Darnton (ed.), *The Kiss of Lamourette: Reflections in Cultural History* (London, 1990), pp. 154–190

Davidoff, Leonore, 'Class and Gender in Victorian England: The Diaries of Arthur J. Munby and Hannah Cullwick', *Feminist Studies* 5 (1979), pp. 87–141

Davis, Jennifer, 'The London Garotting Panic of 1862. A Moral Panic and the Creation of a Criminal Class in Mid-Victorian England', in V.A.C. Gatrell, Bruce Lenman and Geoffrey Parker (eds), *Crime and the Law: The Social History of Crime in Western Europe since 1500* (London, 1980), pp. 190–213

——————, 'A Poor Man's System of Justice: The London Police Courts in the Second Half of the Nineteenth Century', *Historical Journal* 27 (1984), pp. 309–335

——————, 'Prosecutions and Their Context: The Use of the Criminal Law in Later Nineteenth Century London', in Douglas Hay, and Francis Snyder (eds), *Policing and Prosecution in England 1750–1850* (Oxford, 1989), pp. 397–426

Davis, Susanne, 'Sexuality, Performance and Spectatorship in Law: The Case of Gordon Lawrence, Melbourne 1888', *Journal of the History of Sexuality* 7, 3 (1997), pp. 389–409

Davis, Tracy C., 'Actresses and Prostitutes in Victorian London', *Theatre Research International* 13 (Autumn 1988), pp. 221–234

De Lauretis, Teresa, 'Queer Theory: Lesbian and Gay Sexualities', *Differences* 2 (1991)

Dixon, Joy, 'Sexology and the Occult: Sexuality and Subjectivity in Theosophy's New Age', *Journal of the History of Sexuality* 7, 3 (1997), pp. 409–433

Duggan, Lisa, 'The Trials of Alice Mitchell: Sensationalism, Sexology and the Lesbian Subject in Turn-of-the-Century America', *Signs* 18, 41 (1993), pp. 791–814

Dyos, H.J., 'The Objects of Street Improvement in Regency and Early Victorian London', in David Cannadine, H.J. Dyos and David Reeder (eds), *Exploring the Urban Past: Essays in Urban History by H.J. Dyos* (Cambridge, 1982), pp. 81–86

Fisher, Trevor, 'Britain's Unpermissive Society 1880–1900', *History Today* 42 (August 1992), pp. 38–44

————, 'Permissiveness and the Politics of Morality', *Contemporary Record* 7, 1 (1993), pp. 149–165

Foucault, Michel, *The History of Sexuality*, 3 vols, trans. Robert Hurley (London, 1979–84)

————, 'Space, Knowledge and Power', in Paul Rabinow (ed.), *The Foucault Reader* (London, 1991), pp. 239–56

————, 'The Eye of Power', in C. Gordon (ed.), *Power/Knowledge: Selected Interviews and Other Writings 1972–1977* (London, 1980), pp. 146–165

————, 'Power and Strategies', in C. Gordon (ed.), *Power/Knowledge: Selected Interviews and Other Writings 1972–1977* (London, 1980), pp. 134–145

————, 'Truth and Power', in C. Gordon (ed.), *Power/Knowledge: Selected Interviews and Other Writings 1972–1977* (London, 1980), pp. 109–133

————, 'The Subject and Power', in Hubert Dreyfus and Paul Rabinow, *Michel Foucault: Beyond Structuralism and Hermeneutics* (Hemel Hempstead, 1982), pp. 211–243

————, 'Governmentality', in Graham Burchell, Colin Gordon and Paul Miller (eds), *The Foucault Effect: Studies in Governmentality* (Hemel Hempstead, 1991), pp. 87–104

Fraser, Derek, 'The Editor as Activist: Editors and Urban Politics in Early Victorian England', in Joel Wiener (ed.), *Innovators and Preachers: The Role of the Editor in Victorian England* (London, 1985), pp. 121–42

Garside, Patricia L., 'Representing the Metropolis: The Changing Relation Between London and the Press 1870–1939', *London Journal* 16, 2 (1991), pp. 156–173

Gatrell, V. A. C., 'The Decline of Theft and Violence in Victorian and Edwardian England', in V. A. C. Gatrell, Bruce Lenman, and Geoffrey Parker (eds), *Crime and the Law: The Social History of Crime in Western Europe since 1500* (London, 1980), pp. 238–337

Gilbert, Arthur, 'The "Africaine" Court Martial: A Study of Buggery in the British Navy', *Journal of Homosexuality* 1, 1 (Fall 1974), pp. 111–122

————, 'Buggery and the British Navy, 1700–1861', *Journal of Social History* 10 (1976–7), pp. 72–98

————, 'Social Deviance and Disaster During the Napoleonic Wars', *Albion* 9 (1977), pp. 98–113

————, 'Sodomy and the Law in Eighteenth and Early Nineteenth Century Britain', *Societas* 8 (Summer 1978), pp. 225–241

————, 'Conceptions of Homosexuality and Sodomy in Western History', *Journal of Homosexuality* 6 (1980–81), pp. 69–70

Goodbody, John, '*The Star*: Its Role in the New Journalism', *Victorian Periodicals Review* (Winter 1987), pp. 141–150

Goodich, Michael, 'Sodomy in Ecclesiastical Law and Theory', *Journal of Homosexuality* 1, 3 (1976), pp. 427–434

————, 'Sodomy in Medieval Secular Law', *Journal of Homosexuality*, 1, 3 (1976), pp. 295–302

Gordon, Colin, 'Governmental Rationality: An Introduction', in Graham

Burchell, Colin Gordon, and Paul Miller (eds), *The Foucault Effect* (Hemel Hempstead, 1991), pp. 1–51

Gray, Donald J., 'Early Victorian Scandalous Journalism: Renton Nicholson's *The Town* (1837–42)', in Joanne Shattock and Michael Wolff (eds), *The Victorian Periodical Press: Samplings and Soundings* (Leicester, 1982), pp. 317–49

Hare, E., 'Masturbatory Insanity, The History of an Idea', *Journal of Mental Science* 108 (January 1962), pp. 1–25

Harris, D., 'The Aesthetic of Drag', *Salmagundi* 108 (Fall 1995), pp. 62–74

Hart, Jennifer, 'The Reform of the Borough Police 1835–1856', *English Historical Review* 70 (July 1955), pp. 411–427

Harvey, A.D., 'Prosecutions for Sodomy at the Beginning of the Nineteenth Century', *Historical Journal* 21 (1978), pp. 939–949

Hay, Douglas, 'Property, Authority and the Criminal Law', in Douglas Hay et al (eds), *Albion's Fatal Tree: Crime and Society in Eighteenth Century England* (New York, 1975), pp. 23–54

————, 'The Criminal Prosecution and its Historians', *Modern Law Review* 47 (January 1984), pp. 1–29

————, 'Prosecution and Power: Malicious Prosecution in the English Courts 1750–1850', in Douglas Hay and Francis Snyder (eds), *Policing and Prosecution in Britain 1750–1850* (Oxford, 1989)

————, 'Controlling the English Prosecutor', *Osgood Hall Law Journal*, 21 (1993), pp. 165–186

Hay, Douglas, and Snyder, Francis, 'Using the Criminal Law 1750–1850: Policing, Private Prosecution, and the State', in Douglas Hay and Francis Snyder (eds), *Policing and Prosecution in Britain 1750–1850* (Oxford, 1989)

Henderson, A. R., 'Prostitution and the City', *Journal of Urban History* 23 (January 1997), pp. 231–239

Hetcher, Kathy, 'Planche, Vestris and the Transvestite Role: Sexuality and Gender in Victorian Popular Theatre', *Nineteenth Century Theatre* 15 (Summer 1987), pp. 9–33

Hilliard, David, 'UnEnglish and Unmanly: Anglo-Catholicism and Homosexuality', *Victorian Studies* 25, 2 (1982), pp. 181–210

Humphreys, Anne, 'G.W.M. Reynolds: Popular Literature and Popular Politics', *Victorian Periodicals Review* 16 (1983), pp. 79–83

————, 'The Geometry of the Modern City: G.W.M. Reynolds and the Mysteries of London', *Browning Institute Studies* 11 (1983), pp. 69–80

————, 'Generic Strands and Urban Twists: The Victorian Mysteries Novel', *Victorian Studies* 34 (Summer 1991), pp. 455–472

Innes, Joanna, 'Politics and Morals: The Reformation of Manners Movement in late 18th Century England', in Eckhart Helmuth (ed.), *The Transformation of Political Culture: England and Germany in the Later Eighteenth Century* (Oxford, 1990), pp. 57–118

Innes, Joanna, and Styles, John, 'The Crime Wave: Recent Writing on Crime and Criminal Justice in Eighteenth Century England', *Journal of British Studies* 25 (October 1986), pp. 380–435

Israel, Kalli, 'French Vices and British Liberties: Gender, Class and Narrative

Competition in a Late Victorian Sex Scandal', *Social History* 22, 1 (January 1997), pp. 1–26

Jones, David, 'The New Police, Crime and People in England and Wales 1829–1888', *Transactions of the Royal Historical Society* xxxiii (1983), pp. 151–168

Katz, Jonathan N., 'The Age of Sodomitical Sin 1607–1740', in Jonathan Goldberg (ed.), *Reclaiming Sodom* (Berkeley, 1994), pp. 43–58

————, 'The Invention of Heterosexuality', *Socialist Review*, 20, 1 (1990), pp. 7–34

Kent, Christopher, 'The Editor and the Law', in Joel Wiener (ed.), *Innovators and Preachers: The Role of the Editor in Victorian England* (London, 1985), pp. 99–119

King, Peter, 'Decision-Makers and Decision-Making in the English Criminal Law, 1750–1800', *Historical Journal* 27,1 (1984), pp. 25–58

Knelman, Judith, 'Class and Gender Bias in Victorian Newspapers', *Victorian Periodicals Review* 26, 1 (1993), pp. 29–35

Krieg, Joanne P., 'Without Walt Whitman in Camden', *Walt Whitman Quarterly Review* 14, 2–3 (1997), pp. 85–112

Manchester, Colin, 'Lord Campbell's Act: England's First Obscenity Statute', *Journal of Legal History* 9, 2 (1988), pp. 223–241

————, 'A History of the Crime of Obscene Libel', *Journal of Legal History*, 12, 1 (1991), pp. 36–57

Maxwell, Richard C., 'G.W.M. Reynolds, Dickens, and the Mysteries of London', *Nineteenth Century Fiction* 32 (1977), pp. 185–213

McEldowney John, 'Crown Prosecutions in Nineteenth Century Ireland', in Douglas Hay and Francis Snyder (eds), *Policing and Prosecution in Britain, 1750–1850* (Cambridge, 1989), pp. 427–457

McIntosh, Mary, 'The Homosexual Role', *Social Problems* 16 (1968/69), pp. 182–192

Micklewight, A., 'The Bishop of Clogher Case', *Notes and Queries* 214 (1969), p. 423

Moore, Lisa, '"Something More Tender Still Than Friendship": Romantic Friendship in Early Nineteenth Century England', *Feminist Studies* 18, 3 (1992), pp. 499–520

Morgan, Thais, 'Reimagining Masculinity in Victorian Criticism: Swinburne and Pater', *Victorian Studies* 36 (Spring 1993), pp. 315–332

Morris, R. J., 'Voluntary Societies and British Urban Elites, 1780–1850: An Analysis', *Historical Journal* 26, 1 (1983), pp. 95–118

Mort, Frank, and Nead, Lynda, 'Sexuality, Modernity and the Victorians', *Journal of Victorian Culture* 1 (1996), pp. 118–130

Nord, Deborah Epstein, 'The City as Theater: From Georgian to Early Victorian London', *Victorian Studies* 31 (Winter 1988), pp. 159–188

Nunokawa, Jeff, 'The Miser's Two Bodies: Silas Marner and the Sexual Possibilities of the Commodity', *Victorian Studies* 36, 3 (Spring 1993)

Oldham, James, 'The Origins of the Special Jury', *University of Chicago Law Review* 50 (Winter 1983), pp. 137–120

Olsen, Donald J., 'Victorian London: Specialisation, Segregation and Privacy, *Victorian Studies* 17, 2 (December 1974), pp. 265–280

Padgug, Robert, 'Sexual Matters: On Conceptualizing Sexuality in History', *Radical History Review* 20 (1979), pp. 3–23

Paley, Ruth, '"An Imperfect, Inadequate and Wretched System"? Policing London before Peel', *Criminal Justice History* X (1989), pp. 95–130

————, 'Thief Takers in London in the Age of the McDaniel Gang, c. 1745– 1754', in Douglas Hay and Francis Snyder (eds), *Policing and Prosecution in Britain 1750–1850* (Oxford, 1989), pp. 301–41

Parker, Graham, 'Is a Duck an Animal? An Exploration of Bestiality as a Crime', *Criminal Justice History* VII (1986), pp. 95–110

————, 'No Angels in the House: The Victorian Myth and the Paget Women', *American Historical Review* 84, 3 (1984), pp. 677–708

Penn, Donna, 'Queer: Theorizing Politics and History', *Radical History Review* 62, 24 (1995), pp. 24–42

Petrow, Stefan, 'The Rise of the Detective in London, 1869–1914', *Criminal Justice History* XIII (1993), pp. 91–108

Philips, David, '"Good men to Associate and Bad Men to Conspire": Associations for the Prosecution of Felons in England 1760–1860', in Douglas Hay and Francis Snyder (eds), *Policing and Prosecution in Britain 1750–1850* (Oxford, 1989), pp. 113–170

Pollak, Vivian R., 'Death as Repression, Repression as Death: A Reading of Whitman's "Calamus" Poems', in Geoffrey Sill (ed.), *Walt Whitman of Mickle Street: A Centennial Collection* (Knoxville, 1994) pp. 179–193

Price, Richard, 'Historiography, Narrative and the Nineteenth Century', *Journal of British Studies* 35 (April 1996), pp. 220–256

Reynolds, Elaine A., 'St Marylebone: Local Police Reform in London 1755– 1829', *Historian* 51, 3 (1989), pp. 446–466

Roberts, M.J.D., 'The Society for the Suppression of Vice and its Early Critics, 1802–1812', *Historical Journal* 26, 1 (1983), pp. 159–176

————, 'Making Victorian Morals? The Society for the Suppression of Vice and Its Critics, 1802–1886', *Historical Studies* 21 (1984), pp. 157–173

————, 'Public and Private in Early Nineteenth Century London: The Vagrant Act of 1822 and its Enforcement', *Social History* 13 (October 1988), pp. 273–294

Rubin, Gayle, 'Thinking Sex: Notes for a Radical Theory of the Politics of Sexuality', in Carol S. Vance (ed.), *Pleasure and Danger: Exploring Female Sexuality* (Boston, 1984), pp. 267–319

Rustigan, Michael, 'A Reinterpretation of Criminal Law Reform in Nineteenth Century England', *Journal of Criminal Justice* 8 (July 1980), pp. 205–219

Salveson, Paul, 'Loving Comrades: Lancashire's Links to Walt Whitman', *Walt Whitman Quarterly Review* 14, 2–3 (1997), pp. 57–84

Seidman, Steven, 'The Power of Desire and the Danger of Pleasure: Victorian Sexuality Reconsidered', *Journal of Social History* 24, 1 (1990), pp. 47–67

Senelick, Laurence, 'The Evolution of the Male Impersonator on the

Nineteenth Century Stage', *Essays in Theatre* 1, 1 (November, 1982), pp. 31–44

————, 'Boys and Girls Together: The Subcultural Origins of Glamour Drag in Nineteenth Century England', in Lesley Ferris (ed.), *Crossing the Stage: Controversies in Cross Dressing* (London, 1994), pp. 80–95

————, 'The Illusion of Sex', *American Theatre* 12 (November 1995), pp. 12–16

Showalter, Elaine, 'Family Secrets and Domestic Subversion: Rebellion in the Novels of the 1860s', in Anthony Wohl (ed.), *The Victorian Family: Structures and Stresses* (London, 1978), pp.101–118

Shubert, Adrian, 'Private Initiative in Law Enforcement: Associations for the Prosecution of Felons, 1744–1856', in Victor Bailey (ed.), *Policing and Punishment in Nineteenth Century Britain* (London, 1981), pp. 25–41

Sindall, Rob S., 'Middle Class Crime in Nineteenth Century England', *Criminal Justice History* IV (1983), pp. 23–40

————, 'The Criminal Statistics of Nineteenth Century Cities: A New Approach', *Urban Studies Yearbook* (1986), pp. 28–36

Smith, F. B., 'Labouchere's Amendment to the Criminal Law Amendment Bill', *Historical Studies*, 67, 17 (October 1976), pp. 165–173

————, 'Sexuality in Britain, 1800–1900: Some Suggested Revisions', in Martha Vicinus (ed.), *A Widening Sphere: Changing Roles of Victorian Women* (Bloomington, 1977), pp. 182–198

Stearns, Claire, and Stearns, Peter, 'Victorian Sexuality: Can Historians Do it Better', *Journal of Social History* 28, 4 (1985), pp. 265–634

Storch, Robert, '"The Plague of Blue Locusts": Police Reform and Popular Resistance in Northern England 1840–1857', *International Review of Social History* 20 (1975), pp. 61–90

————, 'The Policeman as Domestic Missionary: Urban Discipline and Popular Culture in Northern England 1850–1880', *Journal of Social History* 9 (Summer 1976), pp. 481–509

————, 'Police Control of Street Prostitution in Victorian London: A Study in the Contexts of Police Action', in D.H. Bayley (ed.), *Police and Society* (London, 1977), pp. 49–73

————, 'Policing Rural Southern England Before the Police: Opinion and Practice, 1830–1856', in Douglas Hay and Francis Snyder (eds), *Policing and Prosecution in Britain 1750–1850* (Oxford, 1989)

Styles, John, 'Sir John Fielding and the Problem of Criminal Investigation in Eighteenth Century England', *Transactions of the Royal Historical Society* xxxiii (1983), pp. 127–150

Sweet, Mathew, 'Outside Swan and Edgar's', *London Review of Books* 20, 3 (5 February 1998), pp. 26–27

Swift, Roger, 'Urban Policing in Early Victorian England 1835–1866', *History* 73 (June 1988), pp. 211–273

Terry, Jennifer, 'Theorizing Deviant Historiography', *Differences* 3, 2 (Summer 1991), pp. 55–74

Tosh, John, 'What Should Historians do With Masculinity? Reflections on

Nineteenth Century Britain', *History Workshop Journal* 38 (1994), pp. 179–202

Townsend, Camilla, '"I am the Woman for Spirit": A Working Woman's Gender Transgression in Victorian London', *Victorian Studies* 36, (Spring 1993), pp. 293–314

Traies, Jane, 'Jones and the Working Girl: Class Marginality in Music-Hall Song 1860–1900', in J. S. Bratton (ed.), *Music Hall: Performance and Style* (Milton Keynes, 1986), pp. 23–48

Trodd, Anthea, 'The Policeman and the Lady: Significant encounters in mid-Victorian fiction', *Victorian Studies* 27 (Summer 1984), pp. 435–460

Trumbach, Randolph, 'London's Sodomites: Homosexual Behaviour and Western Culture in the Eighteenth Century', *Journal of Social History* 10 (Fall 1977), pp. 1–33

————, 'Sodomitical Subcultures, Sodomitical Roles and the Gender Revolution of the Eighteenth Century: The Recent Historiography', *Eighteenth Century Life*, 9 (1985), pp. 109–121

————, 'The Birth of the Queen: Sodomy and the Emergence of Gender Equality in Modern Europe 1660–1750', in George Chauncey, Martin Duberman and Martha Vicinus (eds), *Hidden From History: Reclaiming the Gay and Lesbian Past* (New York, 1989), pp. 129–140

————, 'London's Sapphists: From Three Sexes to Four Genders in the Making of Modern Culture', in Gilbert Herdt (ed.), *Third Sex, Third Gender: Beyond Sexual Dimorphism in Culture and History* (New York, 1994), pp. 111–136

————, 'The Origin and Development of the Modern Lesbian Role in the Western Gender System: Northwestern Europe and the United States 1750–1950', *Historical Reflections* 20, 2 (1994), pp. 288–320

Valverde, Mariana, 'The Love of Finery: Fashion and Fallen Women in Nineteenth Century Social Discourse', *Victorian Studies* 32 (Winter 1989), pp. 169–188

Vicinus, Martha, '"They Wonder to Which Sex I Belong": The Historical Roots of Modern Lesbian Identity', in Henry Abelove, Michele Aina Barale, David M. Halperin (eds), *The Lesbian and Gay Studies Reader* (London, 1993), pp. 432–452

————, 'Turn of the Century Male Impersonation: Rewriting the Romance Plot', in Andrew H. Miller and James Eli Adams (eds), *Sexualities in Victorian Britain* (Bloomington, 1996), pp. 187–213

————, 'Lesbian Perversity and Victorian Marriage: The 1864 Codrington Divorce Trial', *Journal of British Studies* 36 (January 1997), pp. 70–98

Vincent, David, 'The Origins of Public Secrecy', *Transactions of the Royal Historical Society* I (1991), pp. 229–248

Wach, Howard. M., 'Civil Society, Moral Identity and the Liberal Public Sphere: Manchester and Boston 1820–1840', *Social History* 21, 3 (October 1996), pp. 28–40

Waters, Sarah, '"The Most Famous Fairy in History": Antinous and Homosexual Fantasy', *Journal of the History of Sexuality* 6, 2 (1995), pp. 194–231

Weber, Gary, 'Henry Labouchere, *Truth* and the New Journalism of Late Victorian Britain', *Victorian Periodicals Review* (Spring 1993), pp. 36–43

Weeks, Jeffrey, '"Sins and Diseases": Some Notes on Homosexuality in the Nineteenth Century', *History Workshop Journal* 1 (1976), pp. 211–219

————, 'Inverts, Perverts and Mary-Annes: Male Prostitution and the Regulation of Homosexuality in the Nineteenth and Early Twentieth Centuries', in George Chauncey, Martin Duberman and Martha Vicinus (eds), *Hidden From History: Reclaiming the Gay and Lesbian Past* (London, 1991), pp. 195–211

————, 'The Late Victorian Stew of Sexualities', *Victorian Studies*, 35, 4 (1992), pp. 409–415

Weinberger, Barbara, 'The Police and the Public in Mid-Nineteenth Century Warwickshire', in Victor Bailey (ed.), *Policing and Punishment in Nineteenth Century Britain* (London, 1981), pp. 65–93

Weir, Lorna, 'Cosmic Consciousness and the Love of Comrades: Contacts Between R.M. Bucke and Edward Carpenter', *Journal of Canadian Studies* 30, 2 (Summer 1995) pp. 39–57

Wiener, Joel, 'Edmund Yates: The Gossip as Editor', in Joel Wiener (ed.), *Innovators and Preachers: The Role of the Editor in Victorian England* (London, 1985), pp. 259–74

Winder, W.H.D., 'The Development of Blackmail', *Modern Law Review* 5 (1941), pp. 21–50

Wolff, Janet, 'The Invisible *Flâneuse*: Women and the Literature of Modernity', in Janet Wolff, *Feminine Sentences: Essays on Women and Culture* (Berkeley, 1990), pp. 34–50

Yeo, Stephen, 'A New Life: The Religion of Socialism in Britain, 1883–1896', *History Workshop Journal* 4 (1977) pp. 5–56

Theses

Cook, Matthew, 'The Inverted City: London and the Constitution of Homosexuality, 1885–1914' (Ph.D., University of London, 2000)

Mauriello, Christopher, 'The Public Sphere and the Liberal Imagination: Public Intellectuals, New Liberalism and the Transformation of Culture 1880–1920' (Ph.D., Brown University, 1995)

Morris, Polly, 'Defamation and Sexual Reputation in Somerset 1733–1850' (Ph.D., Warwick University, 1985)

Simpson, Anthony, 'Masculinity and Control: The Prosecution of Sex Offences in Eighteenth Century London' (Ph.D., University of Michigan, 1984)

Index